THE CRAFT COCKTAIL COMPENDIUM

CONTEMPORARY INTERPRETATIONS AND INSPIRED TWISTS ON TIME-HONORED CLASSICS

WARREN BOBROW
"THE COCKTAIL WHISPERER"

FAIR WINDS

Quarto is the authority on a wide range of topics.
Quarto educates, entertains and enriches the lives of
our readers—enthusiasts and lovers of hands-on living.
www.QuartoKnows.com

First published in the United States of America in 2017 by
Fair Winds Press, an imprint of
Quarto Publishing Group USA Inc.
100 Cummings Center
Suite 406-L
Beverly, Massachusetts 01915-6101
Telephone: (978) 282-9590
Fax: (978) 283-2742
QuartoKnows.com
Visit our blogs at QuartoKnows.com

21 20 19 18 17   1 2 3 4 5

ISBN: 978-1-59233-762-0

Library of Congress Cataloging-in-Publication Data available

The content in this book originally appeared in *Apothecary Cocktails* (Fair Winds Press 2013), *Whiskey Cocktails*
(Fair Winds Press 2014), and *Bitters & Shrub Syrup Cocktails* (Fair Winds Press 2015), all by Warren Bobrow.

Design: Sussner Design Company
Photography: Glenn Scott Photography

Printed in China

The information in this book is for educational purposes only. It is not intended to replace the advice of a physician or
medical practitioner. Please see your health-care provider before beginning any new health program.

DEDICATION

*To my late grandmother Sophia Bobrow who
lived until 104.5 and with whom I toasted
her longevity with her favorite drink, bourbon,
mere days before her departure.*

CONTENTS

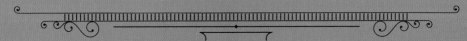

INTRODUCTION

THESE DAYS, DRINKERS THE WORLD OVER HAVE AN EXCELLENT REASON TO LIFT THEIR GLASSES WITH GOOD CHEER. WHY? WELL, YOU'D HAVE TO BE LIVING (AND DRINKING) UNDER A ROCK TO HAVE MISSED THE COCKTAIL RENAISSANCE THAT'S TAKEN THE TWENTY-FIRST CENTURY BY STORM. GONE ARE THE DAYS WHERE A "COCKTAIL" MEANT A HEFTY SLUG OF POOR-QUALITY BOOZE TOSSED OVER FREEZER-BURNT ICE AND TOPPED WITH A SUGARY, ADDITIVE-LADEN COLA OR RUBBISHY TONIC WATER. NO, SIR: DISCERNING DRINKERS PRIZE QUALITY OVER QUANTITY NOWADAYS, AND THAT ETHOS HAS SPREAD FAR AND WIDE—TO PROFESSIONAL MIXOLOGISTS AND HOME BARTENDERS ALIKE.

First of all, though, let's define our terms. In general, craft cocktails (and mocktails, too: alcohol-free cocktails don't have to be boring) value three things: top-quality spirits; fresh, often handmade mixers; and well-made ice that's hand-cut where possible. Do drinks made from these ingredients tend to take a little more time and effort—and, perhaps, a little extra money—to prepare? Sometimes. Are they worth it? Absolutely.

Enter *The Craft Cocktail Compendium*, a collection of nearly 200 cocktail recipes for every occasion. They're very different to one another, but they all have one thing in common: They take their inspiration from the history of mixology, a subject that's close to my heart. See, cocktails originated as medicinal cures that old-time pharmacists doled out to their customers long before the widespread production of synthetic drugs, and I've been interested in the history of patent medicines and apothecaries for as long as I can remember. My grandfather was in the patent pharmaceutical business and, even as a child, the world of patent medicines and quack cures were a part of my day-to-day life. (In fact, they were impossible to ignore, since I was fed a teaspoon of spirit-based vitamin tonic along with my chewable vitamins and orange juice at breakfast every day.) Hence my fascination with, and passion for, the world of mixology.

Since cocktails were first created to be curatives, it's no surprise that some of the recipes in this book draw inspiration from the apothecary. Back in the day, pharmacists would have used alcohol to preserve herbs' healing properties and to prevent them from rotting. And said pharmacists would have administered these spirits along with, say, a little fizzy water and a final flourish of herb-laden bitters. There you have it: a template for the contemporary cocktail. These days, naturally, drinkers are more interested in the ingredients and the lore of apothecary-inspired cocktails, and don't necessarily visit cocktail bars to be cured of an illness. Instead, they're enthralled by the histories of many older brands of liquors, some of which were originally created to be medicines or tonics. And they appreciate the use of herbal ingredients that would have been apothecary staples centuries ago. All of this reflects the fact that healthful, authentic eating and drinking are top priorities of twenty-first century tipplers.

Similarly, artisan spirits are experiencing a massive boom both in the United States and abroad. Small producers are creating truly exceptional handcrafted spirits, like gins, vodkas, and, of course, whiskies. (Purists, take note: If you think that there's only one way to drink whiskey—neat, no ice—prepare to be astounded. Lots of the cocktails in this book provide delicious, artfully-created backdrops for the many varieties of American, Scotch, Irish, Japanese, and Indian whisk(e)ys that grace the market today.)

What's more, this book will also show you how to make and use superior mixers, bitters, and garnishes for your drinks, since these are vital components of memorable cocktails. For instance, you'll learn to make a variety of shrubs, which are flavorful mixtures of vinegar, sugar, and fruits or vegetables: their bright acidity and intense flavour profiles make them must-have ingredients for all your homemade drinks. Shrubs are easy to make, too; once you combine the ingredients, the natural fermentation that follows does all the hard work for you. And I've also included recipes for homemade simple syrups, fruit purees—and even handmade bitters!—to use in your drinks (and in the kitchen, too).

Whether you're after a mouthwatering aperitif, an old-fashioned curative taken straight from the apothecaries of yore, a cold-weather cocktail to warm your hands and lift your spirits, or the perfect drink to serve at your next party, you'll find what you're looking for in the pages that follow. I hope you enjoy these handmade drinks as much as I've enjoyed creating them.

CH. 1 NO.

APERITIFS:

CRAFT COCKTAILS TO WHET YOUR APPETITE

• • •

"ONE CANNOT THINK WELL, LOVE WELL, SLEEP WELL, UNLESS ONE HAS DINED WELL," WROTE VIRGINIA WOOLF. SHE WAS RIGHT—BUT SHE FORGOT ONE THING: ONE MUST DRINK WELL, TOO. AND THAT'S WHERE APERITIFS COME IN. A PERFECTLY-CRAFTED PRE-DINNER COCKTAIL CAN ACCOMPLISH WHAT NEARLY AMOUNTS TO MAGIC: IT CAN PREPARE YOUR PALATE (AND YOUR STOMACH) FOR AN EXCELLENT MEAL; IT CAN RESTORE DROOPING SPIRITS AFTER A LONG DAY AT THE OFFICE (AFTER ALL, YOU CAN'T ENJOY DINNER WHEN YOU'RE STRESSED OUT, CAN YOU?); AND IT'S A GREAT POTABLE PARTNER FOR FINGER FOOD LIKE TAPAS, HORS O'OEUVRES, OR OTHER NIBBLES.

And aperitifs have long been part of the fabulous food cultures of France and Italy, where diners might enjoy pastis or an Aperol spritz before a leisurely lunch or dinner. Historically, though, aperitifs weren't created only to be pleasurable complements to food; they were also a way to administer medicinal herbs and spices that could ease the effects of the many belly-related maladies that plagued our ancestors before the age of refrigeration, such as indigestion and food poisoning. These valuable (and often expensive) botanicals were preserved in a suspension of alcohol, and the resulting liqueur would often have been bitter to the taste—which is why so many aperitifs have such strong, bracing flavors. Other alcoholic "tonics" were created in days gone by in order to cure a specific ailment: for instance, Dubonnet, a type of quinine-laden vermouth, was developed by a French chemist and wine merchant of the same name in the mid-nineteenth century in order to combat malaria. But since quinine's taste was so bitter, Monsieur Dubonnet concocted a secret recipe of botanicals to mask its flavor (it's closely-guarded to this day), and voila!—a popular pre-prandial tipple was born.

Want to get in on the action? You've come to the right place. This chapter shows you how to make mouthwatering aperitifs that are sure to put you in the mood for food. Some are tried-and-true classics, like the Pretty-Close-to-Normal Manhattan on page 10 or the Classic Old-Fashioned on page 18, while others feature a couple Cocktail-Whisperer-style twists, like the Oblique Manhattan on page 10 (hint: it involves absinthe!) or the Bitter, Twisted Sidecar on page 16, which adds a dash of my homemade Italian Blood Orange and Charred Rosemary Shrub to the traditional triumvirate of brandy, Cointreau, and freshly squeezed lemon juice. And there are a couple surprises, too: for instance, if you haven't been making beer cocktails yet, now's the time to start—and for "now" read "before dinner," because beer actually makes an excellent aperitivo (in the right hands, of course). Or, if rum's your thing, invest in a good bottle of Rhum Agricole and whip up the Ginger-Lime Rum Daiquiri on page 26: there's no better way to rouse a recalcitrant appetite, especially on a sultry summer's evening.

Word to the wise, though: Be sensible when it comes to enjoying aperitifs, especially if you're planning on drinking alcohol with dinner, too. Stick to a single drink, or two at the most: there's no point giving that hangover a headstart.

LET'S START MIXING!

A PRETTY-CLOSE-TO-NORMAL MANHATTAN

Since it's a twentieth-century classic, you're probably already familiar with the Manhattan, at least in theory. Perhaps your mom drank one on the rocks every evening before dinner. Or maybe your beer-loving great-uncle used to mix himself a straight-up Manhattan once in awhile, on special occasions. Just like Mom and Great-Uncle Harold, the Manhattan is one of my favorite "normal" cocktails (for "normal," read "un-Cocktail-Whisperified"). Its ingredients are as simple as could be, and it's just as easy to prepare. Aside from the rye whiskey, there's nothing at all to add but bitters and sweet vermouth—but do feel free to play the field when it comes to the vermouth. Whichever way you craft your Manhattan, as long as you make it with rye whiskey, all will be well.

INGREDIENTS

_ 2 OUNCES (60 ML) RYE WHISKEY

_ 1/2 OUNCE (15 ML)
SWEET VERMOUTH

_ SEVERAL SHAKES OF
AROMATIC BITTERS

_ EASY HOME-CURED COCKTAIL
CHERRY (SEE PAGE 311)

DIRECTIONS

Fill a cocktail mixing glass three-quarters full with ice. Add the rye, vermouth, and a few shakes of the aromatic bitters. Stir well, and then strain into either a rocks glass or a martini glass. (Some people add ice at this point, but I am not one of them.) Add an Easy Home-Cured Cocktail Cherry to finish. Serve one to an appreciative friend—then mix up another one for yourself. Beware, though: You may have to repeat the process several times!

AN OBLIQUE MANHATTAN →

Every bartender knows how to make a Manhattan—but the beauty of its simplicity is that it can sustain so many variations. Its recipe is a template that creative mixologists love to tinker with. And I'm one of them. While the standard version is usually made with whiskey, sweet vermouth, and bitters, my Oblique Manhattan combines bourbon, a dose of my delectable Spiced Cherry Shrub, and a whisper of absinthe. (According to some sources, very early versions of the Manhattan originally included absinthe, so I like to think that my variation on the theme tips its hat to a proto-Manhattan now lost to the mists of time.) Bitters and an orange zest twist are a traditionally inspired finish to my twisted Manhattan. It's a peerless pre-dinner drink: Serve it with just about any kind of hors d'oeuvre—or be a purist, and enjoy it on its own.

INGREDIENTS

- 2 OUNCES (60 ML) GOOD-QUALITY BOURBON, SUCH AS FOUR ROSES YELLOW LABEL
- 1/4 TEASPOON ABSINTHE
- 1 OUNCE (30 ML) COLONIAL SOUR CHERRY SHRUB (SEE PAGE 210)
- 1 OUNCE (30 ML) VERMOUTH, SUCH AS CARPANO ANTICA
- 2-4 DROPS AROMATIC BITTERS
- ORANGE ZEST TWIST

DIRECTIONS

Fill a cocktail mixing glass three-quarters full with ice. Add all the liquid ingredients except the bitters, and stir slowly about 30 times. (Never, ever shake a Manhattan! Bad things will happen.) Strain, using a Hawthorne strainer, into a short rocks glass and garnish with the orange zest twist. Top with 2–4 drops of aromatic bitters.

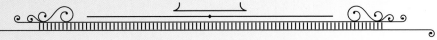

VIEUX CARRÉ COCKTAIL

Rye whiskey, sweet vermouth, and a dash of bitters: sounds like a Manhattan, doesn't it? Not quite. The Vieux Carré may be a cousin of the Manhattan, but it's got a charm all its own—and it dates back to an original recipe from the historic Hotel Monteleone in New Orleans, where perking up flagging appetites with carefully-concocted, alcoholic curatives was the order of the day.

INGREDIENTS

_ 1 OUNCE (25 ML) RYE WHISKEY

_ 1 OUNCE (25 ML) COGNAC

_ 1 OUNCE (25 ML) SWEET VERMOUTH

_ 2 TO 3 SHAKES PEYCHAUD'S BITTERS

_ 2 TO 3 SHAKES ANGOSTURA BITTERS

_ 1/2 OUNCE (15 ML) BÉNÉDICTINE

_ LEMON ZEST TWIST

DIRECTIONS

Add the rye whiskey, cognac, vermouth, bitters, and Bénédictine to a mixing glass over a couple handfuls of ice. Mix well, then strain into a short rocks glass. Twist the lemon zest over the edge of the glass, and sip slowly. Hungry yet?

SIDENOTE

⇒ **Peychaud's bitters** are a New Orleans–based brand of aromatic bitters that were originally intended to heal stomach maladies of all sorts. And they've been around for nearly two centuries. French-born pharmacist Antoine Peychaud developed his recipe for bitters in 1830—long before safe food-handling practices became de rigueur—and his soothing recipe contained anise, cloves, cinnamon, and nutmeg (along with copious amounts of brandy, of course). For a time, Peychaud's combination of herbs, spices, and alcohol was available only in pharmacies, and was even meant to ease the symptoms of more serious diseases such as dysentery and ulcers.

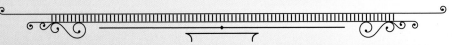

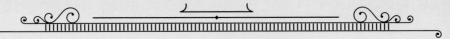
THE GRENADIER COCKTAIL

Need to add a little Vitamin C to your pre-prandial diet? The Grenadier Cocktail is just what the doctor ordered, and it's based on a combination that's been around since time immemorial. Like the classic Tequila Sunrise cocktail, it combines tequila, citrus juice and grenadine—but it's not your everyday mix of budget tequila, concentrated orange juice, and bottled, artificially colored grenadine syrup. No way, man. Reposado tequila, three types of freshly squeezed citrus juice, and homemade grenadine mean serious mixological business is happening here. And a final flourish of homemade bitters turns the Grenadier into a truly elegant aperitif. Relax: Making your own grenadine is really easy, and it's so much better than the stuff you get from a bottle or a can.

INGREDIENTS

- 2 OUNCES (60 ML)
  REPOSADO TEQUILA

- 1/4 OUNCE (7 ML) HOMEMADE
  GRENADINE SYRUP (SEE PAGE 312)

- 1/4 OUNCE (7 ML) EACH
  FRESHLY SQUEEZED LEMON,
  LIME, AND ORANGE JUICES

- 3 DROPS COCKTAIL WHISPERER'S
  RAW HONEY AROMATIC
  BITTERS (SEE PAGE 311)

DIRECTIONS

Add all the ingredients except the bitters to a Boston shaker. Top the ingredients with enough ice to fill the shaker three-quarters full. Cover and shake hard for 15 seconds. Strain the mixture into a coupe glass and dot the bitters over the top.

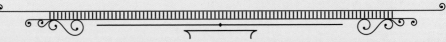

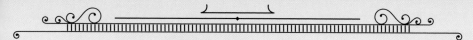

ALMOND PASTIS

Pastis is one of the most popular drinks in France, especially in the nation's southern and southwestern regions, where scorching heat can accompany the summer months. The French, undisputed masters of all things gastronomic, rely on this simple cocktail of aniseed-flavored liqueur diluted with water and served over ice to keep that stifling, appetite-muffling heat at bay. It can be enjoyed as an aperitif, digestif, or even on its own during those long, warm afternoons. Here, an infusion of orgeat—that is, almond-flavored—syrup acts as a delicious foil to the liqueur's bitter edge. If you like, you can substitute Turkish raki for the Pernod—both work equally well.

INGREDIENTS

_ 3 OUNCES (90 ML) FRENCH
  PERNOD OR TURKISH RAKI

_ 2 OUNCES (60 ML) ORGEAT SYRUP

_ 6 OUNCES (175 ML) COOL WATER

_ ICE CUBES

DIRECTIONS

Add a handful of ice cubes to a 12-ounce (355-ml) glass. Add the Pernod or raki, followed by the orgeat syrup. Pour the cool water over the liqueur and syrup, and mix gently. It's just what the apothecary ordered to restore wilting appetites before a meal—especially alongside hors d'oeuvres or a Turkish mezze platter of olives, cheeses, dips, and fresh fruits and vegetables.

BITTER, TWISTED SIDECAR

We all know and love the Sidecar, a tart threesome of brandy, Cointreau, and freshly squeezed lemon juice. Named for the motorcycle attachment (although the reasons for this are nothing if not obscure), the sidecar is a staple of twenty-first century cocktail bars everywhere. And it's guaranteed to get your appetite up and running. I like to add a few variations to the theme, though. Here, a whisper of absinthe coats the glass; my Italian Blood Orange and Charred Rosemary Shrub replaces the traditional Cointreau; and a couple drops of my homemade bitters round things off nicely. And don't forget to frost the rim of the glass. Pour a little freshly squeezed lemon juice into a saucer; dunk the rim in the juice; and then dunk it into a saucer of sugar that's been mixed with the tiniest pinch of cayenne pepper.

INGREDIENTS

- FEW DROPS TENNEYSON ABSINTHE ROYALE
- 2 OUNCES (60 ML) COGNAC
- 1 OUNCE (30 ML) ITALIAN BLOOD ORANGE AND CHARRED ROSEMARY SHRUB (SEE PAGE 22)
- 1/4 OUNCE (7 ML) FRESHLY SQUEEZED LEMON JUICE, STRAINED
- 2 DROPS COCKTAIL WHISPERER'S RAW HONEY AROMATIC BITTERS (SEE PAGE 311)

DIRECTIONS

Swirl a few drops of the absinthe around a coupe glass, then pour the absinthe out (into your mouth: no wasting good liquor!) Set aside. Fill a cocktail mixing glass three-quarters full with ice. Add the cognac, the shrub, and the lemon juice, then stir 40 times to cool. Using a Hawthorne strainer, strain the mixture into the absinthe-cured coupe glass. Dot with my Raw Honey Aromatic Bitters, and serve to an appreciative friend. Then make another for yourself. Guests first, of course!

SIDENOTE

⇥ **What are shrubs?** Don't be misled by the name: the kind of shrubs we're talking about here bear little relation to the decorative bushes in your front yard. Shrubs truly were the original energy drinks, and they were especially popular during the nineteenth and early twentieth centuries. These early shrubs consisted of little more than a sweetening agent, like honey or sugar, combined with water and vinegar, but that simple combination of sweet, tart, and savory makes for a really refreshing, revitalizing beverage. Thirst-slaking shrubs were the soft drinks of their era, before fizzy, sugary soda pop exploded onto the market.

Today, shrubs have captured the attention of top mixologists, many of whom are interested in how cocktail history can be re-imagined in contemporary craft cocktails. Professionals and home bartenders alike are attracted by shrubs' deep, concentrated flavors and their funky, sweet-tart aromatics. And the best part is, shrubs are really easy to make at home. Just about any type of fruit or vegetable you can think of can be made into a shrub— and, while there are usually several steps in the shrub-making process, it's actually pretty simple. The process generally goes like this: Fruits or vegetables are combined with sugar or simple syrup and spices in a nonreactive bowl. After leaving them to sit for about twenty-four hours in order to promote natural fermentation, the fruit-sugar mixture is crushed or pressed to release the intensely flavored juices. Then the juices are mixed with vinegar and left to sit for up to several weeks to combine. (Not always, though: some shrub recipes, like the ones in this chapter, can be made much more quickly.) The result? A concentrated, flavorful "liqueur" that adds layers of character to each sip of your homemade cocktails.

THE CLASSIC OLD FASHIONED

The main ingredient in a perfectly crafted Old Fashioned cocktail is love. Sure, there's been a lot of disagreement among mixologists in recent years over the recipe: lots of fruit, or no fruit at all? Whichever camp you might be in, the keys to a great Old-Fashioned—a drink that's truly an integral part of American cocktail culture—are patience and passion. My version calls for a slice of thickly cut orange rind, instead of the traditional chunks of citrus fruit; singeing the rind with a lit match releases its aromatic essential oils, soaking the sugar cube with flavor. And the bitters are an important component of this drink, so feel free to experiment a bit. There are so many different varieties on the market these days—and some yield fascinating results! I enjoy the process of making an Old-Fashioned almost as much as I enjoy sipping one before a leisurely meal.

INGREDIENTS

_ 1 ROUGH-CUT BROWN SUGAR CUBE

_ 2 DASHES AROMATIC BITTERS
OF YOUR CHOICE

_ 2 OUNCES (60 ML) RYE WHISKEY

_ 1 THICKLY CUT ORANGE ZEST TWIST
(USE A PARING KNIFE, NOT A PEELER)

_ HAND-CUT ICE CUBES

DIRECTIONS

Place the sugar cube in an old-fashioned glass. Wet the cube with the aromatic bitters. Singe the orange zest twist by holding it firmly behind a lit match and pinching it to release its natural citrus oils. Be careful to spritz the citrus oils into the glass. Place the orange zest twist into the glass; using a muddler or the end of a wooden spoon, press it gently against the sugar cube. Then add the rye whiskey and stir gently. Add a couple large hand-cut ice cubes to the glass; stir gently again. Garnish with another orange zest twist, and serve. It's restrained, potable elegance in a glass.

SLIGHTLY ASKEW OLD-FASHIONED

You're familiar with the Classic Old-Fashioned. Now, here's the Cocktail Whisperer's twisted take on it! After all, not to experiment with the Old-Fashioned paradigm would be a crime against creativity. At first glance, this cocktail may seem a bit on the complicated side, but it's actually a snap to make. In addition to rye whiskey and belly-friendly Fernet, my version of the Old Fashioned involves organic sage tea liqueur, which is a distinctive American liquor made from a combination of restorative herbs. Instead of using a flamed orange zest twist, I make this cocktail Slightly Askew by using orange wedges that have been soaked in Earl Grey tea overnight. Italian vermouth brings up the rear here, while the Mexican mole bitters lend the drink an earthy simplicity. The finished product is a combination of flavors that's just astonishing.

INGREDIENTS

_ 1 ORANGE, CUT INTO 1-INCH (2.5-CM) WEDGES AND SOAKED OVERNIGHT IN EARL GREY

_ 1 OUNCE (30 ML) RYE WHISKEY

_ 1 OUNCE (30 ML) FERNET BRANCA

_ 1/4 OUNCE (7 ML) ITALIAN VERMOUTH

_ 1/4 OUNCE (7 ML) ORGANIC SAGE TEA LIQUEUR

_ 3 DROPS MEXICAN MOLE BITTERS, OR AROMATIC BITTERS

_ EASY HOME-CURED COCKTAIL CHERRIES (SEE PAGE 311)

DIRECTIONS

Place two Earl Grey–soaked orange segments in the bottom of a Boston shaker. Add the rye whiskey, then muddle with a muddler or the end of a wooden spoon. Add the Fernet Branca, Italian vermouth, and sage tea liqueur. Then fill the shaker three-quarters full with ice. Shake for about 15 seconds. Place a couple of large ice cubes in a rocks glass, and strain the mixture into the glass. Drip the bitters into the glass, and garnish with an Easy Home-Cured Cocktail Cherry. Quite a newfangled take on an old-fashioned classic!

ITALIAN BLOOD ORANGE AND CHARRED ROSEMARY SHRUB

The combination of orange and rosemary is a match made in heaven, but what sets my Italian Blood Orange Shrub apart from the crowd is its use of charred rosemary, which intensifies the shrub's flavor, and blood oranges, a spunky fruit with blood-red flesh and a taste that lies somewhere between sweet and tart. Bound with citrusy yuzu vinegar and Demerara sugar, this shrub can be used in cocktails after just 24 hours. Or, if you've got the patience, you can age it in the fridge or at cellar temperature for a month or two before using it. (Your friends may try to grab a bottle when you're not looking. Just let them try.) Try it in my Bitter, Twisted Sidecar on page 16.

INGREDIENTS

_ 3-4 BLOOD ORANGES, PEELED (REMOVE AS MUCH OF THE WHITE PITH AS POSSIBLE: IT'S BITTER) AND QUARTERED. SLICE THE PEEL INTO NARROW STRIPS—AGAIN, REMOVING AS MUCH OF THE BITTER WHITE PITH AS POSSIBLE.

_ 1 CUP (200 G) DEMERARA SUGAR

_ 2-3 STALKS OF ROSEMARY, HELD ABOVE A FLAME AND LIGHTLY CHARRED, THEN COOLED

_ 1 CUP (235 ML) YUZU VINEGAR (AVAILABLE AT YOUR LOCAL ASIAN MARKET)

DIRECTIONS

Time: 24 hours. *Combine the oranges, the peels, sugar, and the charred rosemary (needles only, no wood, please!). Stir to coat the oranges and zest with the charred rosemary. Cover with plastic wrap and let it sit overnight so that the oranges will release their delicious juices. Then add the yuzu vinegar and stir. Let the mixture sit for another 12 hours in the fridge, stirring every hour or so. Then strain the mixture through a nonreactive strainer into a second bowl, pressing as much of the orange pulp through the strainer as possible. Discard the pulp (or serve it alongside fresh scones instead of jam or marmalade). Funnel the liquid into sterilized bottles or jars. Use immediately: or, if you like, leave it in the fridge and forget about it for a month or so, shaking the bottle every so often to combine the sugar, vinegar, and fruit. That'll concentrate the flavors (and intensify the colors, too).*

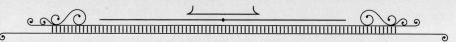

INSTANT BLOOD ORANGE SHRUBB COCKTAIL

This shrubb cocktail is the accelerated version of my Italian Blood Orange Shrub on page 22, except it takes minutes, not hours, to make. It's great with rum, but rye whiskey works just as well. And it's a wonderfully simple, no-fuss aperitif: instant gratification in a glass!

INGREDIENTS

_ 3 OUNCES (120 G) BLOOD
ORANGE MARMALADE

_ 1 OUNCE (30 ML) WHITE
BALSAMIC VINEGAR

_ 1 OUNCE (30 ML) BASIC SIMPLE
SYRUP (SEE PAGE 311)

_ 1 OUNCE (30 ML) 100-PROOF RHUM
AGRICOLE OR RYE WHISKEY

_ DASH OF SELTZER WATER

_ 1-2 SHAKES ORANGE BITTERS

DIRECTIONS

Combine the marmalade, vinegar, simple syrup, and rum or rye whiskey over ice in a Boston shaker. Shake like crazy, and then strain into an coupe glass. Top with the seltzer water and the orange bitters. Done.

SIDENOTE

⇒ **Instant shrubs.** It's true that shrubs—flavorful mixtures of fruit, sugar, and vinegar—benefit from time and patience, since the aging process helps their flavors concentrate and improve. But what if your patience just won't hold out? No problem! Shrubs can be ready in as little as a few minutes, since you don't necessarily need to concoct your shrub before you make your cocktail: you can actually make the shrub right into your cocktail. Here's how: Replace the fruit and sugar with marmalade, and balance it out with the vinegar's acidity—combined, they'll fool your palate into thinking this instant shrub spent weeks aging in the fridge.

VISIONARIA COCKTAIL

This boozy twist on the famous Arnold Palmer iced tea-lemonade combo is truly the stuff of dreams. It combines graciously exotic jasmine tea (don't use jasmine green tea, though: that's different!) with homemade ginger syrup in a tall glass—and it's the perfect showcase for Tennessee sipping whiskey (that is, straight bourbon whiskey produced in the state of Tennessee). Fresh lemon juice and a hit of seltzer water give it a refreshing kick—and if you make your ice with jasmine tea, too, you can be sure your Visionaria won't get watered down along the way. Although its taste is sophisticated, there's nothing complicated about this cocktail; it's as easy to make as its ingredients are to find. The Visionaria is a great match for salty snacks, so it makes a very nice aperitif. Alternatively, enjoy it on its own; it's just the thing to accompany a lazy afternoon of daydreaming.

INGREDIENTS

_ ICE MADE FROM STRONGLY
BREWED JASMINE TEA

_ 2 OUNCES (60 ML) TENNESSEE
SIPPING WHISKEY

_ 1 OUNCE (30 ML) LEMON JUICE

_ 1/2 OUNCE (15 ML) GINGER
SIMPLE SYRUP (SEE PAGE 312)

_ 2 OUNCES (60 ML) STRONGLY-BREWED,
COOLED JASMINE TEA

_ 1 OUNCE (30 ML) SELTZER WATER

_ LEMON PINWHEELS DRIZZLED WITH
A LITTLE GINGER SIMPLE SYRUP

DIRECTIONS

Add the jasmine tea ice to a tall Collins-style glass, and then add the whiskey. Top the whiskey with the lemon juice, and pour the chilled Ginger Simple Syrup and cooled jasmine tea over the mixture. Finish with the seltzer water, and garnish with the syrupy lemon pinwheel. Then, just kick back and relax.

THE CLASSIC ROB ROY COCKTAIL

My grandfather was very fond of a pre-dinner Rob Roy. For him, there was no better way to stimulate the appetite and to relax before a family meal. Well, times change, but the effects of good Scotch don't, and this cocktail is as delicious as it was when it was first created in the late nineteenth century in New York City. A kissing cousin of the Manhattan—the Manhattan calls for rye whiskey, where the Rob Roy employs Scotch—this drink is named after the eighteenth-century Scottish hero Rob Roy MacGregor, and it's as noble as its namesake. Here's the time-honored recipe. It's exactly how my grandfather enjoyed them back in the day, and it'll be just as popular a hundred years from now.

INGREDIENTS

_ 3 OUNCES (90 ML) BLENDED
SCOTCH WHISKY

_ 1/2 OUNCE (15 ML) SWEET VERMOUTH

_ ANGOSTURA BITTERS

DIRECTIONS

Chill a Martini glass until frosty by filling it with ice water, and then pour the ice water out. Shake a dash or two of the Angostura bitters into the martini glass. Then, fill a cocktail mixing glass three-quarters full with ice. Add the Scotch and the sweet vermouth. Stir and strain into the pre-chilled, bitters-drizzled martini glass. Serve immediately—then get to work preparing a second round.

THE CLASP KNIFE COCKTAIL

Back in the day, a seaman would have used his clasp knife to repair the ship's rigging and cordage—which meant he'd have to climb high up onto the yardarms above the roiling sea. This strong, tart cocktail takes its name from that essential tool. And beware: like its namesake, it's got a surprisingly sharp edge. Be sure to make it with Belgian-style "sour" ale, not traditional ale. Sour ale is a beer with an acidic taste that's made by introducing various yeasts into the brewing process, unlike "regular" ale, which is brewed in a sterile environment. Its flavor is a great partner for my Ginger-Lime Shrubb, and together they balance the potency of Rhum Agricole and Pineau des Charentes (a sweet, fortified wine). Landlubbers who indulge in too many of these little firecrackers may need to be dosed with Angostura bitters the next morning to make the pain go away. So stick with just one, preferably before a hearty meal.

INGREDIENTS

_ 2 OUNCES (60 ML) PINEAU DES CHARENTES

_ 2 OUNCES (60 ML) 100-PROOF RHUM AGRICOLE

_ 2 OUNCES (60 ML) GINGER-LIME SHRUBB (SEE PAGE 82)

_ 1 OUNCE (30 ML) BELGIAN-STYLE "SOUR" ALE

_ 2 DASHES LIME BITTERS (FOR PREVENTING SCURVY, OF COURSE)

DIRECTIONS

Add the Pineau and the Rhum Agricole to a beer goblet. Add the Ginger-Lime Shrubb and mix well (you can use ice, if you like, although ice wouldn't have been available in the great age of sail). Pour the sour ale over the mixture, and finish with the lime bitters.

GINGER-LIME RUM DAIQUIRI →

Have you ever had a real daiquiri? I don't mean that syrupy, pseudo-fruity red stuff topped with rubbishy rum. The classic daiquiri, which has been around since the early twentieth century, has nothing to do with the artificially colored variety that comes in bottles or cans. I'm talking about the real thing: a trinity of handcrafted white rum, freshly squeezed lime juice, and a little simple syrup. If this doesn't sound familiar already, consider yourself introduced. But instead of starting you off with the traditional recipe, I'm going to throw you into the deep end with my twisted version of the rum daiquiri. Here, a mere ounce (30 ml) of my Ginger-Lime Shrubb adds extra tartness and pep to the rum-lime-sugar combination. The result is a straight-up, ginger-laced cocktail that's as bracing as a margarita—and as refreshing and reinvigorating on a warm day.

INGREDIENTS

_ 2 OUNCES (60 ML) RHUM AGRICOLE

_ 1 OUNCE (30 ML) GINGER-LIME
SHRUBB (SEE PAGE 82)

_ 3/4 OUNCE (20 ML) FRESHLY
SQUEEZED LIME JUICE

_ 1/2 OUNCE (15 ML) BASIC SIMPLE
SYRUP (SEE PAGE 311)

_ LIME WHEEL, FOR GARNISH

DIRECTIONS

Fill a Boston shaker three-quarters full with ice. Add all the liquid ingredients to the shaker, and shake hard for about 15 seconds. Strain into a martini glass, garnish with a lime wheel, and serve.

MR. STRAHAN'S SEVERED EAR

Named after a fictional seaman who slices off a portion of his own ear, this potent cocktail really packs a punch, thanks to un-aged tequila (a great partner for spelt whiskey) and grilled grapefruit juice, which lends it a subtle, charred flavor. A distant cousin of the tequila sunrise, Mr. Strahan's Severed Ear makes a most animating aperitif.

INGREDIENTS

_ 2 OUNCES (60 ML) CASA NOBLE JOVEN, OR OTHER YOUNG, POTENT, AND "MOONSHINE-LIKE" TEQUILA

_ 1 OUNCE (30 ML) SPELT WHISKEY

_ 2 OUNCES (60 ML) GRILLED GRAPEFRUIT JUICE (SEE PAGE 301)

_ 1 OUNCE (30 ML) SPICY SIMPLE SYRUP (TRY ROYAL ROSE'S SIMPLE SYRUP OF THREE CHILES, OR MAKE YOUR OWN: SEE PAGE 313)

_ 2 OUNCES (60 ML) GRAPEFRUIT-FLAVORED SPARKLING NATURAL MINERAL WATER

_ 3 DROPS MEXICAN MOLE BITTERS

DIRECTIONS

Fill a Boston shaker three-quarters full with ice. Add the first four ingredients to the shaker, and shake for about 15 seconds. Pour into a coupe glass, top with the sparkling water, and add the bitters. Serves two. Try not to have more than two rounds of these: If you do, the Cocktail Whisperer will not be responsible for the fate of your own ears.

I BEG YOUR PARDON, SIR?

If you haven't discovered the pleasures of beer cocktails, brace yourself, because your life is about to change: They make fabulous (and fabulously effective) aperitifs. Refreshing and full of joie de vivre, the assertive, interrogative, straight-talking I Beg Your Pardon, Sir? is just what you want pre-barbeque on a hot summer's day.

INGREDIENTS

_ 2 OUNCES (60 ML) RHUM AGRICOLE

_ 4 OUNCES (120 ML) OAK BARREL-AGED BELGIAN ALE, SUCH AS RODENBACH ALE

_ 3 DROPS THAI BITTERS

_ SPRIG OF THAI BASIL, SLAPPED

DIRECTIONS

Add the Rhum Agricole to a goblet or large Burgundy wine glass. Top with the ale, and dot the bitters over the top of the drink. Place the sprig of Thai basil in the palm of your hand and slap it with your other hand, releasing its essential oils. Float the slapped basil in the cocktail, and serve immediately.

SIDENOTE

⇒ **Rhum Agricole** is a type of handmade white rum that hails from the West Indian island of Martinique, where it was used in lots of traditional curatives, since it would've acted as a preservative for delicate herbs and spices (and might have given the patient a much-needed buzz at the end of an interminable—and possibly expensive—curative session!) But what's with the "h" in "Rhum?" Well, in rum parlay, "Rhum" signifies an appellation d'origine contrôlée (AOC), or "controlled designation of origin," which means that your bottle of Rhum has met certain standards of production, and will always be made from freshly cut sugarcane instead of the ubiquitous molasses. That said, don't worry if you can't find Rhum Agricole: use any good quality spiced rum in its place.

OLD GNAW

Sometimes, a strong drink is exactly what the doctor ordered. If that's where you're at, look no further than an Old Gnaw. Paired with freshly squeezed lemon juice and a simple syrup made with smoky chiles, it showcases hopped whiskey, which adds a beer-flavored spark to just about any cocktail. Why? Because, while all whiskeys begin life as "beer" (though you wouldn't want to drink it before it becomes whiskey, that's for sure), they're usually made sans hops. (Hops are the flowers of the hop plant, and they're used in beermaking to lend your favorite brew its distinctive bitterness and aroma.) Hopped whiskey, on the other hand, is made with hops: Hence the name, and the unmistakable beer-like flavor. With its palate-lifting citrus and spice and a pinch of tongue-tickling sea salt, the Old Gnaw is the ideal aperitif.

INGREDIENTS

_ 2 OUNCES (60 ML) HOPPED WHISKEY

_ 1/2 OUNCE (15 ML) SPICY SIMPLE SYRUP (SEE PAGE 313)

_ 1/2 OUNCE (15 ML) LEMON JUICE

_ 1 EGG WHITE

_ 1 SCANT PINCH OF SEA SALT

_ 1/4 OUNCE (7 ML) CLUB SODA

_ DASH OF GRAPEFRUIT BITTERS

DIRECTIONS

Fill a Boston shaker three-quarters full with ice. Add the whiskey, Spicy Simple Syrup, lemon juice, egg white, and sea salt. Shake hard for about 15 seconds. Strain into a coupe glass, top with the club soda, and shake a few drops of grapefruit bitters over the top to finish.

⇒ **Whiskey's frisky history.** Whiskey is fiery, soothing, and stimulating all at once. It's been treasured as a valuable curative—but it's also been seen as physically and morally toxic: During Prohibition, the nationwide American ban on the production and consumption of alcoholic beverages that was in place between 1920 and 1933, it was verboten, along with all beer, wine, and liquor. But what is whiskey, anyway?

Simply put, whiskey is a distilled beverage that begins life in the same way that beer does: as a mixture or "mash" of one or more grains, including corn, rye, barley, and wheat. Then it's aged in wooden, usually oak, barrels before it's bottled and sold. Whiskey normally clocks in at around forty percent alcohol by volume (ABV), or eighty proof, and it's made in just about every country in which grain can be grown. Ireland and Scotland are its ancestral homes: in fact, the word "whiskey" is derived from the Scots-Gaelic phrase uisge beatha, or "water of life." Over hundreds of years, uisge beatha (pronounced ISH-geh BAH-hah) eventually evolved into the word whisky (for reasons lost to the mists of time, the Scottish dropped the "e" in the word: these days, drinkers in Japan, India, and Canada also spell the word sans "e," while the Irish and American spellings still retain it).

Don't ask. Just drink it.

THE CLASSIC WHISKEY SOUR

According to legend, while the author Ernest Hemingway was living in France, he used whiskey sours as a substitute for medicine. He was a man who—to use a gross understatement—knew his liquor, and I tend to agree with him. Well, on this point, at least. Anyway, I've made whiskey sours for years now, and I used to love them with bourbon—but then I discovered that it makes much more sense to use rye in this classic drink. That's because rye whiskey's natural spiciness makes for a drier cocktail. For an alternative take on the whiskey sour, try adding a few drops of bright-red Peychaud's bitters as a final touch; they look gorgeous when dashed over the drink's snow-white foam, and they lend depth and balance to this sweet-and-sour libation. It's what cocktail hour was made for.

INGREDIENTS

_ 1 PIECE THICKLY SLICED LEMON ZEST

_ 1 EGG WHITE

_ 11/2 OUNCES (45 ML) RYE WHISKEY

_ 1 OUNCE (30 ML) BASIC SIMPLE SYRUP (SEE PAGE 311)

_ 3/4 OUNCE (22 ML) FRESHLY SQUEEZED LEMON JUICE

_ EASY HOME-CURED COCKTAIL CHERRY (SEE PAGE 311)

_ 1 CHUNK LEMON

DIRECTIONS

Rub the inside of a cocktail shaker with the lemon zest, and then add the egg white. Dry shake—that is, shake without adding ice—for about 10 seconds to create the meringue-like foam that's essential to a whiskey sour. Then fill the shaker three-quarters full with ice. Add the simple syrup, rye whiskey, and lemon juice. Shake for another 10 seconds or so. Strain the mixture into an old-fashioned glass, and garnish with the lemon chunk and an Easy Home-Cured Cocktail Cherry. Magnificent.

SHERRY PEPPER INFUSION →

On the island of Bermuda, a British protectorate that boasts a long history of shrub-making, residents preserve hot chili peppers with sherry and aromatic bitters for a table-to-glass condiment that's intensely hot and powerful. My Sherry Pepper Infusion is delicious in cool, savory cocktails like Bloody Marys (especially as a prelude to brunch), and it adds a piquant flourish to cooked fish dishes when served tableside. You can make this with a darker, older variety of sherry with a more robust mouthfeel, like oloroso or Pedro Ximénez, but it'll take several months (or even up to a year) to mature—whereas this version, made with crisp, aromatic, refreshing fino sherry, takes only a month. Word to the wise: Wear gloves when you chop insanely hot bird's eye chilies. Otherwise, their essential oils will cling to your skin, even after you wash your hands.

INGREDIENTS

_ 6 OUNCES (175 ML) FINO
  (VERY DRY) SHERRY

_ 6 OUNCES (175 ML) SHERRY VINEGAR

_ 2 TABLESPOONS (30 G)
  CHOPPED FRESH THAI BIRD'S
  EYE CHILI PEPPERS

_ 2 TEASPOONS ANGOSTURA BITTERS

DIRECTIONS

*Combine all ingredients in a sterilized bottle or jar, then cap
and store in a cool, dry place, or the refrigerator, for a month or
more before using. Then, use (sparingly!) in dishes or drinks
that are served cool, like jellied madrilène soup, or in a batch
of Bloody Marys.*

THE ROBERT BURNS COCKTAIL

Scotch whisky is an essential ingredient in the Robert Burns cocktail, a tipple that honors Scotland's most famous poet. (Some drinkers think that this classic cocktail was named after a cigar salesman of the same name, but I prefer the literary association. So there!) Every sip of the Robbie Burns is pure elegance, whether it's served straight up in a martini glass with a flamed orange zest twist, or over a crystal-clear chunk of hand-cut ice. That said, if you're a "wee tim'rous beastie," as Burns himself wrote, steer clear: This cocktail is not for the faint of heart. If you can handle it, though, it's a truly luxurious way to start an evening. Try it as an aperitif with a sweet-and-smoky hors d'oeuvre, like bacon-wrapped dates.

INGREDIENTS

_ 2 OUNCES (60 ML) SCOTCH WHISKY

_ 3/4 OUNCE (22 ML) ITALIAN VER-
MOUTH, SUCH AS CARPANO ANTICA

_ DASH OF ORANGE BITTERS

_ DASH OF ABSINTHE

_ ORANGE ZEST TWIST (OPTIONAL)

DIRECTIONS

Fill a cocktail shaker three-quarters full with ice. Pour all the ingredients over the ice. Using a long-handled bar spoon, stir gently to combine. Strain this into a martini glass. Singe the orange zest twist by holding it firmly behind a lit match and pinching it to release its natural citrus oils. (Be careful to spritz the citrus oils into the glass.) Or, pour the mixture over a large chunk of hand-cut ice in a rocks glass, serve, and lift your glass to auld Scotland.

A TWISTED NEGRONI

The Negroni has been on my mind for years. Maybe that's because it's one of the first cocktails I ever tried—and I drank it in Rome, at the top of the famous Spanish Steps. There, in the Italian sunshine, impossibly well-dressed people were sipping short, bright-red cocktails: I quickly followed suit. And it didn't take long for me to become bewitched by the vivid Negroni. Like the bitter Italian soda I just couldn't get enough of, a Negroni tastes sharp and acerbic, and it's a classic aperitif, guaranteed to lift your palate and sharpen your appetite before a great meal. My version maintains the traditional 1:1:1 ratio of Campari, vermouth, and gin—but it benefits from the last-minute addition of dark, brooding chocolate bitters. Incredibly civilized.

INGREDIENTS

_ 1 OUNCE (30 ML) CAMPARI

_ 1 OUNCE (30 ML) SWEET VERMOUTH, SUCH AS CARPANO ANTICA

_ 1 OUNCE (30 ML) LONDON DRY GIN

_ 2-3 DROPS CHOCOLATE BITTERS

DIRECTIONS

Fill a cocktail mixing glass three-quarters full with ice. Add the Campari, the vermouth, and the gin, and stir gently until combined. Strain the mixture into a rocks glass, either with or without ice. Dot with the chocolate bitters, serve, and dream of a Roman holiday.

SHALL WE TALK OF BUSINESS, MADAM?

The Madam in question is Mrs. McRankine, a venerable Scottish widow with a formidable amount of spice in her language in Robert Louis Stevenson's unfinished novel, St. Ives. Like Mrs. McRankine herself, this cocktail certainly speaks its mind. If you like classic whisky sours, you'll love this spiced-up kissing cousin of the classic drink.

INGREDIENTS

_ 2 OUNCES (60 ML) SCOTCH WHISKY

_ 2 DROPS SHERRY PEPPER INFUSION (SEE PAGE 32-33)

_ 1 OUNCE (30 ML) RAW HONEY SIMPLE SYRUP (SEE PAGE 312-313)

_ 1 OUNCE (30 ML) FRESHLY SQUEEZED LEMON JUICE

_ 2 DROPS COCKTAIL WHISPERER'S RAW HONEY AROMATIC BITTERS (SEE PAGE 311)

DIRECTIONS

Fill a Boston shaker three-quarters full with ice. Add the whisky, the Sherry Pepper Infusion, the simple syrup, and the lemon juice, and then cap and shake vigorously for 10 seconds. Strain the mixture into a rocks glass over a single cube of hand-cut ice. Drip the bitters over the top, and serve.

SIDENOTE

⇒ **Food-friendly cocktails.** Great aperitifs like the Shall We Talk Of Business, Madam? can happily be enjoyed on their own, but they make wonderful accompaniments to pre-dinner nibbles, too, since they're usually short drinks with brightly-acidic or bitter flavor profiles that rouse the appetite and slice right through savory, salty, or oily antipasti. Hungry yet? Serve just about any aperitif alongside these simple snacks:

- ○ Handfuls of sea-salted, roasted almonds
- ○ Thin slices of prosciutto, or Serrano or Parma ham
- ○ Sweet Medjool dates stuffed with bleu cheese
- ○ Salty nicoise olives
- ○ Spiced, oven-roasted Brussels sprouts

OLD SHIPS OF BATTLE

Is the classic Rob Roy one of your true loves? If so, now drink this. Old Ships of Battle is my Cocktail Whisperer's twisted take on the Scottish legend. It replaces the sweet vermouth with the old-fashioned cherry liqueur known as Cherry Heering. (First produced in the early nineteenth century, Cherry Heering is a spiced, cherry-based liqueur that isn't terribly sweet, and it's also used in drinks like the Singapore Sling. On the off chance you can't find it, try cherry brandy instead.) Then it calls for a whack of dry vermouth. Instead of plain old Angostura bitters, it kicks things up with a dash or three of strangely beguiling lemon bitters for a citrusy, aromatic finish. In a shout-out to the great British age of sail, I've named this drink Old Ships of Battle, and I think it's best enjoyed before lunch on a blustery spring day.

INGREDIENTS

_ 2 OUNCES (60 ML) BLENDED
SCOTCH WHISKY

_ 1/2 OUNCE (15 ML) CHERRY HEERING

_ 1/2 OUNCE (15 ML) DRY VERMOUTH

_ SEVERAL SHAKES OF LEMON BITTERS

_ CLUB SODA

DIRECTIONS

Fill a Collins glass with a couple hand-cut ice cubes. Add the Scotch, Cherry Heering, and the dry vermouth. Stir with a bar spoon. Add the lemon bitters, and top with club soda. Sip, and while you're at it, toast the iron-sided ships and the ironmen who sailed them.

CRAFT CURATIVES:

REVIVING, UPLIFTING LIBATIONS FROM THE APOTHECARY

◆ ◆ ◆

BEFORE THE ADVENT OF MODERN MEDICINE, HOW DID ORDINARY PEOPLE—WITH MINIMAL ACCESS TO QUALIFIED DOCTORS—HEAL WHAT AILED THEM? THE ANSWER IS SIMPLE: THEY TURNED TO THEIR LOCAL PHARMACIST, OR APOTHECARY, WHO COULD ADMINISTER HEALING POTIONS TO THEIR PATIENTS (USUALLY IN VERY SMALL, CAREFULLY-MEASURED AMOUNTS). APOTHECARIES MANUFAC-TURED TINCTURES, BITTERS, ELIXIRS, AND TONICS FOR ALL KINDS OF AILMENTS; USING PRIMITIVE INGREDIENTS, SOME OF THESE RECIPES WERE OLD AS SPOKEN HISTORY. IN MANY CASES, THESE CURATIVE, HOMEMADE POTIONS MAY HAVE BEEN LACED WITH COPIOUS AMOUNTS OF DISTILLED ALCOHOL, THEN STIRRED OR SHAKEN BEFORE BEING POURED DIRECTLY INTO A GLASS AND GIVEN TO THE PATIENT ON THE SPOT AS A PRESCRIPTIVE. THE EARLIEST KNOWN PHARMACIST-PREPARED TREATMENTS CALLED FOR FRAGILE HERBS, FLOWERS, FRUITS, AND EVEN VEGETABLES—ALONG WITH THE AFOREMENTIONED SUBSTANTIAL QUANTITIES OF ALCOHOL, WHICH PREVENTED THEM FROM ROTTING, AND PRESERVED THEIR HEALING QUALITIES. MOST OF THESE BOTANICALS WOULD HAVE BEEN GROWN RIGHT IN THE APOTHECARIES' OWN KITCHEN GARDENS, TO ENSURE FRESHNESS AND POTENCY. EACH FORMULARY WOULD HAVE BEEN CUSTOM-MADE, DEPENDING ON THE INDIVIDUAL PATIENT'S COMPLAINT, AND WAS HAND-PREPARED FROM START TO FINISH.

Asuccessful pharmacist had to earn his customers' trust, and that meant delivering curatives that would actually work. Many of the most effective curatives in the United States were introduced by immigrants from Europe, Asia, and the Caribbean islands, who brought some of their healing methods (and their exotic ingredients) with them. Folk treatments using herbs suspended in alcohol had been commonplace in all of these locations for hundreds of years, so the methods these immigrant healers practiced would have dated back centuries—if not millennia. And that includes alcoholic bitters—highly concentrated herbal concoctions that were prescribed to treat a multitude of afflictions, like malaises of the stomach and respiratory systems. Like their European counterparts, American pharmacists came to view them as reliable curatives—especially in the absence of modern pharmaceutical companies that could produce and distribute synthetic drugs.

Folks didn't just consult their local pharmacist for physical complaints, either. Before the advent of powerful, synthetic antidepressants in the mid-twentieth century, sufferers would have turned to herbal cures for relief from stormy moods. And pharmacists had a variety of remedies at their disposal. Teas made from valerian root or chamomile could relieve anxiety and irritation, and could help the patient fall into a restorative sleep that would ease peevishness. The natural oils in sage can promote a sense of calm and content, which could have taken the nervous edge off the stressed and the restless. And of course, alcohol was recommended as an antidote to glum moods, and as a way to restore flagging energy. Rest assured that very few of the apothecary's patients would've resisted a healing dose of sherry or brandy to "calm the nerves!" Using alcohol would've helped preserve the healing power of the pharmacist's botanicals, too. It truly was essential for medicinal purposes.

These days, we know to avoid overconsumption of alcohol, and we turn to qualified doctors or other medical professionals for health advice. But the spirit (no pun intended!) of these traditional curatives lives on in the cocktails in this chapter. Digestive woes troubling you? Make yourself a small-but-powerful Sazerac, which features Peychaud's bitters and absinthe—both of which were said to be great for uneasy tummies. Or, mix up a batch of Dr. Arrow's Strong Water Shrub; it's packed with nutritious beets, Asian spices, and vinegar, which promotes digestive health. If you've got a stubborn cold, treat yourself to a Hot Buttered Rum to ease those aches and pains. And if it's your mood that needs tweaking, try a Mead Refresher: it's a sparkling combination of mead (wine made from fermented honey), plus lemonade and fizzy water, and it's nothing short of good cheer in a glass.

Read on for more restorative craft cocktails inspired by days gone by! But do try to avoid overindulging—or you'll have to head back to your local apothecary for a hangover cure.

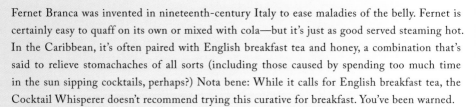

FERNET BRANCA WITH ENGLISH BREAKFAST TEA AND RAW HONEY →

Fernet Branca was invented in nineteenth-century Italy to ease maladies of the belly. Fernet is certainly easy to quaff on its own or mixed with cola—but it's just as good served steaming hot. In the Caribbean, it's often paired with English breakfast tea and honey, a combination that's said to relieve stomachaches of all sorts (including those caused by spending too much time in the sun sipping cocktails, perhaps?) Nota bene: While it calls for English breakfast tea, the Cocktail Whisperer doesn't recommend trying this curative for breakfast. You've been warned.

INGREDIENTS

_ 3 OUNCES (90 ML) FERNET BRANCA

_ POT OF STRONG ENGLISH BREAKFAST TEA (ABOUT 2 CUPS [475 ML])

_ 2 TABLESPOONS (40 G) RAW HONEY

DIRECTIONS

Preheat two mugs by filling them with boiling water; discard the water after a few seconds. Add 1 1/2 ounces (45 ml) of Fernet Branca to each mug. Fill the mugs with tea, and stir a tablespoon (20 g) of honey into each mug. Lean back, sip slowly, and let the healing begin. **Serves 2.**

DR. ARROW'S STRONG WATER SHRUB

Dr. Arrow's Strong Water Shrub transforms lemons, spices, pickled beets, sugar, and vinegar into a syrup that's fragrant, intense, and intoxicating. It's a fabulous match for clear spirits like vodka or gin. Remember, vinegar is great for the digestive system, so this savory shrub will have you healthy as a handsome goat in no time.

INGREDIENTS

_ 4-5 LEMONS, WELL WASHED AND PEELED (REMOVE AS MUCH BITTER PITH AS YOU CAN FROM THE PEELS, THEN RESERVE THEM)

_ 1 CUP (200 G) DEMERARA SUGAR

_ 1 POUND (455 G) BEETS, OVEN-ROASTED FOR AN HOUR AT 400°F (200°C, OR GAS MARK 6) IN FOIL UNTIL SOFT, COOLED, AND PEELED UNDER WATER

_ 1 TEASPOON EACH SWEET PICKLING SPICES, SUCH AS CHINESE FIVE STAR PODS, CORIANDER, CLOVES, CARDAMOM, AND/OR 1 CINNAMON STICK

_ 1 CUP (235 ML) RICE WINE VINEGAR

DIRECTIONS

Time: 2-3 weeks. *Quarter the peeled lemons, and place them in a nonreactive bowl with their peels. Add the sugar, the assorted spices, and the cooked, peeled beets. Stir well to cover the beets and lemons with the sugar. Cover tightly and let sit at room temperature for 24 hours. Mash as much pulp as you can from the lemons and beets, and then strain the liquid from the mixture. Add the vinegar to the liquid, and let sit tightly covered either in the fridge or in a cool, dark place for 2–3 weeks. Funnel your shrub to sterilized bottles, and be sure to shake them every 1–2 days.*

ULYSSES LEFT ON ITHACA COCKTAIL

Smoked American whiskey is a wonderful match for a citrus-oil-tinged tea like Earl Grey. Don't worry, I'm not suggesting you start spiking your morning pick-me-up; this delicate cocktail proves that Earl Grey isn't just for breakfast anymore. Bound together by homemade ginger simple syrup (don't forget that ginger is a well-known curative for nausea), the Ulysses is named for the Greek hero of the epic poem, The Odyssey. Reluctant to leave his homeland of Ithaca, he pretended to be insane by sowing his fields with salt instead of grain. In his honor, the final touch to the Ulysses is a pinch of sea salt, which adds an unexpected, crunchy kick. It's a delicious finish. The ingredients for this cocktail are simplicity themselves, but the sum of the parts is truly bewitching.

INGREDIENTS

_ 4 OUNCES (120 ML) FRESHLY-BREWED EARL GREY TEA, COOLED

_ 3 OUNCES (90 ML) SMOKED AMERICAN WHISKEY

_ 2 OUNCES (60 ML) SPICY GINGER SIMPLE SYRUP (SEE PAGE 313)

_ 1 OUNCE (30 ML) CLUB SODA

_ 2 PINCHES OF SEA SALT

_ 2 SPRIGS OF THYME

DIRECTIONS

Brew and cool the Earl Grey Tea. Fill a mixing glass three-quarters full with ice. Pour the whiskey, tea, and the Spicy Ginger Simple Syrup over the ice, and then stir to combine. Taste for sweetness: If it's not sweet enough, add a bit more simple syrup. Place a chunk of hand-cut ice into each of two short rocks glasses. (If you really want to bring out the gingery taste of the simple syrup, make ginger ice in advance: Freeze slices of fresh ginger root into your homemade ice.) Add the splash of club soda to each glass, and top each with a pinch of sea salt to add a welcome "crunch" to each sip. Garnish with the thyme sprigs—and get ready to pour a second round.

SAZERAC COCKTAIL

Created in New Orleans early in the twentieth century, the Sazerac Cocktail still occupies a well-deserved spot in our cabinet of healing cocktails. It calls for Peychaud's bitters, which were originally intended to heal stomach sicknesses, as well as the infamous liqueur, absinthe—also known as the Green Fairy or La Fée Verte, due to its bright-green hue. Back in the day, the wormwood in absinthe would have placed this cocktail as a curative, since it was reputed to be both an antispasmodic and a digestive aid. (Licorice-scented anisette is a good replacement for absinthe if you can't find it.) This version of the Sazerac calls for rye whiskey instead of traditional cognac, and it's a powerfully sweet, strikingly colorful, deliciously healing concoction.

INGREDIENTS

_ 1 OUNCE (25 ML) ABSINTHE
  (OR ANISETTE)

_ 2 1/2 OUNCES (75 ML) RYE WHISKEY

_ 4 TABLESPOONS (60 ML) SIMPLE
  SYRUP (SEE PAGE 311)

_ ICE CUBES

_ SEVERAL DASHES OF
  PEYCHAUD'S BITTERS

_ 2 LEMON TWISTS

DIRECTIONS

*Wash two rocks glasses with the absinthe by pouring 1/2 ounce (15 ml) absinthe into each glass, swirling it around, and pouring it out—preferably into your mouth! Divide the rye whiskey between the two glasses. Add 2 tablespoons (30 ml) of simple syrup to each glass. Pop 1 large ice cube into each cocktail, and top each with a dash or two of bitters. Garnish the drinks with lemon twists. Lift your glasses high, and drink to happier bellies. **Serves 2.***

⇒ **Absinthe-minded.** Known as the Green Fairy because of the high chlorophyll levels of the botanicals originally used in its production— and because the psychoactive substances that were also present in them could allegedly make heavy drinkers hallucinate—absinthe used to contain the leaves and blossoms of the wormwood plant, Artemisia absinthium. It's been used in traditional medicine since ancient times to ease headaches and general malaise, and to soothe stomachs made ornery from exposure to spoiled food.

And it inspired—and, in some cases, ruined—dozens of nineteenth- and early twentieth-century artists and writers. Absinthe, or la feé verte, was popular among people of all social classes in nineteenth-century France, and it became more popular still once it was mass-produced around the turn of the twentieth century. Its reputed health dangers (plus, perhaps, its bohemian associations?) caused many countries to ban it, but today, it's regarded as neither more nor less dangerous than any other type of spirit. (Of course, it's important to enjoy spirits of all types sensibly. Just sayin'!) Famous devotees of absinthe included Oscar Wilde, Charles Rimbaud, Vincent van Gogh, Ernest Dowson, and Ernest Hemingway.

DR. ARROW'S STRONG WATER ELIXIR

Wondering what to do with that batch of Dr. Arrow's that's been aging happily in your fridge? Start with a savory Strong Water Elixir. It makes an excellent aperitif, especially in the winter, when your palate needs a lift before tackling comfort foods like short ribs, garlic smashed potatoes, and root vegetables: Fresh dill, a twinkling of fleur de sel, and a lemon zest twist keep things light and fresh.

INGREDIENTS

_ 3 OUNCES (90 ML)
  GOOD-QUALITY VODKA

_ 4 OUNCES (120 ML) DR. ARROW'S
  STRONG WATER SHRUB (SEE PAGE 48)

_ 2 OUNCES (60 ML) SELTZER

_ 2-3 SHAKES LEMON BITTERS

_ LEMON ZEST TWISTS

_ 2 SPRIGS FRESH DILL

_ PINCH OF FLEUR DE SEL

DIRECTIONS

Add the vodka and the shrub to a cocktail mixing glass. Mix gently and use a Hawthorne strainer to divide the mixture between two coupe glasses. Top each glass with 1 ounce (30 ml) of seltzer, and 2–3 shakes of lemon bitters. Garnish each glass with a lemon zest and a sprig of fresh dill. Finish each drink with a pinch of fleur de sel. **Serves 2.**

SIDENOTE

⇒ **Beet benefits.** If you're looking for a reason to mix up a couple rounds of Dr. Arrow's Strong Water Elixir, chew on this: Beets are nutritional powerhouses, full of compounds that may prevent liver and cardiovascular disease—and that, as the saying goes, can't do any harm and may do some good. Plus, they're staggering sources of vitamins and minerals, like folate and manganese. (And when you're making the Strong Water Shrub, don't throw out the beet greens. Boil or sauté them, as you would with spinach: They're packed with valuable dietary fiber, calcium, and magnesium.)

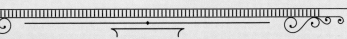

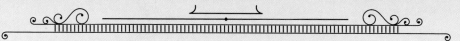

CHARTREUSE ELIXIR APPLICATION

The legendary Chartreuse Vegetal Elixir is not imported into the United States—and perhaps for good reason, since its alcohol content approaches a blistering 140 proof. (Feel free to substitute regular chartreuse for this recipe instead.) Chartreuse contains over 130 different herbs, but the recipe is guarded as if it were the Holy Grail: Produced in the French Alps by the Péres Chartreux monks, the mystical powers of the ingredients are guarded so closely that only three monks at a time are trusted with the original recipe for the Chartreuse Vegetal Elixir. Although the monks only produce a small amount of the liqueur today, Chartreuse Vegetal Elixir is sold in the same liquid form today as it was originally distilled, and is best served straight from a teaspoon or dripped onto a sugar cube to balance its bitter flavor. The Péres Chartreux monks believe that the key to their long life is facilitated through the careful—and regular—application of these potent herbal ingredients.

INGREDIENTS

- 1 TEASPOON CHARTREUSE VEGETAL ELIXIR (OR CHARTREUSE VEP—THAT IS, CHARTREUSE AGED FOR AN EXCEPTIONALLY LONG TIME)

- 1 SUGAR CUBE

- DASH OF SELTZER WATER, ABOUT 1/4 OUNCE (7 ML)

DIRECTIONS

Using a teaspoon, slowly drip the chartreuse onto a sugar cube. Place the sugar cube in your mouth, under the tongue, if desired, until dissolved. Or, place the chartreuse-soaked sugar cube into a bit of seltzer water, and muddle to a soft paste with a cocktail stick. Top with a bit more seltzer and drink quickly to good health. A spoonful of sugar really does help the medicine go down.

RYE WHISKEY SLUSHEE WITH ROASTED STRAWBERRIES

Strawberry and rhubarb is a combination that just smacks of summer. But there's no need to wait for those long July evenings to indulge in one of these slushy, R-rated cocktails: This icy drink is refreshing—and bewitching—just about any time of year, and it's a great way to begin a meal, too. Here, organic rhubarb tea liqueur, simultaneously tart and sweet, acts as a tasty counterpoint to caramelized strawberries, and rye whiskey is the boozy glue that binds them together. Like rye whiskey itself, rhubarb has a history that's as old as the United States, and then some: In the eighteenth century, American pharmacists would have recommended it as a digestive aid (as Asian herbal healers had been doing for thousands of years). Plus, rhubarb packs a hefty wallop of vitamin C, which boosts the immune system. So don't wait: Mix up a Rye Whiskey Slushee for a tantalizing taste of days gone by.

INGREDIENTS

_ 2 OUNCES (60 ML) RYE WHISKEY

_ 1 OUNCE (30 ML) ORGANIC RHUBARB TEA LIQUEUR

_ 2 TABLESPOONS (30 ML) ROASTED STRAWBERRIES AND RHUBARB (SEE PAGE 313)

_ 1 OUNCE (30 ML) BASIC SIMPLE SYRUP (SEE PAGE 311)

_ CLUB SODA

_ PINCH OF SEA SALT

_ SOFT, SLUSHY CRUSHED ICE

DIRECTIONS

Add the Roasted Strawberries to a Boston shaker. Using a muddler or the end of a wooden spoon, muddle them to release their perfume. Add the rye whiskey, rhubarb tea, and the Basic Simple Syrup. Shake for 20 seconds or so, and strain the mixture into a coupe glass filled half full with the slushy ice. Top with a splash or two of club soda, and a pinch of sea salt.

MINT JULEP CURIOSITY

This Mint Julep Curiosity is a quirky take on the classic M.J. Sure, it includes fresh mint, rye whiskey, and simple syrup—but it's also spiked with root tea liqueur, an instant orange shrub, bittersweet chocolate syrup (it works, trust me!) and mint bitters. I'm sure my Southern friends rue the day that chocolate bitters made their way into a mint julep, but—unless you're a staunch purist—fear not: this curative Curiosity is intriguing, refreshing, and delicious.

INGREDIENTS

_ 2 OUNCES (60 ML) SCOTCH WHISKY

_ 5-6 FRESH MINT LEAVES

_ 4 DROPS MINT BITTERS

_ 1/2 OUNCE (15 ML) BASIC
SIMPLE SYRUP (SEE PAGE 311)

_ 2 OUNCES (60 ML) RYE WHISKEY

_ 1/2 OUNCE (15 ML) ORGANIC
ROOT TEA LIQUEUR

_ 1/4 OUNCE (7 ML) BITTERSWEET
CHOCOLATE SYRUP

_ 1 OUNCE (30 ML) INSTANT ORANGE
SHRUB (SIMPLY COMBINE 1
TABLESPOON (15 G) ORANGE
MARMALADE WITH 1 TABLESPOON
(15 ML) CIDER VINEGAR)

_ CRUSHED ICE

DIRECTIONS

Place the mint in your grandpappy's sterling silver julep cup. Muddle the mint with 2 drops of the mint bitters, the Basic Simple Syrup, and a bit of the crushed ice. Then add the rye whiskey, the root tea liqueur, the chocolate syrup, and the orange shrub. Add more ice (and a little more rye, if you like) and mix until the julep cup is nicely frosted, inside and out. Finish with 2 more drops of the mint bitters, and then serve. Kentucky Derby optional.

SIDENOTE

⇒ **Rejuvenating juleps.** When I say "julep," what's the first thing that pops into your mind? I bet it's "mint." And with good reason, too: the all-American mint julep has quite a pedigree, and dates back at least to the eighteenth century. But juleps didn't always involve mint: In fact, the term "julep" (which stems from the Arabic word for "rosewater") referred to a curative mixture of water, sugar, and spirits that could be used as a vehicle for medicines, or for steeping herbs in. The moral of the story? A spoonful of sugar—and one of liquor—really does help the medicine go down!

MOCK MINT JULEP

Did you know that a great mint julep doesn't need to be heavy on the booze? In fact, it doesn't really need booze at all. Say hello to my Mock Mint Julep, one of the most exciting mocktails I've ever met. I've added an aromatic and addictive twist in the form of my Dr. Arrow's Strong Water Shrub.

INGREDIENTS

_ 4 LEAVES FRESH SPEARMINT

_ 2 OUNCES (60 ML) DR. ARROW'S STRONG WATER SHRUB (SEE PAGE 42)

_ 2 OUNCES (60 ML) ICED ENGLISH BREAKFAST TEA

_ 1 OUNCE (30 ML) SUGARCANE-BASED GINGER BEER

_ 1 OUNCE (30 ML) BASIC SIMPLE SYRUP (SEE PAGE 311)

_ 4 DASHES COCKTAIL WHISPERER'S RAW HONEY AROMATICS BITTERS (SEE PAGE 311)

_ CRUSHED ICE

DIRECTIONS

Place the fresh mint in a silver julep cup. Using the back of a wooden spoon, muddle the mint to release its natural oils. Add a handful of the crushed ice. Then add the Dr. Arrow's Strong Water Shrub, stir, and add another handful of ice. Now add the English breakfast tea and the ginger beer. Stir, and add a third handful of ice. Finally, add the simple syrup, and stir some more. Top with my homemade Raw Honey Aromatic Bitters. Garnish with a sprig of fresh mint and a drizzle of Dr. Arrow's Strong Water Shrub over the top for an extra burst of color and flavor.

COCKTAIL WHISPERER'S VERY TWISTED OAT WHISKEY MINT JULEP

Three mint julep recipes in row? You must think I'm joking. Not at all: Each version is unique, and each really deserves its spot in the limelight. Over the years, I've experimented with mint juleps of all sorts, and I love the dry, peppery finish that oat whiskey lends to this drink—not to mention the absinthe wash, which brings this time-honored cocktail into another dimension.

INGREDIENTS

_ 3 OUNCES (90 ML) OAT WHISKEY

_ 1 TEASPOON (5 G) RAW BROWN SUGAR (OR DEMERARA SUGAR)

_ 1/2 OUNCE (15 ML) ABSINTHE

_ CRUSHED ICE

_ FRESH MINT

_ AROMATIC BITTERS OF YOUR CHOICE

DIRECTIONS

Wash your favorite julep cup by filling it with a mixture of cold water, ice, and absinthe, and then pour it out. Add a few table-spoons of crushed ice to the cup, a few sprigs of mint, and lightly crush the mint into the ice to release its oils and perfume. Then, add half the whiskey and half the sugar. Mix gently and thoughtfully: You're connecting with the mint julep's venerable tradition, so take care while you're doing it. Add the rest of the whiskey, then a bit more crushed ice, followed by the rest of the sugar: Mix carefully with a non-metallic stirrer until the outside of the julep cup is frosted over. Step back and admire your work, and then finish with a shake or two of aromatic bitters for an extra-savory finish.

- -

SIDENOTE

⇒ **Freshly minted cocktails.** Handmade cocktails like mint juleps truly need fresh mint in order to shine. (Do *not* use dried mint or bad things will happen: marching armies, horses, cannon fire … don't go there! Mint bitters are acceptable in a pinch, however.) If you aren't growing mint in your garden, or in a pot by the windowsill, you should start—you can easily grow mint indoors, even in winter. Place your mint plant in a location where it'll get morning sun and partial afternoon shade, and keep the soil moist but not too wet. Or, at the very least, keep a package of fresh mint in your fridge in case the craving for a Twisted Oat Mint Julep strikes!

GERMAN PAVILION COCKTAIL

Smoked whiskey has an assertive flavor and aroma, like the German rauch, or smoked, beers that I enjoyed as a college student. But herbal, citrusy, Campari-like Sanbitter, an Italian soda with a bright-red hue, is more than a match for it—as is the dash of mezcal that rounds out this minimal-ist-but-mesmerizing drink. (Look for Sanbitter in specialty food shops.)

INGREDIENTS

_ 2 OUNCES (60 ML) SMOKED
AMERICAN WHISKEY

_ 1 BOTTLE OF SANBITTER SODA
(4 OUNCES, OR 120 ML)

_ 1/4 OUNCE (7 ML) MEZCAL

_ 1 THINLY SLICED LEMON
WHEEL, HALVED

DIRECTIONS

Wash a Collins glass with the mezcal, and then pour the mezcal out (into your mouth, perhaps?) Add the smoked whiskey to the washed glass, and top with a chilled bottle of Sanbitter, and garnish with a very thin half-round of lemon. It's supernaturally good.

SIDENOTE

⇒ **What's smoked whiskey?** Don't try to stick a lit match into your whiskey bottle: Smoked whiskey is distilled from grains that have been pre-smoked, sometimes using a combination of fuels such as wood and peat. Like the strikingly smoky suds for which the German Pavilion cocktail is named, some alternative-grain whiskeys have such emphatic flavors that enjoying them takes some practice, but don't give up right away. Try a couple different cocktails featuring smoked whiskey—or try tempering it with a little plain water or tonic water.

NECTARINE, CELERY, AND BLACK PEPPER SHRUB

Does the idea of a celery-flavored drink make you wince? Keep calm: It's good for you. Celery seed has been used as a pain reliever for thousands of years, and may even help lower blood pressure. Plus, celery-flavored soft drinks have been on the market since the late nineteenth century, so a precedent has definitely been set for this delicious shrub. (That said, celery allergies are no joke, and can be potentially life threatening, so if you happen to have a celery allergy or sensitivity, skip this one.) Nectarine and celery juices are brightened with fresh lime juice and sweetened with simple syrup, then combined with a dose of white balsamic: And in two weeks, you'll have a bracing tonic that's also highly refreshing when used—judiciously—in all sorts of cocktails.

INGREDIENTS

_ 1 POUND (455 G) NECTARINES, PEELED, STONES REMOVED

_ 1/2 CUP (120 ML) FRESHLY PRESSED CELERY JUICE

_ 1 CUP (200 G) DEMERARA SUGAR

_ 3 OUNCES (90 ML) YELLOW CHARTREUSE

_ 1/2 TEASPOON BLACK PEPPERCORNS

_ 4 LIMES, PEELED AND QUARTERED (BE SURE TO REMOVE ALL THE BITTER WHITE PITH)

_ PINCH OF FLEUR DE SEL

_ 1/2 CUP (120 ML) WHITE BALSAMIC VINEGAR

_ 1/2 CUP (120 ML) WHITE WINE VINEGAR

DIRECTIONS

Time: 2 weeks. *Combine the nectarines with the celery juice, Demerara sugar, yellow chartreuse, peppercorns, lime quarters, and the fleur de sel in a nonreactive bowl. Cover and let sit at room temperature for 24 hours. Place a strainer over a second nonreactive bowl, and transfer the mixture to the strainer, extracting as much liquid from the nectarines as possible by mashing with a wooden spoon. Discard the nectarines and lime segments or cook into a pot roast. (You may want to strain the liquid through two pieces of cheesecloth to remove all the peppercorns: That'll prevent them from getting caught in your teeth later on.) Add both the vinegars and stir. Let the mixture sit for a few hours, and then funnel into sterilized bottles or Mason jars. Store in the fridge and shake daily to help the flavors mellow and combine. After 2 weeks your shrub will be ready to use. Store in the fridge for about 6 months: If it becomes foamy, discard immediately.*

CAPTAIN JOHN SILVER'S CELERY-NECTARINE FIZZ

In Robert Louis Stevenson's *Treasure Island*, Captain Silver's men were about to attack and loot a mercantile ship when Silver called to them, "I'm only interested in the wine and the pickles." I couldn't agree more: Who needs hordes of gold and silver bullion when you've got wine and pickles? There's no wine involved in this Celery-Nectarine Fizz, but there sure are pickles—plus 100-proof hand-crafted white rum, yellow chartreuse and lemon bitters. Finishing touches of *fleur de sel* and seltzer water make for a memorable cocktail that's sure to revive tired palates.

INGREDIENTS

_ 1/2 OUNCE (15 ML) YELLOW CHARTREUSE

_ 2 OUNCES (60 ML) 100-PROOF RHUM AGRICOLE BLANC (OR ANY GOOD 100-PROOF WHITE RUM)

_ 2 OUNCES (60 ML) NECTARINE, CELERY, AND BLACK PEPPER SHRUB (SEE PAGE 58)

_ 1 OUNCE (30 ML) SELTZER WATER

_ PINCH OF FLEUR DE SEL

_ 3 DROPS LEMON BITTERS

_ SEVERAL SHARDS OF CAPTAIN JOHN SILVER'S QUICK CELERY PICKLE (SEE PAGE 311)

_ CRUSHED ICE

DIRECTIONS

Fill a coupe glass with water, crushed ice, and the aromatic yellow chartreuse. When the glass is chilled, pour out the chartreuse and water mixture (down your throat, ideally: No need to waste good liquor!) Add the rum to the glass, and pour the shrub over it. Top with the seltzer and a pinch of fleur de sel: then add the bitters, garnish with the celery pickle, sip, and lift your glass to the Captain.

HOT BUTTERED RUM: THE SAILOR'S CURE-ALL →

Ships' doctors of yesteryear may have delivered doses of this classic hot buttered rum to sailors in order to relieve aching bones and flagging spirits. Four magic ingredients—hot tea, sugar, butter, and rum—connect every sailor who's ever had to head face-first into a full gale while out at sea. Today, this curative is a treat that goes down smoothly after a long day of skiing, hiking, or just sitting by the fire.

INGREDIENTS

_ HOT BLACK TEA

_ 6 OUNCES (175 ML) RUM

_ DARK BROWN SUGAR

_ 2 TEASPOONS BUTTER
   (ABOUT 2 ACORN-SIZED LUMPS)

_ FRESHLY GRATED NUTMEG

DIRECTIONS

Prepare a pot of strong black tea. While the tea is steeping, preheat mugs by filling them with boiling water; discard the water after a few seconds. Add 3 ounces (90 ml) of rum to each mug. Fill each mug with tea and mix gently. Sweeten to taste with dark brown sugar. Add a walnut-sized lump of butter to each mug, and dust each drink with fresh nutmeg. Anchors aweigh!
Serves 2.

POMPIER COCKTAIL

Vermouth served chilled over ice is another famous warm-weather refresher. Vermouth comes in two forms: sweet or dry, and each is delicious when served on its own over ice or with the addition of other liquors such as rye whiskey or Scotch. Historically, pharmacists may have prescribed vermouth as a remedy for afflictions that were exacerbated by hot weather, including intestinal disorders and gout. Created by my fellow cocktail scribe, Gary Regan, this cocktail was based on the Pompier Highball that's detailed in the fabulous *Gentleman's Companion: An Exotic Drinking Book* by Charles Baker, Jr., published in 1946. It features a dash of vitamin-laden citrus, and a tot of gin to make the medicine go down, as they say, "with a grin of sin on your face." It's fairly low in alcohol, so add a bit more gin to it, if you like, but avoid using more than one ounce (25 ml), since it's really the herbs in the vermouth that make this drink a healing treat.

INGREDIENTS

_ 2.5 OUNCES (75 ML) DRY VERMOUTH

_ 1/2 OUNCE (15 ML) GIN

_ 1/4 OUNCE (7 ML) CRÈME DE CASSIS

_ LEMON TWIST

DIRECTIONS

Fill a Boston shaker three-quarters full with ice. Add the liquid ingredients one at a time, stir gently, and strain into a chilled cocktail glass. Garnish with the lemon twist. Take one each time the temperature hits ninety!

iii

"READING THE PAPER" →

There's nothing better for the constitution than a little R&R, so curl up in your favorite easy chair with the Sunday paper or a great book--then kick back and relax with this Drambuie and mezcal-laced cocktail by your side.

INGREDIENTS

_ 1 OUNCE (30 ML) DRAMBUIE

_ 2 OUNCES (60 ML) MEZCAL

_ 1 OUNCE (30 ML) BROILED GRAPEFRUIT JUICE (SPRINKLE HALF A GRAPEFRUIT WITH A TEASPOON OF DEMERARA SUGAR AND BROIL UNTIL BUBBLY—THEN COOL AND JUICE)

_ 1 OUNCE (30 ML) BROILED ORANGE JUICE (SPRINKLE HALF AN ORANGE WITH A TEASPOON OF DEMERARA SUGAR AND BROIL UNTIL BUBBLY—THEN COOL AND JUICE)

_ 2 DROPS BLACK WALNUT BITTERS

_ 2 DROPS PLUM BITTERS

DIRECTIONS

Fill a Boston shaker three-quarters full with ice. Add all the ingredients except the bitters: cover, shake, and pour into an 8 ounce (235-ml) old-fashioned glass over a cube of hand-cut ice. Dot with two drops each of black walnut and plum bitters. Serve alongside a sigh of satisfaction.

- -

SIDENOTE

⇒ **Broil, then squeeze.** Fresh citrus juices pop up in lots of cocktails—and with good reason, because they're super-versatile (and because their tart acidity is a good match for all sorts of spirits). You can use them to make shrubs; you can add them directly to your drinks; and you can use citrus rinds as judicious garnishes. But have you ever tried broiling your citrus fruit before juicing it? If not, it's time to start: Broiling the fruit, as in "Reading the Paper," lends it a toasty, caramelized finish.

LEMONADE AND BEET JUICE "SHRUB"

The Lower East Side of New York City has long been a creative center when it comes to liquid refreshments, and my instant Lemonade and Beet Juice "Shrub" takes its inspiration from a shrub made at Russ and Daughters' Lower East Side delicatessen. Early twentieth-century Eastern European immigrants would have added sweet pickled-beet juice, apple cider vinegar,

iiiiiiiiiiiiiiiiiiiiiiiiiiiiiiiiiiiiiiiiiiiiiiiiiiiiiiiiiiiiiiiiiiiiiiiiiiiiiiiiiiiiiii

spices, sugar, and vegetables to tart, homemade lemonade for a healthy, revitalizing quaff. It's an aesthetic treat, too: The beet juice gives the lip-smacking lemonade a bright-red stain. It's darned good, and best of all, it's packed with vitamins. My version is booze-free, but if you need a little hair of the dog, add 2 ounces (60 ml) of good-quality vodka. Serve this faux "shrub" with fresh bagels, lox, and cream cheese for brunch.

INGREDIENTS

_ 1 OUNCE (30 ML) JUICE FROM
  SWEET PICKLED BEETS (AVAILABLE
  AT A KOSHER DELI)

_ 2 OUNCES (60 ML) BASIC SIMPLE
  SYRUP (SEE PAGE 311)

_ 8 OUNCES (235 ML) FRESHLY MADE
  HOMEMADE LEMONADE (SEE PAGE 312)

_ 3 DROPS CELERY BITTERS

_ PINCH OF SEA SALT

DIRECTIONS

Fill a Collins glass with crushed ice. Add the beet juice and the simple syrup, and then top with the lemonade and stir. Top with a pinch of sea salt and a couple drops of the celery bitters to finish. A sure cure for whatever ails you!

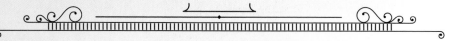

MEAD REFRESHER

Do your spirits need a bit of a lift? We've all been there. Make yourself a Mead Refresher. This bubbly cocktail combines sweet mead with tart, refreshing lemonade, a splash of fizzy water, and a dash of remedial bitters into a prescriptive that's sure to cheer and heal at the same time.

INGREDIENTS

_ 6 OUNCES (175 ML) MEAD

_ 6 OUNCES (175 ML) FRESH LEMONADE

_ 4 DASHES OF AROMATIC BITTERS
   (ANY KIND: IT'S UP TO YOU)

_ 4 OUNCES (120 ML) SELTZER WATER

DIRECTIONS

Combine the mead, lemonade and bitters ingredients in a mixing glass or pitcher. Stir to combine, and pour into four short glasses. Top each glass with about 1 ounce (25 ml) of seltzer water. Serves four, so it won't be long before you and three friends feel like the proverbial bee's knees.

SIDENOTE

⇒ **Honey for health.** Everyone knows that royal jelly, which is produced by worker bees and fed to their hive-mates, is an important curative in health preparations. But raw—that is, unprocessed —honey is also deeply curative, and what's more, the distillation of spirits using raw honey is an ancient, well-regarded technique. Honey has been used medicinally at least since ancient Egyptian civilization, and beverages produced from honey, such as mead, have been enjoyed since time immemorial. "Mead is good," wrote the nineteenth-century German herbalist, Sebastian Kneipp, because it "increases the hunger, stimulates digestion, purifies and strengthens the stomach, and frees the body of bad substances." He wasn't wrong: Raw honey may possess antibacterial qualities, and is said to promote weight loss, reduce cholesterol, and relieve symptoms of intestinal disorders.

GRILLED TANGERINE SHRUB

It really doesn't take long to bring out the best in hardy, versatile tangerines. I like to grill my tangerines first to add a bit of char to their bright acidity. Then I coat them in simply syrup before combining them with yuzu vinegar, that Japanese kitchen staple—and a day later they're ready for use in cocktails

INGREDIENTS

_ 10 SMALL TANGERINES, PEELED AND HALVED, AND SEARED IN A CAST-IRON PAN, THEN COOLED, SEGMENTED AND CHOPPED (RESERVE THE PEELS, REMOVE AS MUCH WHITE PITH AS POSSIBLE, AND SLICE INTO THIN STRIPS)

_ 1 CUP (235 ML) DEMERARA SIMPLE SYRUP (SEE PAGE 311)

_ 2-4 CUPS (475-940 ML) YUZU VINEGAR

DIRECTIONS

Time: 48 hours. *Combine the chopped tangerine segments and the sliced tangerine peels with the Demerara Simple Syrup in a nonreactive bowl, and stir to combine. Cover the bowl tightly and let the mixture sit for 24 hours, stirring several times to encourage fermentation and flavor development. Then add enough yuzu vinegar to cover the fruit mixture, and let it steep for another 24 hours. Finally, muddle the mixture a bit with a wooden spoon to release as much juice as possible from the tangerine segments, and strain the shrub into sterilized bottles or jars. Use immediately—or, if you have time, age in the fridge for a month. It's wonderful with rum, vodka, and whiskey cocktails.*

JUST DOWN THE WAY FROM PARIS, TEXAS →

What I'm about to tell you will change your life. Here it comes: bitters are marvelous in beer. And the Just Down The Way From Paris, Texas is living proof. There's nothing complicated about it, but it does feature a couple of clever twists. The first is a little absinthe; the second, a portion of my Grilled Tangerine Shrub. When you combine the two with a good lager and a few drops of my homemade bitters, you get a cocktail that's guaranteed to quench your thirst, even in the face of desert-level temperatures.

INGREDIENTS

_ 8 OUNCES (235 ML) LAGER BEER

_ 1/2 OUNCE (15 ML) TENNEYSON ABSINTHE ROYALE (FRANCE)

_ 2 OUNCES (60 ML) GRILLED TANGERINE SHRUB (SEE ABOVE)

_ 4 DROPS COCKTAIL WHISPERER'S RAW HONEY AROMATIC BITTERS (SEE PAGE 311)

_ THYME LEAVES, FOR GARNISH

DIRECTIONS

Add the Grilled Tangerine Shrub to a beer glass. Top with the beer and mix with a swizzle stick (I use a Belgian triple-style ale with a bit more alcohol). Pour the Absinthe over the top. Finish with 4 drops of the homemade cocktail bitters for good health and a garnish with a few leaves of fresh thyme.

TWENTY-CUBIC-FEET OF SAIL

As the old song goes, there's nothing like a fresh'ning breeze. Well, there's no doubt about it: This bracing cocktail is sure to put wind in your sails. It matches dry, spicy rye whiskey with an organic ginger liqueur that's reminiscent of old-fashioned gingerbread—the kind made with plenty of fresh ginger, and lashings of blackstrap molasses. (Use a good organic ginger liqueur; you won't want to adulterate this cocktail with anything sugary and sickly-sweet.) Then a dose of fresh lemon juice supplies a citrusy edge, while seltzer and bitters give the whole shebang a fizzy lift. I think it's a great way to boost a flagging appetite, so try serving a round of Twenty-Cubic-Feet of Sail alongside *hors d'oeuvres* to get your next dinner party off to a rousing start. Anchors aweigh!

INGREDIENTS

_ 2 OUNCES (60 ML) RYE WHISKEY

_ 1/2 OUNCE (15 ML) ORGANIC
  GINGER LIQUEUR

_ 1/2 OUNCE (15 ML) FRESHLY
  SQUEEZED LEMON JUICE

_ 4 OUNCES (120 ML) SELTZER

_ AROMATIC BITTERS

DIRECTIONS

Add a couple hand-cut ice cubes to a Collins glass. Pour the rye whiskey over the ice, and then add the ginger liqueur, followed by the lemon juice. Stir gently with a cocktail spoon to combine. Top with the seltzer, and finish with a dash or two of the aromatic bitters. Serve with a straw.

DOWN EAST MOCKTAIL

Fresh berries—like my favorite variety, the Maine Wild Blueberry—boast a lip-smacking acidity that's just dazzling in alcohol-free libations. With its touch of balsamic vinegar, grilled orange juice, and lush Blueberry Simple Syrup, my Down East Mocktail involves making an instant-shrub-of-sorts right in your cocktail glass—then topping the mixture up with a celebratory sparkle of seltzer water. This zesty, colorful mocktail is just the thing to whip up if you're planning, say, a festive weekend brunch, a relaxed birthday lunch, or an early-afternoon engagement party. Sometimes you just don't feel like downing mimosas or Bloody Marys before noon, so opt for a Down East instead: It's got all the jubilance of a champagne-based cocktail minus the (not-so-jubilant) aftereffects.

INGREDIENTS

_ 1 OUNCE (30 ML) BLUEBERRY
SIMPLE SYRUP (SEE PAGE 311)

_ 1 TEASPOON BALSAMIC VINEGAR

_ 1 OUNCE (30 ML) GRILLED ORANGE
JUICE (SLICE ORANGES INTO
1/2-INCH ROUNDS: GRILL LIGHTLY
OVER CHARCOAL OR ON A GRILL PAN
UNTIL GENTLY COLORED, THEN JUICE)

_ SELTZER WATER

_ 1/2 INCH (1.3 CM) GRILLED
ORANGE ROUND, FOR GARNISH

_ AROMATIC BITTERS

DIRECTIONS

Combine the simple syrup, vinegar, and orange juice in a champagne flute, then top with enough seltzer to fill the glass. Garnish with a round of grilled orange, and dot with the bitters.

TENNESSEE LAMENTATION

The Jack-and-ginger combination is much maligned. While it has all the stuffing for a flavor-driven experience that's redolent of spice and smoke, it's often ruined, unfortunately, by the use of super-sweet, cloying, corn syrup–based ginger ale instead of spicy, heady ginger beer. It's time to draw the Jack-and-ginger into the twenty-first century, via the olden days of ships and sails. How? Implement a spicy, homemade ginger simple syrup that's made with a dash of cayenne pepper and chunks of fresh ginger. That's when the J-and-G metamorphoses into something ethereal, sophisticated—and exceptionally perilous. This recipe replaces sugary, mass-produced ginger ale with a homemade ginger beer of sorts—a radical step that turns the Tennessee Lamentation into an all-out celebration.

INGREDIENTS

- 2 OUNCES (60 ML) TENNESSEE SIPPING WHISKEY

- 1/2 OUNCE (15 ML) SPICY GINGER HONEY SIMPLE SYRUP (SEE PAGE 313)

- 2 OUNCES (60 ML) FRESH SELTZER WATER

- 1 DASH LEMON BITTERS

- 1 EASY HOME-CURED COCKTAIL CHERRY (SEE PAGE 311)

DIRECTIONS

Fill a cocktail shaker three-quarters full with ice. Add the Spicy Ginger Simple Syrup and the Tennessee sipping whiskey, and shake like crazy for about ten seconds. Strain the mixture over a single two-inch (5 cm) cube of ice (remember, hand-cut ice is best) in an old-fashioned glass. Top with the seltzer water, and add the dash of lemon bitters. Garnish with an Easy Home-Cured Cocktail Cherry. Makes a fabulous aperitif.

OTHER ASSORTED TALES OF WOE

You've probably enjoyed a Dark and Stormy cocktail at some point in your drinking life. It's usually made with a popular, brand name black rum from Bermuda and a very recognizable Bermudan ginger beer, and it has a sweet and sassy personality. You might be familiar with Dark and Stormy weather, but I bet you've never immersed yourself in assorted tales of woe. This variation on the D-and-S theme replaces the black rum with rye whiskey, and mixes it with spicy, cane sugar–based ginger beer, plus a shot of thickly sweet, Cuban-style espresso coffee. It's a great pick-me-up for those fuzzy-headed days when you can't decide whether to have a cocktail or a coffee. Now, you can mix business with pleasure and have them both at once. And I guarantee the tales of woe will change the way you think about rye whiskey—for the better, of course.

INGREDIENTS

_ 4 OUNCES (120 ML) RYE WHISKEY

_ 1 OUNCE (30 ML) FRESHLY
SQUEEZED LIME JUICE

_ 1 OUNCE (30 ML) FRESHLY
SQUEEZED LEMON JUICE

_ 2 OUNCES (60 ML) SWEETENED,
CUBAN-STYLE ESPRESSO, COOLED:
COMBINE 1 OUNCE (30 ML) OF
ESPRESSO WITH 1 OUNCE (30 ML)
BASIC SIMPLE SYRUP (SEE PAGE 311)

_ 4 OUNCES (120 ML) CANE
SUGAR-BASED GINGER BEER

_ 2 TO 3 DROPS BLACK WALNUT BITTERS

DIRECTIONS

Add all the liquid ingredients except the ginger beer and bitters to a tall mixing glass with a few hand-cut cubes of ice. Stir to chill and combine. Then, place a cube or two of hand-cut ice into each of two Collins glasses. Strain the mixture over the ice, and drip the black walnut bitters over the top of each drink. Add two tall straws, and you're done. Serves 2 woeful drinkers. Plan accordingly.

BILL MONROE'S KENTUCKY COOLER

No one who's a fan of bluegrass music needs to be educated upon the merits of the late, great Bill Monroe, the Kentucky mandolinist who helped establish bluegrass as a genre. I can only imagine the various kinds of liquor that may—or may not—have been served in the early days of Monroe's career as a performer. After all, he was active in the years just before Prohibition ended, and I'm sure folks didn't always stick to sweet iced tea or milk while listening to his music! As tart and sweet as bluegrass itself, this cocktail balances white whiskey with lush peach and apricot nectars, plus a dose of iced tea and a dash of bitters. Of course, it's just the thing for sipping on a long summer's evening—but truth be told, it's wonderful any time of the year.

INGREDIENTS

_ 1 OUNCE (30 ML) PEACH NECTAR

_ 1 OUNCE (30 ML) APRICOT NECTAR

_ 1/2 OUNCE (15 ML) LEMON JUICE

_ 2 OUNCES (60 ML) SWEET ICED TEA

_ 2 OUNCES (60 ML) WHITE WHISKEY

_ 2 TO 3 SHAKES ANGOSTURA BITTERS

DIRECTIONS

Fill a mixing glass three-quarters full with ice. Add the fruit juices and the sweet iced tea, and then the white whiskey. Mix gently and carefully. Place a few hand-cut ice cubes into a Collins glass, and pour the mixture over the ice. Top with a few drops of bitters, and serve with a colorful straw!

SIDENOTE

⇒ **What's white whiskey?** Otherwise known as White Dog or moonshine, white whiskey is un-aged whiskey. Historically, white whiskey has had a reputation for being rough. (Or, perhaps, ruff! Get it? White Dog? Ruff? Ahem, sorry.) It's been thought of as a rough-and-ready kind of drink, likely to be served in a pail, still hot, drained off a backwoods still just a few minutes prior to consumption. And, of course, it's been rumored to be ridiculously, unbelievably, mythologically intoxicating. Indeed, true "White Dog" was practically pure ethyl alcohol, exceeding 180 proof (that's a staggering ninety percent ABV). Obviously, no liquor like the White Dog of days gone by is sold legally today. Thus, modern-day liquor producers have created new versions of the White Dog mystique: Some of them even pretty up their "moonshine" with candied fruits such as cherries or peaches, or suggest combining White Dog with soda to make it palatable. These products are not on my menu, and you won't find them in this book. That's not to say that there aren't good white whiskeys on the market—there are, and they bear no resemblance to the awful stuff called moonshine. Try Tuthilltown Spirits's Hudson New York Corn Whiskey, which is distilled from 100 percent New York corn.

NIX BESSER COCKTAIL

Nix besser means "none better" in Amish, and this cocktail lives up to its name. On a sweltering Saturday afternoon in August, there's little else that can refresh and rejuvenate quite like the Nix Besser. Here, fresh, roasted peaches partner with the summery flavors of chiles, simple syrup, and Thai basil—and they make a run for bibulous infamy when combined with rye whiskey and freshly squeezed-citrus juices. Apothecaries might have recommended this cocktail because it is said to help heal a number of maladies, including heatstroke—plus, the peach has been used in traditional Chinese medicine for centuries to improve circulation and to relieve the symptoms of allergies. Purely from a gourmand's POV, this body- and spirit-cooling preparation is also delicious as an aperitif before a leisurely meal on a summer evening.

INGREDIENTS

_ 2 TABLESPOONS (30 ML) OF ROASTED PEACHES (SLICE ABOUT A POUND (455 G) OF FRESH PEACHES INTO CHUNKS, THEN ROAST FOR ABOUT 25 MINUTES AT 400°F (200°C), OR UNTIL CARAMELIZED AND SOFT. SET ASIDE TO COOL. PUREE IN A FOOD PROCESSOR UNTIL THEY BECOME A SOFT PULP)

_ 4 OUNCES (120 ML) RYE WHISKEY

_ 3 OUNCES (90 ML) SPICED RUM

_ 4 TABLESPOONS ROYAL ROSE SIMPLE SYRUP WITH CHILIES

_ 3 OUNCES (90 ML) FRESHLY SQUEEZED LIME JUICE

_ 3 OUNCES (90 ML) FRESHLY SQUEEZED ORANGE JUICE

_ SEVERAL THAI BASIL LEAVES, SLICED

_ 2 TABLESPOONS (30 ML) AROMATIC BITTERS

_ ICE CUBES

DIRECTIONS

Put all of the ingredients except the bitters and ice cubes into a tall mixing glass. Stir gently—but whatever you do, don't shake! Add the bitters to the mixture. Put four ice cubes into two Collins glasses. Divide the mixture between the two glasses, and you'll see how this cocktail got its name: There really is nothing better for keeping the heat at bay.

CH. 3 NO.

HOT WEATHER HEALERS:

CHILLED OUT COCKTAILS TO CLEANSE AND REFRESH

• • •

WHO DOESN'T LOVE SUMMER? SUNNY DAYS SPENT AT THE BEACH, SURROUNDED BY THE SCENTS OF SALTWATER, HOT SAND, AND SUNSCREEN; FOURTH OF JULY PICNICS, COMPLETE WITH SPARKLERS, S'MORES, AND POTATO SALAD; BARBEQUES THAT STRETCH LATE INTO THE EVENING. BUT WHEN THE TEMPERATURE—AND THE HUMIDITY—SKYROCKETS, IT'S TRULY TOUGH TO BEAT THE HEAT. THAT'S WHEN WE ALL SCURRY INDOORS, CRANK UP THE AC, AND RAID THE FRIDGE IN SEARCH OF COLD DRINKS.

Sure, you want to cool down, and fast—but don't reach for a beer or a sugary soda. Try a craft cocktail instead. As the pharmacists and apothecaries of yore would have known, there are plenty of handmade preparations that can help cool down sweaty bodies from the inside out. These curatives had to heal as well as refresh, so they'd have been made with herbs, spices, citrus fruits, and even fresh, garden-grown vegetables. (Traditionally, pharmacists would have used alcohol as a preservative to protect delicate herbs and spices from sweltering heat and spoilage.) We all know that it's important to drink plenty of plain water year-round in order to stay healthy (especially when you're drinking alcohol), but there are other ways to get your H20: the fresh citrus juices used in hot-weather cocktails, such as orange, lemon, lime, and pineapple, also offer a hit of hydration in addition to a dose of vitamin C. And drinks that call for fizzy water, such as club soda or seltzer, help you feel cooler a bit quicker thanks to those refreshing little bubbles, and they can help pep up flagging appetites, too.

Using exotic spices and flavorful ingredients such as hot chiles in cocktails can help bring down body temperature and aid healing. When we eat spicy foods such as chiles, we tend to sweat, which creates moisture on the surface of the skin. When the wind blows across damp skin, you feel cooler immediately. That's why the Roasted Tomato and Chile Bloody Mary on page 96, enjoyed in the warmth of the sun, is so effective against overheating (not to mention hangovers). And anise, a key ingredient in anisette, one of the key ingredients in the Orange Zest Oasis on page 80, is renowned as a relaxant for both body and mind, and as a cure for all manner of digestive disorders. It's no accident that it's often enjoyed before or after meals: it soothes the belly and calms the brain. Fresh coconut water, which takes center stage in the Coconut Cooler on page 87, carries precious potassium, which is a valuable electrolyte that's depleted through sweating. (Maybe that's why the pina colada is such a popular beach-side tipple!)

But cooling cocktails aren't necessarily all about exotic flavors. Fruits and vegetables from your own garden pack powerful healing properties, too. Use your harvest to make a batch of the English Pea and Mint Shrub on page 94, then combine it with Rhum Agricole, lime juice, bitters, and a dash of appetite-boosting nutmeg it in a Last-Minute Rumpus. Or, if you've got rhubarb—also known as "pie plant"—in your garden, put it to good use in your cocktails. Old-time pharmacists certainly would have, since rhubarb has been used in healing for centuries. And it's delicious in cool drinks like the Rhubarb Fizz with Charred Strawberries on page 84–85. If you'd rather skip the booze altogether, go ahead: try my Tiki Mocktail on page 88–89, or Mr. Rankeillor's Door—a simple concoction of my Cucumber-Basil Shrub plus a little soda water, bitters, and sea salt—on page 113. Never fear: these mocktails are so flavorful that you won't miss the booze, not even a little bit.

Don't let the dog days of summer get you down! Embrace the heat with these rejuvenating craft cocktails.

ORANGE ZEST OASIS

Pharmacists of old might have treated hot, parched bodies with anise, which is said to be both calming and cooling to the overheated constitution, plus other herbs and spices—and, of course, the whole lot would have been preserved in a hefty dose of high-proof alcohol. This sweet-and-bitter cocktail takes its inspiration from just such a combination: Here, muddled oranges bathed in dry sake offset the fragrant anisette.

INGREDIENTS

_ 2 ORANGE SLICES, CUT INTO QUARTERS

_ 1/2 TABLESPOON (7 ML) ROOT TEA SYRUP (SEE PAGE 313)

_ 1/4 OUNCE (7 ML) ANISETTE

_ 3 OUNCES (90 ML) DRY SAKE

_ 4 DROPS THAI BITTERS

_ 1 EGG WHITE

_ ORANGE ZEST TWIST

DIRECTIONS

Put the orange slices in the bottom of a Boston shaker, and muddle with a cocktail stick or the long end of a wooden spoon. Then add the remaining ingredients, one at a time. Shake them well for thirty seconds. Strain the frothy mixture into a coupé glass. Garnish with a flamed orange zest twist (pinch the zest firmly and hold it behind a lit match to release the citrusy oils). It's the perfect way to beat the heat.

THE RUNAWAY MOUNTAIN TRAIN →

If you're like me, the mere mention of muddled blueberries makes your mouth water: think plucking sun-warmed wild blueberries straight from the bush and popping them straight into your mouth; think freshly baked blueberry pie topped with vanilla ice cream. Sigh. This cocktail mixes those summertime pleasures with smoky millet whiskey and a fragrant hit of maple syrup for a lightly fizzy drink that's delicious any time of year (although it's best made with wild blueberries, if you can get them!) As in life, so in the art of mixology: You need the salt and the bitters to balance the cocktail's luscious sweetness.

INGREDIENTS

_ 1/4 CUP (35 G) BLUEBERRIES (PREFERABLY WILD MAINE BLUEBERRIES)

_ 3 OUNCES (90 ML) MILLET WHISKEY

_ 1 TEASPOON (5 ML) MAPLE SYRUP

_ HAND-CUT ICE

_ 2 OUNCES (60 ML) CLUB SODA

_ PINCH OF SEA SALT

_ DASH OF CITRUS BITTERS

DIRECTIONS

Muddle the blueberries in a Boston shaker. Add the millet whiskey and the maple syrup. Fill the shaker three-quarters full with ice. Cap and shake for about 15 seconds. Place one cube of hand-cut ice into each of two rocks glasses, and then split the contents of the shaker between the two glasses. Top each with a splash of club soda; add a pinch of sea salt to each; and then finish with a few drops of citrus bitters. Serves 2 parched passengers.

GINGER-LIME SHRUB

It's likely that a version of this luscious shrub would have been served aboard sailing ships in days of yore, so that thirsty sailors could escape scurvy. Fragile citrus fruit wouldn't have lasted long, but luckily, the apple cider vinegar in this recipe acts as a powerful preservative. These days, a Ginger-Lime Shrub is a flavorful addition to dozens of thirst-quenching cocktails—especially ones involving rum. Hard to starboard, lads!

INGREDIENTS

_ PEELED ZEST OF 4 WELL-WASHED
LIMES (DISCARD THE PITH:
IT'S VERY BITTER)

_ 4 LIMES (RESERVE THE ONES
FROM THE ZEST), QUARTERED

_ 1 CUP (200 G) DEMERARA SUGAR

_ 6 TABLESPOONS (48 G) FRESHLY
GRATED GINGER ROOT

_ 1–2 CUPS (235–475 ML) APPLE
CIDER VINEGAR (DEPENDING ON
THE HEIGHT OF THE INGREDIENTS
WHEN PLACED IN A BOWL)

DIRECTIONS

Time: 3–4 weeks. *In a nonreactive bowl, combine the sugar, lime peels, lime chunks, and the ginger. Stir to combine and coat all the fruit with sugar. Cover and leave at room temperature at least overnight or for 1–2 days. (Slow, cool fermentation gives a shrub its trademark bite.) Now prepare your shrub for aging. Set a strainer over another nonreactive bowl and pour the lime and ginger chunks into the strainer. Use a stout wooden spoon to extract as much juice as possible from the limes and the softened ginger chunks. Let the mixture sit for a few more hours. Stir again, and discard the fruit chunks. Stir in the vinegar, and then use a funnel to transfer the shrub syrup to a sterilized bottle. Seal, and then shake well to combine. Store the bottles in the refrigerator or at cellar temperature for 3–4 weeks before using. Shake each bottle once or twice daily to help the sugar dissolve. When it's mostly dissolved, your shrub is ready to use. Makes 11/2 cups. Keep refrigerated, and use within about 6 months. (If the bottle gets foamy, changes radically in color, or if you suddenly notice small sea animals gorging themselves on thin wafers inside the bottle, just throw it out. If you don't tell anyone about the sea animals or the thin wafers, I promise I won't, either.)*

GINGER-LIME SHRUB WITH RHUM AGRICOLE AND SALTY LEMONADE

This easy-to-make but very grown-up glass of lemonade also showcases that classic ginger-lime-rum combination. I make mine with a healthy portion of 100-proof Rhum Agricole (which, if drunk on its own, is guaranteed to put hair on your eyeballs). *Rhum Agricole* is handmade on the French island of Martinique, and it's never factory-produced, which is why I prefer it. But, in a pinch, any good white rum will do. Add a toothsome crunch to your lemonade by sprinkling a little *fleur de sel*, or sea salt, into it. The salt-lemon combination will make you thirsty, but the sugar and vinegar in the shrub syrup will quench your thirst in double time. This cocktail makes a great summertime *aperitif*. Mix up a batch at your next barbeque.

INGREDIENTS

_ 2 OUNCES (60 ML) 100-PROOF RHUM AGRICOLE BLANC

_ 2 TABLESPOONS (30 ML) GINGER-LIME SHRUB (SEE PAGE 82)

_ 3 OUNCES (90 ML) FRESHLY MADE LEMONADE SWEETENED WITH RAW HONEY OR SIMPLE SYRUP

_ 1/2 OUNCE (15 ML) SELTZER WATER

_ 1 PINCH FLEUR DE SEL

_ 2-3 DROPS LIME BITTERS

_ HAND-CUT ICE SPEAR

DIRECTIONS

Add the Ginger-Lime Shrub to a Collins-style glass. Then add the ice spear. Top with the Rhum Agricole Blanc, the lemonade, and a splash of seltzer water. Sprinkle a pinch of fleur de sel into the drink, and finish with a couple drops of lime bitters. It's ridiculously refreshing.

RHUBARB FIZZ WITH CHARRED STRAWBERRIES

Fizzes are delicious, revitalizing preparations that suspend healing botanicals, liquors, and/or juices in seltzer water, and the Rhubarb Fizz is a famous—or infamous—example. Add some botanical gin, the effervescence of seltzer water, and plenty of crushed ice, and you've got a cooling cocktail that's powerfully restorative. (Gin is an analgesic, by the way, so this is just the thing for that heat-induced headache.)

INGREDIENTS

_ 1/4 CUP (40 G) CHARRED STRAWBERRIES
(SEAR STRAWBERRIES IN A CAST-IRON
PAN OVER VERY HIGH HEAT, THEN
SET ASIDE UNTIL COOL)

_ 3 OUNCES (90 ML) 80-PROOF RHUBARB
TEA LIQUEUR (PREFERABLY ORGANIC)

_ 1 OUNCE (25 ML) BOTANICAL GIN

_ ICE CUBES

_ 1 OUNCE (25 ML) SIMPLE
SYRUP (SEE PAGE 311)

_ SELTZER WATER

_ CRUSHED ICE

DIRECTIONS

Add about 2 tablespoons (30 ml) of the charred strawberries and the simple syrup to a Boston shaker. Muddle them until they make a fragrant pulp. Then add the rhubarb tea liqueur and the botanical gin, and pile the crushed ice over the liquors and strawberries until the shaker is three-quarters full. Shake well for twenty seconds, scoop some of the crushed ice into a coupé glass (its texture will have become slushy), strain the mixture over the ice, and top with seltzer water. Prepare to be healed!

SIDENOTE

⇒ **Rhubarb as a remedy.** Rhubarb has been used in folk medicine for thousands of years, and, legend has it, first arrived in the United States when Benjamin Franklin brought rhubarb seeds from Europe in the late eighteenth century. Famed for its powerful purgative, laxative qualities, rhubarb (the stems, not the leaves: rhubarb leaves are toxic. Consider yourself warned) has been known to ease blockages of the digestive tract that may stem from poor diet. And it's rich in vitamin C, vitamin A, and potassium, too. Plus, according to legend, it's an aphrodisiac. But there's only one way to find out if that's true: Whip up a pair of Rhubarb Fizzes next time you've got someone special over on a sultry summer's night, and see where the evening takes you.

MAPLE SYRUP SWITCHEL

Switchel originated in the Caribbean, and quickly became popular in the United States. And, like shrubs, it's definitely making a comeback. Top a portion with a couple drops of my Cocktail Whisperer's Raw Honey Aromatic Bitters (see page 311), and a little soda water, if you like. It's a great way to chill out during hot, humid weather.

INGREDIENTS

_ 3 TABLESPOONS (45 ML)
APPLE CIDER VINEGAR

_ 4 TABLESPOONS (60 ML) GRADE B (OR
DARK AMBER/COOKING) MAPLE SYRUP

_ 1 TABLESPOON (8 G) OF GRATED
FRESH GINGER ROOT

_ 1 CUP (235 ML) OF COOL SPRING
WATER (WHATEVER YOU DO, DON'T
SUBSTITUTE TAP WATER!)

DIRECTIONS

Time: 24 hours. *Combine all the ingredients in a sterilized Mason jar. Cover tightly and store in the fridge for at least 24 hours, shaking to combine the ingredients. This lasts for several months in the fridge.*

SIDENOTE

⇒ **Switchel: The original energy drink.** Also known as haymaker's punch, thirsty farmers relied on switchel for centuries in order to stay hydrated while working outdoors under the sun, long before manufactured energy drinks were available on the market. It's a close cousin of shrubs: in fact, the only difference between them is that shrubs contain fermented fruit or vegetables, while switchel doesn't. Like shrubs, it's powerfully thirst-quenching, thanks to the vinegar in it—plus, since it's made with maple syrup, which is a natural source of sugar, it can give you a much-needed energy boost on sweltering summer afternoons. (That's no bad thing—especially if you're an iced-coffee addict trying to cut back on the hard stuff.) And, of course, switchel is free from all the colorings, additives, preservatives, and synthetic sweeteners that most of us try to avoid. That's a win-win!

These days, switchel is popping up in cutting-edge cocktail bars around the country. But if you don't fancy heading to your local bar—or relying on pre-made versions—here's some good news: It's so easy to make your own. All it takes is four ingredients, and it's ready to use very quickly, either on its own or in craft cocktails: it takes just 24 hours in the fridge. Then you can strain your switchel into rocks glasses filled with ice and an ounce (30 ml) of either brandy or dark rum for an instant pick-me up.

COCONUT COOLER

In the Caribbean islands, old-time pharmacists might have been called on to help patients counter the effects of too much sun. Their solution was probably a simple one, relying on potassium-packed coconut water for hydration and for a much-needed blast of potassium, and local rum to ease the sufferer's body and mind. Pharmacists may have packed their coconuts in ice overnight to ensure that the coconut water—the nutrient-dense, milky liquid inside the fruit—was well-chilled before punching holes in them in order to pour a healthy dose of rum inside. Since coconut water has plenty of potassium and other electrolytes, it's a speedy way to replenish much-needed nutrients in the midst of mind-boggling heat. And the best part is, there's no glass to wash afterwards.

INGREDIENTS

_ ONE LARGE COCONUT, CHILLED

_ 6 OUNCES (175 ML) RHUM AGRICOLE

DIRECTIONS

Chill the coconut by keeping it on ice overnight, or by storing it in the refrigerator. Using a drill, puncture three holes into the coconut (but don't discard the precious water inside!) (In the islands, a machete is often used to punch holes into coconuts. Some people who use machetes are missing their fingertips. I'm not one of them.) Add the Rhum Agricole through one of the holes, using a funnel if necessary. Stick a straw into each of the holes, and sip the contents while cheek-to-cheek with a close friend. **Serves 2.**

TIKI MOCKTAIL

Get ready to stage a return to the 1940s and 50s, when tiki culture reigned supreme—especially in matters of food and drink. This velvety, coconut-scented, tropically influenced mocktail will take you there in a jiffy. Buy yourself a bottle of orgeat: it's a softly textured syrup that's enlivened with almonds, pure cane sugar, and either rose- or orange-flower water. In my Tiki Mocktail, it's combined with the usual tiki-esque suspects: lemon, lime, orange, and grapefruit juices, plus coconut cream and the requisite pineapple juice. But there's a twist: Toasty, smoky chicory powder adds the richness of rum to the mix, even though this drink is liquor-free. Decadent and slightly kitschy, you'll be thrilled that you can drink as many of these as you like with no fear of the consequences. Best served alongside a grass skirt and a lei.

INGREDIENTS

_ 1 OUNCE (30 ML) FRESHLY
SQUEEZED ORANGE JUICE

_ 1 OUNCE (30 ML) GOOD-QUALITY
ESPRESSO POWDER (FOR QUICK ENERGY)

_ 1 OUNCE (28 G) CHICORY POWDER
(ELIMINATES INTESTINAL WORMS,
IN CASE YOU WERE CURIOUS)

_ 1 OUNCE (30 ML) FRESHLY
SQUEEZED GRAPEFRUIT JUICE

_ 1 OUNCE (30 ML) FRESHLY
SQUEEZED PINEAPPLE JUICE

_ 1 OUNCE (30 ML) FALERNUM
OR ORGEAT SYRUP

_ 1 OUNCE (30 ML) COCONUT CREAM

_ 1/2 OUNCE (15 ML) FRESHLY
SQUEEZED LEMON JUICE

_ 1/2 OUNCE (15 ML) FRESHLY
SQUEEZED LIME JUICE

_ FRESH MINT SPRIGS

_ COCKTAIL WHISPERER'S RAW HONEY
AROMATIC BITTERS (SEE PAGE 311)

_ FRESHLY SCRAPED NUTMEG

DIRECTIONS

Fill a blender half full with ice, then add all the ingredients except the mint, bitters, and the nutmeg. Blend on high for 20 seconds, and pour into tiki-style mugs. Dot the top of each drink with 2 drops of my Raw Honey Aromatic Bitters, a sprig of fresh mint, and a little of the freshly grated nutmeg for a colorful, aromatic finish. Serve with a spoon, if desired. Serves 2, with a refill.

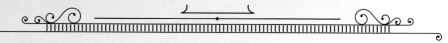

TWISTED CACHAÇA SOUR

Bitters aren't for savory cocktails only. They've long been key features of tropical libations, like the famous Peruvian Pisco Sour. In this twisted version of that classic, I've replaced the Pisco with Cachaça, a kind of sugarcane-based, barrel-aged, distilled spirit that's the very soul of Brazil. Don't indulge in more than two of these, though; they're treacherously smooth.

INGREDIENTS

_ 3 OUNCES (90 ML) CACHAÇA

_ 1/2 OUNCE (15 ML) GREEN CHARTREUSE

_ 1 OUNCE (30 ML) GINGER-LIME SHRUB (SEE PAGE 82)

_ 1/2 OUNCE (15 ML) FRESHLY SQUEEZED LIME JUICE

_ 1 EGG WHITE

_ 3 DROPS GRAPEFRUIT BITTERS

_ SMASHED ICE

DIRECTIONS

Mix the Cachaça and chartreuse with the Ginger-Lime Shrub. Add the fresh lime juice, the simple syrup, and the egg white to your Boston Shaker, and then add enough bar ice to fill to shaker three-quarters full. Cap and shake hard for 15 seconds. Put a fistful of smashed ice into a coupe glass, and pour the mixture over. Dot grapefruit bitters directly on top of the egg white foam, and serve.

SIDENOTE

⇒ **Crush your ice in a Lewis bag.** If you're a rabid home mixologist, you probably find yourself crushing or smashing ice for your cocktails all the time. Do you resort to sticking it into a plastic bag and whacking it with a rolling pin, only to have the bag burst—again? Well, quit it. Invest in a Lewis bag instead. Lewis bags are made of heavy-duty canvas, and they can really take a beating: Fill yours with ice, close it, then pound it with a wooden mallet until the ice has reached the right texture, and you're done. The bag helps wick the moisture away from the smashed ice, and it's easy to store in a kitchen drawer or cupboard, too.

SUNSET OVER THE GANGES COCKTAIL

Ice is the major consideration here, so please make your coconut water ice the day before—or at least eight hours before—you plan to enjoy one of these. The ice must be perfectly firm so that it can be shaved properly. How does one shave ice, you ask? Buy or borrow a woodworker's rasp (if you decide to do the latter, please remove all wood splinters, oils, et cetera, before you attempt to shave the ice!) The consistency you're going for is a sort of a fine, slushy, coconutty gravel. Combined with whisky and a dash of spice from Teapot Bitters, this mysterious combination of South Asian ingredients mimics India's sweet-and-spicy chai tea. Remember, don't use the cheap stuff: Use only a high-quality brand of single-malt Indian whisky for this cocktail.

INGREDIENTS

_ 3 OUNCES (90 ML) INDIAN WHISKY

_ 1 OUNCE (30 ML) BASIC SIMPLE
SYRUP (SEE PAGE 311)

_ SHAVED ICE, MADE FROM
COCONUT WATER

_ 1/2 OUNCE (15 ML) CLUB SODA

_ 5 DROPS TEAPOT BITTERS

DIRECTIONS

Shave the coconut water ice with a woodworking rasp (if it's not brand-new, make sure it's absolutely clean of any wood shavings or oils). The ice should be the consistency of the Italian ices you loved as a kid. Keep the coconut water ice dry by placing a dry cloth over it. Fill a mixing glass three-quarters full with plain ice. Add the whisky and the simple syrup. Stir well until chilled. Pack an old-fashioned glass with the shaved coconut water ice, and strain the mixture on top of the shaved ice. Top with the club soda, and drip 5 drops of the Teapot Bitters over the top of the drink. Garnish with two small bar straws. Sip, and watch the sun go down.

CHINESE ICED TEA WITH STAR ANISE

Strangely enough, star anise isn't related to aniseed—although the two herbs share a distinctive, licorice flavor, and both are used to alleviate upset stomachs and freshen breath. Star anise is frequently used in traditional Chinese medicine to warm the body and stimulate circulation. It's also said to possess antibacterial and antifungal qualities, and is often added to hot tea in order to relieve persistent colds, coughs, and other flu symptoms. This curative, an Asian-influenced take on the classic iced tea, is a great way to lift flagging spirits and refresh hot, tired bodies on a sultry summer day. Anise, ginger, and lemon are flavorful complements to one another, while antioxidant-rich Chinese black tea may be good for heart health. Top it off with botanical gin, and you've got a cocktail that's as tasty and invigorating as it is healing.

INGREDIENTS

_ 1 SMALL POT (ABOUT 2 CUPS [475
ML]) ICED CHINESE BLACK TEA

_ 2 PODS CHINESE STAR ANISE

_ 4 TABLESPOONS (60 ML) GINGER
SIMPLE SYRUP (SEE PAGE 312)

_ 3 OUNCES (90 ML) FRESHLY
SQUEEZED LEMON JUICE

_ 6 OUNCES (175 ML) BOTANICAL GIN

_ SPRIG OF FRESH MINT FOR GARNISH

DIRECTIONS

Brew the pot of Chinese black tea; then let it cool. Add the star anise, ginger simple syrup, lemon juice, and gin to the pot, and mix well. Pack two Collins glasses with ice; then fill them with the iced tea, and garnish each glass with fresh mint. Serves 2 tired tipplers.

ENGLISH PEA AND MINT SHRUB

Shrubs don't need to be fruit-based—and neither do cocktails. Ready in just a day and a half, sweet peas and fragrant mint take center stage in this toothsome shrub that's inspired by your springtime vegetable garden. They're mixed with richly textured Demerara sugar, and then quickly preserved in luxurious champagne vinegar, and the result is a most beguiling, bright-green syrup that's a surprising, refreshing complement to white rum, or even to plain seltzer water. If you can tie yourself to the mast and avoid the shrub's siren call, go ahead and age it in the fridge for a month—but I bet you won't be able to restrain yourself from using it the minute it's ready.

INGREDIENTS

_ 1 POUND (455 G) FRESH PEAS, SHELLED, THEN BLANCHED (ADD A PINCH OF BAKING SODA TO BOILING WATER, AND THEN SUBMERGE THE PEAS IN THE WATER FOR A FEW SECONDS: THE BAKING SODA WILL ENHANCE THEIR VIVID GREEN COLOR) AND LIGHTLY CRUSHED

_ 1 CUP (235 ML) DEMERARA SUGAR SIMPLE SYRUP (SEE PAGE 311)

_ 1 CUP (235 ML) CHAMPAGNE VINEGAR

_ 1 CUP (95 G) FRESH MINT, WASHED AND SLAPPED TO RELEASE ITS ESSENTIAL OILS

DIRECTIONS

Time: 36 hours. *Combine the blanched, lightly crushed peas and simple syrup in a nonreactive bowl, and let them sit at room temperature overnight. The next morning, stir the mixture well with a wooden spoon, and then add the champagne vinegar and slapped mint. Stir again, and keep in the fridge for 24 hours so that the flavors combine (be sure to keep your bowl well-covered: You don't want your delicate flavors ruined by that bowl of leftover garlic pasta that lives on the other side of the fridge!). Place a sieve over another nonreactive bowl, and transfer the mixture to the sieve, pressing down so as to extract as much juice and pea solids as possible. Funnel the mixture into sterilized bottles or jars, and use immediately. Or, let it ferment for up to another month or two in the fridge, shaking the bottles daily so that the sumptuous flavors combine.*

LAST-MINUTE RUMPUS →

Try serving this savory libation alongside a first course, like a simple salad of avocado, citrus, and chopped hazelnuts. Or, indulge in a little daytime drinking, and mix up a Last-Minute Rumpus on one of those late Saturday afternoons when a lazy brunch with a couple of friends stretches right into cocktail hour.

INGREDIENTS

_ 2 OUNCES (60 ML) RHUM AGRICOLE
  BLANC (100 PROOF)

_ 2 OUNCES (60 ML) ENGLISH
  PEA AND MINT SHRUB

_ 2 OUNCES (60 ML) COOL SPRING WATER

_ 2 DROPS SARSAPARILLA BITTERS

_ SQUEEZE OF FRESH LIME JUICE

_ SCRAPING OF FRESH NUTMEG

DIRECTIONS

Add the first two ingredients to a rocks glass (no ice necessary). Pour the cool spring water over the top, and mix with your (clean) finger. Add the bitters, followed by the lime juice, and then scrape a little fresh nutmeg into the drink as a final flourish—serve immediately.

ROASTED TOMATO AND CHILI BLOODY MARY

One of the best things about summertime is that gardens and farmers' markets overflow with juicy melons, succulent strawberries, delicate lettuces, and firm, deep-red tomatoes. It's the perfect time to cool down with this spicy twist on the classic Bloody Mary. Trust me, the rich flavor of roasted tomatoes really makes it worth turning on the oven, even in sizzling heat.

INGREDIENTS

_ 6 OUNCES (175 ML)
GOOD-QUALITY VODKA

_ 6 OUNCES (175 ML) ROASTED
TOMATO PUREE (SEE PAGE 313)

_ 3 OUNCES (90 ML) LEMON JUICE

_ 2 TABLESPOONS (30 ML) HOT CHILI
SAUCE (A SWEET-AND-SPICY ONE WORKS
BEST, SUCH AS VIETNAMESE SRIRACHA)

_ ICE CUBES

_ DASH OF CELERY SALT

DIRECTIONS

Combine all the ingredients except the celery salt in a large glass, and mix gently (with a celery stick, perhaps?). Just before serving, sprinkle the celery salt over the top of the drink. Garnish with a lemon wedge. Find a spot in the shade, sip slowly, and cool down from the inside out. **Serves 2.**

HEIRLOOM TOMATO, PEAR, AND SAGE SHRUB

One evening I found myself sampling a large selection of French *eau de vie*—strong, clear fruit brandy—at the New York restaurant Rouge Tomate. One of the many liquors I tried that night was made with—count 'em—62 different varieties of heirloom tomato. The haunting tomatoey taste and fragrance infused each sip. Then my thoughts turned to Poire William, an eau de vie that's made from impossibly tart pears. What if, I thought, it were possible to combine those tart pears with a portion of the tomato eau de vie—combined, say, with a touch of vinegar, crumbled sage, and simple syrup? Stop right there: Before you object, "Where on earth am I going to get tomato *eau de vie*?" I have the answer: Skip the *eau de vie*, and make a batch of my Heirloom Tomato, Pear, and Sage Shrub instead. It's an incredible partner for gin-based cocktails.

INGREDIENTS

_ 1 CUP (255 G) DICED
HEIRLOOM TOMATOES

_ 3-4 SAGE LEAVES, CRUMBLED

_ 1 CUP (235 ML) BOSC
PEAR "SHRUB" SIMPLE
SYRUP (SEE PAGE 311)

_ 1 CUP (235 ML) APPLE
CIDER VINEGAR

DIRECTIONS

Time: 24 hours. *Combine the diced tomatoes, sage, and Bosc Pear "Shrub" Simple Syrup in a nonreactive bowl. Stir to combine, then cover the bowl and let the mixture sit at room temperature overnight or for 12 hours. Add the vinegar, stir, cover, and refrigerate for another 12 hours to combine the flavors. Place a nonreactive strainer over a second bowl, and transfer the mixture to the strainer, pressing down on the tomato-sage pulp to extract as much flavor as possible. Funnel into sterilized bottles or jars, and use immediately—or, store in the fridge for a month to let the flavors combine.*

THE ENLIGHTENER

Although some say that mezcal's smoky scent and flavor make it a less versatile spirit than its close relative, tequila, I disagree. The Enlightener is proof positive: it's a great way to showcase mezcal's merits. A distant relative of the margarita, this cooling cocktail brightens up mezcal with sweet agave syrup, a trio of citrus juices, and a dash of fizzy water, creating a crisp, fragrant, vitamin C-laced tipple that's sure to banish the sweat from your brow. And, naturally, palate-stimulating Mexican bitters top off this memorable slurp. It's a refreshing route to good cheer, Cocktail Whisperer-style.

INGREDIENTS

_ 3 OUNCES (90 ML) MEZCAL

_ 2 OUNCES (60 ML) AGAVE SYRUP

_ 1 OUNCE (25 ML) FRESHLY
SQUEEZED ORANGE JUICE

_ 1 OUNCE (25 ML) FRESHLY
SQUEEZED GRAPEFRUIT JUICE

_ 1 OUNCE (25 ML) FRESHLY
SQUEEZED LIME JUICE

_ 2 OUNCES (60 ML) SELTZER WATER

_ 4 DROPS MEXICAN BITTERS

_ LIME WHEEL FOR GARNISH

DIRECTIONS

Add the mezcal, agave syrup, and fruit juices to a Boston shaker filled three-quarters full with ice. Shake for about twenty seconds, until the vessel is frosty. Strain into a coupé glass, and top with the seltzer water and then the bitters. Pop the lime wheel over the edge of the glass for garnish. Lift your glass, and say goodbye to the blues.

ANOTHER THOR COCKTAIL

You might not think that Scotch is a match for Tiki-style drinks, with their fresh citrus juices and coconutty sweetness—but now is the time to think again. The saline, smoky finish of, say, an Islay Scotch whisky makes it just as desirable in tropical cocktails as hearty, barrel-aged rum. Named for the Norse god of thunder, Another Thor mixes good Islay Scotch with orange, pineapple, lemon, and lime juices, as well as a little orgeat syrup (orgeat is a sweet, almond-flavored syrup that's used in lots of cocktails, such as the Mai Tai). A dash of curried bitters and a splash of palate-lifting club soda make for a surprising finish to this sultry summery cocktail. It's just the thing for sipping poolside—or, if you're on vacation, at brunch.

INGREDIENTS

_ 2 OUNCES (60 ML) ISLAY-STYLE SCOTCH WHISKY

_ 1 OUNCE (30 ML) FRESHLY SQUEEZED ORANGE JUICE

_ 1 OUNCE (30 ML) FRESHLY SQUEEZED PINEAPPLE JUICE

_ 1/4 OUNCE (7 ML) FRESHLY SQUEEZED LEMON JUICE

_ 1/4 OUNCE (7 ML) FRESHLY SQUEEZED LIME JUICE

_ 1 OUNCE (30 ML) SWEETENED COCONUT CREAM (SWEETENED)

_ 1/2 OUNCE (15 ML) ORGEAT

_ 3 DROPS CURRIED BITTERS

_ SPLASH OF CLUB SODA

DIRECTIONS

Fill a Boston shaker three-quarters full with ice. Add all the ingredients except the club soda and the bitters. Shake for about 15 seconds. Strain the mixture over a single hand-cut ice cube in a rocks glass. Add the splash of club soda, and drip the curried bitters over the top of the drink. Serve, wearing a grass skirt.

CHANCES IN THE FOG COCKTAIL

Feel like you've been groping your way through the day? We've all been there. Reward yourself for making it to quitting time with a Chances in the Fog Cocktail. London-style dry gin and fizzy seltzer water set off my savory, tangy Heirloom Tomato, Pear, and Sage Shrub to great effect.

INGREDIENTS

- 2 OUNCES (60 ML) LONDON DRY GIN

- 1 OUNCE (30 ML) HEIRLOOM TOMATO, PEAR, AND SAGE SHRUB (SEE PAGE 97)

- 1/2 OUNCE (15 ML) SELTZER WATER

- 3 DASHES AROMATIC BITTERS (SUCH AS MY COCKTAIL WHISPERER'S RAW HONEY AROMATIC BITTERS: SEE PAGE 311)

DIRECTIONS

Fill a cocktail glass three-quarters full with ice. Add the gin and the Heirloom Tomato, Pear, and Sage Shrub. Use a long cocktail spoon to stir the mixture for about 30 strokes. Use your Hawthorne strainer to strain the mixture into a coupe glass. Top with the aromatic bitters (try my Cocktail Whisperer's Raw Honey Aromatic Bitters: see page 311).

A CHORUS OF VOICES COCKTAIL

This deliciously twisted take on the gin and tonic calls upon a variety of piquant flavors: a little rum, a dose of my Nectarine, Celery, and Black Pepper Shrubb, and a good dry tonic water—or even plain seltzer. And they make beautiful music together. So what's the perfect finale to such a chorus? Two types of bitters, including grapefruit bitters, which add an astringent, assertive finish, plus the crunch of a pinch of fleur de sel, not to mention an elegant grapefruit twist in place of the typical (read: ho-hum) lime wheel. The finished product is so memorable that you'll be through with those boring old G&Ts for good.

INGREDIENTS

_ 2 OUNCES (60 ML) OLD TOM-STYLE GIN

_ 1/2 OUNCE (15 ML) RHUM AGRICOLE

_ 1 OUNCE (30 ML) NECTARINE, CELERY, AND BLACK PEPPER SHRUBB (SEE PAGE 58)

_ 1 OUNCE (30 ML) CANE-SUGAR BASED TONIC WATER (OR SELTZER, FOR A DRIER FINISH)

_ 2 DASHES WEST INDIAN ORANGE BITTERS

_ 2 DASHES GRAPEFRUIT BITTERS

_ LARGE CUBES OF HAND-CUT ICE

_ PINCH OF FLEUR DE SEL

_ GRAPEFRUIT ZEST TWIST

DIRECTIONS

Add two cubes of hand-cut ice to a large goblet. Add the gin, the Rhum Agricole, and the Nectarine, Celery, and Black Pepper Shrubb. Top with the tonic water, then the bitters. Finish with the fleur de sel, and garnish with a long grapefruit zest twist—then wait for your guests to demand an encore.

SIDENOTE

⇨ **Gin origins.** Gin probably evolved sometime in the late Middle Ages in Holland, when distillers first produced a spirit from malt wine, then flavored it with juniper (or genever) berries and other botanicals—perhaps angelica, anise seeds, cassia bark, coriander seeds, and citrus peel. It was originally sold in pharmacies, since juniper berries were reputed to have valuable medicinal benefits: they were thought to aid digestion, ease rheumatism, and to act as an antibacterial. But by the mid-eighteenth century, gin had lost its reputation as a stimulating curative, and gained notoriety as a social poison. Because it was cheaply produced and sold, it was easy for members of every social class to overindulge, and by the nineteenth century, it earned the nickname "mother's ruin," since it led so many young men (and women) into lives of debauchery.

Today, thankfully, gin has shed its seedy reputation at last, and artisan distillers are making small-batch pot-still versions of old-time gin styles—both dry and sweet—and restoring them to their former glory. Take, for example, Old Tom gin: Wildly popular in eighteenth-century London, it's enjoying a renaissance these days. It's sweeter than most contemporary gins, and that means it doesn't need a sugar-laden tonic water to balance it out—which is why it works so well in A Chorus of Voices. Don't be afraid to do your own research: head to your local "gin palace," and try a few of the many excellent craft gins on the market.

GRILLED PEACH AND THAI BASIL SHRUB

Whenever I find myself with less-than-perfect-looking produce on hand, I head straight to the grill. Grilling is a great way to harness the flavors of slightly overripe fruits and vegetables. It transforms their flavor profiles by bringing out their natural sugars. And grilled produce is lovely when it's turned into a shrub. Try to let this shrub age for a full month before you use it, since it definitely improves with age. (And as always, I implore you to use fresh ingredients—always. If a recipe calls for produce that's out of season, replace it with a similar seasonal ingredient, and change the recipe accordingly. Never ever use the canned or frozen variety if you can help it.)

INGREDIENTS

_ 2-3 POUNDS (1-1.5 KG) PEACHES, QUARTERED, THEN GRILLED OVER HARDWOOD CHARCOAL UNTIL LIGHTLY CHARRED (OR ROASTED FOR 30 MINUTES AT 400°F (200°C, OR GAS MARK 6) UNTIL LIGHTLY BROWNED), THEN COOLED AND CHOPPED

_ 1 CUP (200 G) DEMERARA SUGAR

_ 1-2 PINCHES OF FLEUR DE SEL

_ 1 CUP (235 ML) SHERRY VINEGAR

_ 1 CUP (24 G) THAI BASIL, LEAVES ONLY

DIRECTIONS

Time: 4 weeks. *Place the peaches in a nonreactive bowl, then cover with the Demerara sugar and sea salt. Stir well to combine, then cover tightly and place the bowl in the fridge or a cool, dark place, stirring several times daily for about 2 days. Place a sieve over another nonreactive bowl, and then transfer the mixture to the sieve. Use a wooden spoon to press the slightly fermented peach solids and liquids through the sieve. Discard the fruit pulp. Add the vinegar and the Thai basil; stir again, then let the mixture sit for a few hours. Funnel the shrub into sterilized bottles or jars, then store in the fridge for a month, shaking the bottle or jar a couple times daily. (Patience is a necessary ingredient in this shrub!) It's delicious in my Mendham Cocktail.*

MENDHAM COCKTAIL

Some of the sweetest peaches I've ever slurped are grown in and around Mendham, a rural New Jersey town, located about an hour north-by-northwest of New York City. Historically, Mendham was the location of the winter encampment for George Washington's Continental Army—and I'll bet my wages that those Mendham peaches were just as delicious two and half centuries ago as they are today. This cocktail puts my Grilled Peach and Thai Basil Shrubb in the driver's seat, alongside a good bourbon like Four Roses and soupcon of Rhum Agricole—its sweetly perfumed flavor profile makes for a haunting, memorable finish. A zap of fizzy water and a few drops of spicy Moroccan-style cocktail bitters—a twenty-first century emendation—and the job's done. The next step? Get ready to make a second round.

INGREDIENTS

_ 2 OUNCES (60 ML) SMALL-BATCH BOURBON WHISKEY, SUCH AS FOUR ROSES

_ 1/2 OUNCE (15 ML) RHUM AGRICOLE

_ 2 OUNCES (60 ML) GRILLED PEACH AND THAI BASIL SHRUBB (SEE PAGE 106–107)

_ SPLASH OF FIZZY WATER

_ MOROCCAN-STYLE BITTERS

_ PINCH OF *FLEUR DE SEL*

DIRECTIONS

Fill a Collins glass with hand-cut ice. Pour the bourbon, the Rhum Agricole, and the shrub over it. Add the fizzy water, and stir gently with a long cocktail spoon. Dash the Moroccan bitters over the top of the cocktail, followed by the fleur de sel. Fin!

LATE SUMMER FIZZ

This refreshing, rye-based cocktail is just the thing to whet your appetite before a good lunch on a late summer's day. In addition to rye, it features Pimm's No. 1 Cup, the citrusy-spicy English liqueur, which is most agreeable when served with fresh juices and Caribbean spices. That's where allspice dram, a liqueur flavored with allspice berries, comes in: Along with the Pimm's, it gives the drink a dark-red stain that's decidedly preppy (it's the exact color of Nantucket Red trousers). If all this sounds terribly exotic, never fear: Rye whiskey and apple cider, that familiar, time-honored combo, are at the heart of this cocktail. An easy-to-make, uncomplicated tipple, there's one tried-and-true way to drink the Late Summer Fizz that I wholeheartedly recommend: with two long straws, and a great deal of relish.

INGREDIENTS

_ 2 OUNCES (60 ML) RYE WHISKEY

_ 1/2 OUNCE (15 ML)
  PIMM'S NO.1 CUP

_ 1/2 OUNCE (15 ML)
  NON-ALCOHOLIC APPLE CIDER

_ SPLASH OF CLUB SODA

_ 1/2 OUNCE (15 ML) SWEET
  WHITE ITALIAN VERMOUTH

_ 1/4 OUNCE (7 ML) ALLSPICE DRAM

_ DASH OF LEMON BITTERS

_ PINCH OF SEA SALT

DIRECTIONS

Fill a Boston shaker three-quarters full with ice. Add the rye whiskey, the Pimm's, and the cider. Shake for 20 seconds. Pour the mixture over a couple hand-cut ice cubes in an old-fashioned glass, and top with a splash of club soda. Float the allspice dram and the Italian vermouth on top of the drink, and then add the dash of lemon bitters. Finish with a pinch of sea salt for a savory kick.

CUCUMBER-BASIL SHRUB

The scent and taste of freshly picked cucumbers straight off the vine is the scent and taste of high summer. When it's concentrated into a summery shrub like this one, it's even more delicious. And it goes so well with Thai basil's fresh bite (I like to use the Thai variety, since it has a bit more spice to it). That's just about all there is to my Cucumber-Basil Shrub, which is breathtakingly easy to assemble, and which matures very quickly—in only about a week. Use European-style seedless cukes to make this shrub: Slimmer and smoother-skinned, they're a slightly different beast to the usual garden-variety ones. You could use it in gin-based cocktails, or in cooling, refreshing virgin tipples, like Mr. Rankeillor's Door (see page 113).

INGREDIENTS

_ 1 EUROPEAN-STYLE SEEDLESS CUCUMBER, SKIN ON, DICED INTO BRUNOISE (VERY TINY CUBES)

_ 1 SMALL BUNCH FRESH THAI BASIL

_ 1/2 CUP (100 G) DEMERARA SUGAR OR RAW HONEY SIMPLE SYRUP (SEE PAGE 311)

_ 1 CUP (235 ML) APPLE CIDER VINEGAR

DIRECTIONS

Time: 1 week. *Combine the cucumber, basil, and sugar or sugar syrup into a bowl and cover with the cider vinegar. Cover tightly, and let it sit in the fridge or at cellar temperature for about a week. Then, place a strainer over a nonreactive bowl, and transfer the cucumber mixture to the strainer. Use a wooden spoon to press the mixture through the strainer, extracting as much liquid from the vegetable pulp as possible. Discard the pulp, and funnel the liquid into sterilized bottles or jars. Use liberally in craft cocktails or mocktails. (Here's a handy hint: Ran out of your favorite aftershave? Slap some of the Cucumber-Basil Shrub onto your cheeks. Seriously! It doubles as an eye-opening, alcohol-free face-freshener.)*

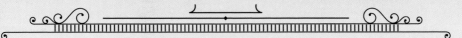

MR. RANKEILLOR'S DOOR

Faced with a thirst so pernicious that plain water, cocktails, sports drinks, and soft drinks all stand helpless before it? Well, help is indeed at hand, because your palate is about to become acquainted with Mr. Rankeillor's Door. Named—with good reason—for "a shrewd, ruddy, kindly, consequential man in a well-powdered wig and spectacles" from Robert Louis Stevenson's Kidnapped, this mocktail is just what you need to revive your spirits and sharpen your appetite for lunch. And, darn it, it's just so easy to make. Here, a flavorsome whack of my Cucumber-Basil Shrub gets pepped up with seltzer water, the barest pinch of sea salt, and my homemade bitters—and that's all there is to it. I drink Mr. Rankeillor's Doors all year round, but it really is the ticket when summer's heat is at its highest.

INGREDIENTS

- 2 OUNCES (60 ML) CUCUMBER-BASIL SHRUB (SEE PAGE 112)
- 6 OUNCES (175 ML) COOL SELTZER WATER
- TINY PINCH OF SEA SALT
- 2 DASHES COCKTAIL WHISPERER'S RAW HONEY AROMATIC BITTERS

DIRECTIONS

Add the shrub and the seltzer water to a tall Collins glass over a spear of hand-cut ice. Top with the bitters, then sprinkle the sea salt over the top of the drink.

TROPICALISTA SUNRISE COCKTAIL

Most cocktails with the word "tropical" in their names call for rum and only rum—but if it's a recipe by the Cocktail Whisperer, anything can happen! This sumptuous drink features wheat whiskey, which is very different to whiskey made from one hundred percent corn. It's softer in the mouth, and the finish goes on and on—and on. It's very elegant stuff. So treat it right: Make your own grenadine (it's not hard), and use good dark rum if you can, since it's such a match for smoky-sweet grilled pineapple juice. (The juice from grilled pineapple has a slightly "charred" taste, which rounds out the necessary acidity in this new American classic.) Go ahead and mix up a second batch, if you like—just don't hold me responsible for your headache the next morning!

INGREDIENTS

_ 3 OUNCES (90 ML) GRILLED PINEAPPLE JUICE (SEE PAGE 312)

_ 1/2 OUNCE (15 ML) HOMEMADE GRENADINE SYRUP (SEE PAGE 312)

_ 2 OUNCES (60 ML) WHEAT WHISKEY

_ 1/2 OUNCE (15 ML) DARK RUM (TRY TWELVE-YEAR-OLD RUM AGED IN BOURBON OAK CASKS, IF AT ALL POSSIBLE. THE DEEP VANILLA-SMOKE FLAVORS IN EACH SIP ARE TOO GOOD TO MISS)

_ 3/4 OUNCE (22 ML) FRESHLY SQUEEZED ORANGE JUICE, STRAINED

_ 1 OUNCE (30 ML) FRESHLY SQUEEZED GRAPEFRUIT JUICE, STRAINED

_ PINCH OF SEA SALT

_ 2 OUNCES (60 ML) CLUB SODA

DIRECTIONS

Add the first six ingredients to a mixing glass with a few chunks of ice. Stir well. Add the pinch of sea salt (don't skip the salt: It's an essential ingredient!) and stir again. Add one large cube of hand-cut ice to a rocks glass. Strain into rocks glasses, top with the club soda, and then garnish each glass with a spear of grilled pineapple and a lemon zest twist, squeezing it gently to release its fragrant oils. Serves two thirsty heads.

SIDENOTE

⇒ **Get grilling.** If you're not charring or grilling your fruit for use in your cocktails (either as garnishes, for muddling, or as soon-to-be-freshly-squeezed juices), now's the time to start. Why? Charring or grilling fruits and vegetables intensifies their flavors; it draws out their natural sugars in the same way that onions become sweeter when you caramelize them. Start with a slightly-underripe stone fruit, like a fresh peach. Slice it into eighths, then place the slices on a hot grill (or grill pan) for a minute or two per side. Let cool, then use judiciously in your craft cocktails.

ROOT AND RYE

The original Rock and Rye cocktail, a mixture of rye whiskey, simple syrup, and citrus fruits, was a nineteenth- and twentieth-century classic. The simple concoction was believed to be a cure for chest congestion, stubborn coughs, and even the common cold. This delicious spin on the Rock and Rye calls for a special ingredient that tips its hat to the early era of medicinal folk healers. It's called root tea, but it's not the kind of tea you'd drink alongside your breakfast bagel. Based on a recipe that's said to have been handed down by Native Americans to pre-colonial settlers, root tea liqueur is a spirit that's been developed to imitate the original flavors and healing techniques of the early apothecary age, using natural materials such as birch bark, sassafras, anise, and cloves. Thanks to root tea liqueur, the Root and Rye gently becalms uneasy bellies, and is especially refreshing on hot summer days.

INGREDIENTS

_ 1 OUNCE (25 ML) ORGANIC
ROOT TEA LIQUEUR

_ 2 OUNCES (60 ML) RYE WHISKEY

_ 1 ROCK CANDY SWIZZLE STICK

_ 6 OUNCES (175 ML) SARSAPARILLA
OR BIRCH BEER

DIRECTIONS

Pack a tall Collins glass with ice. Add the root tea liqueur and the rye whiskey, followed by the sarsaparilla or birch beer. Mix well with the rock candy swizzle stick, sip slowly, and let the Root and Rye settle down that sour stomach.

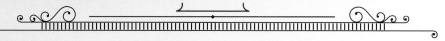

WHERE'S THE DOG STAR?

This simple cocktail features three of my favorite ingredients: white whiskey, organic root tea liqueur, and frozen hot chocolate. With its crunchy, slushy texture, Where's the Dog Star? is more than a mere tipple: It's also a healing tonic of the highest order. That's because root tea liqueur is a combination of hand-selected medicinal spices and extracts of healing roots, suspended and preserved in alcohol. Add a healthy dose of white whiskey to the mix, plus some homemade frozen hot chocolate, and you've got a fortifying cocktail that'll keep your spirits up despite blustery weather and howling gales. Try it on its own on a stormy afternoon; as a dessert (in all weathers); or, best of all, as a nightcap. It's a fabulous restorative for both body and soul.

INGREDIENTS

_ 2 OUNCES (60 ML) WHITE WHISKEY

_ 1 OUNCE (30 ML) ORGANIC
ROOT TEA LIQUEUR

_ 3 OUNCES (90 ML) BEST HOT
CHOCOLATE (SEE PAGE 313), FROZEN
AND CRUSHED INTO PEBBLES

DIRECTIONS

Prepare the Best Hot Chocolate, and let it cool a little. Pour into an ice-cube tray, and freeze 8 hours or overnight. Pop the hot chocolate ice cubes into a blender and crush, or place them into a Lewis bag—a canvas bag especially made for crushing ice—and crush by hand by banging them with a wooden mallet. (It's actually a lot of fun!) Spoon the crushed, frozen hot chocolate into a parfait glass, and then add the white whiskey and the root tea liqueur. Mix gently. Serve with both a straw and a long-handled spoon.

COOL-WEATHER COCKTAILS:

HANDMADE DRINKS TO WARM AND SOOTHE

• • •

WITH THEIR SHORT DAYS AND LONG NIGHTS, AUTUMN AND WINTER HERALD THE YEAR'S END, BUT THERE'S SO MUCH TO LOVE ABOUT BOTH SEASONS. CRISP FALL WEATHER, WITH ITS NOSTALGIC SCENT OF FALLING LEAVES, GIVES WAY TO WINTER'S SHARP, BRACING CHILL— AND TO THE HOLIDAYS, WITH THEIR PARADE OF PARTIES AND DELICIOUS FOOD AND DRINKS. THERE'S NO DOUBT ABOUT IT: THE COOLER MONTHS ARE JUST THE RIGHT TIME TO ENJOY WELL-MADE COCKTAILS—ESPECIALLY THOSE THAT CAN WARM YOU FROM THE INSIDE OUT.

Healing, warming drinks are wonderful remedies for the deep-down kind of cold that really gets into your bones. Apothecaries of old would have had a thorough knowledge of the effects of cold weather upon the body—and they'd have been well versed in how to treat those effects. In chilly climates, of course, it's not just the low temperatures that make the cold difficult to bear; it's also the lack of sunlight, which makes winter days nearly as dark as winter nights, and can lead to sluggishness and sinking spirits. It's not surprising, then, that the pharmacies in Scandinavian countries, for instance, carry many varieties of herbal elixirs, bitters, and tonics—many of them are based on special combinations of botanicals that are specifically designed to warm the body from within. Some of these elixirs can be combined with liquids that are already hot, such as strong, black tea or homemade soups for double the chill-fighting power.

And, as early pharmacists knew well, a single cure can treat a range of maladies—which is why the ingredients in these warming winter cocktails do more than just counteract the cold. Citrus fruits and their juices, for example, are powerful assets to the immune system, as sailors of days gone by would have known: without precious vitamin C, sailors would have been subject to life-threatening diseases such as scurvy. (Cranberries, too, pack a wallop of vitamin C as well as antioxidants.) The warming taste and fragrance of cardamom is wonderful in wintry desserts—have you ever tried it in a chocolate tart?—but it's also said to be an effective antidote to nausea and other tummy troubles. Plus, tasty, frost-battling winter warmers need not be highly alcoholic in order to banish the chills, so go ahead and amend the amount of alcohol in them if you like.

The drinks in this chapter have been created to thaw shivery bodies, and to revive tired, numbed spirits. So, if you're looking for an enlivening aperitif before a mid-fall feast, try a Rye and Cider Mulligatawny Cocktail: in it, rye whiskey and hard apple cider partner up before getting pepped up by warming curried bitters. Or, if extra-strength healing is what you're looking for, reach for a ration of citrusy Navy Grog: its combination of rum, citrus, and tea far exceeds the sum of its parts. If you're in the mood for a drink that's refreshing and warming all at once, make a Cardamom and Rum Elixir, which features a cardamom-laced simple syrup, rum, and a hit of fizzy water. And you've got to try my spice-laden "Cranberry Sauce" shrub: sweet, tart, and fragrant, it's a great match for all kinds of whiskies.

So, if the temperature's headed south, you're battling the sniffles—again—and the weather outside is frightful, take heart: The delicious, soothing handmade cocktails in this chapter are sure to warm you right down to your toes.

RYE AND CIDER MULLIGATAWNY COCKTAIL

In America's early days, apples were an important autumn crop for the Northeastern states, and whiskey—usually rye whiskey—was the only tipple available to the average drinker. Rye whiskey would have been added to apple cider to give it a bit of kick, a combination that lives on in this cocktail. As usual, though, there's a twist: Curried bitters (or, in a pinch, curry powder added to "regular" aromatic bitters) is a tip of the hat to a warm, spicy bowl of mulligatawny stew, which features both apples and curry. Sound weird? Don't worry: It isn't. Dry, spicy rye is the perfect foil to sweet apples—and the curried bitters bind it all together beautifully. Makes an animating late-autumn aperitif.

INGREDIENTS

_ 1 APPLE, PREFERABLY ONE WITH
CRISP FLESH SUCH AS A MACINTOSH
OR A MACOUN, SLICED THICKLY
AND SEARED ON A CAST-IRON PAN
UNTIL SOFT, BUT NOT MUSHY

_ 1/2 TEASPOON ABSINTHE

_ 2 OUNCES (60 ML) RYE WHISKEY

_ 1/4 OUNCE (7 ML) ITALIAN
SWEET VERMOUTH

_ 1 OUNCE (30 ML) HARD APPLE CIDER
(OR APPLE BRANDY, OR CALVADOS [A
TYPE OF APPLE BRANDY FROM THE
NORMANDY REGION OF FRANCE])

_ 4 DROPS CURRIED BITTERS
(ALTERNATIVELY, USE YOUR BASIC
AROMATIC BITTERS, AND ADD A VERY
SMALL PINCH OF CURRY POWDER)

_ HAND-CUT ICE CUBE

DIRECTIONS

Muddle a couple of grilled, softened apple slices with the absinthe in an old-fashioned glass. Add the ice, rye whiskey, and the sweet vermouth. Then add the apple cider or apple brandy, and drip the curried bitters over the top of the glass for a spicy, savory, mulligatawny finish.

CARDAMOM AND RUM ELIXIR

In this invigorating cocktail, the warming, purifying spice cardamom is steeped in simple syrup and combined with cane-sugar rum before it's bathed in fizzy water for a flavorful, powerful curative that's as tasty as it is healing. It's sure to boost the spirits and brush the cobwebs away. Treat yourself to a Cardamom and Rum Elixir when you're recovering from a pesky midwinter cold.

INGREDIENTS

_ 2 OUNCES (60 ML) RHUM AGRICOLE

_ 1/2 OUNCE (15 ML) CARDAMOM
    SIMPLE SYRUP (SEE PAGE 311)

_ 4 OUNCES (120 ML) SELTZER WATER

_ 2 DASHES ANGOSTURA BITTERS

DIRECTIONS

Combine the rum and cardamom simple syrup in a Boston shaker filled three-quarters full with ice. Shake until combined and chilled (about fifteen seconds). Place one ice cube in a short rocks glass; then strain the mixture over the ice. Top with the seltzer water and add the bitters. Sip slowly, and let the ice melt into the cocktail. By the time your glass is empty, that melancholy mood will be ancient history. r.)

SIDENOTE

⇒ **Curative cardamom.** A member of the ginger family, cardamom is frequently used in Asian cuisine, and it also appears regularly in Ayurvedic preparations and traditional Chinese medicine. It promotes the flow of *chi*, or life-energy, which means it's warming and invigorating, and it's reputed to help the kidneys rid the body of harmful impurities. Cardamom is also said to stimulate the nervous system, reduce inflammation, and to act as an expectorant. Early pharmacists in America would have used cardamom and other exotic spices extensively (if they could get them) when treating patients with stubborn flu symptoms—not least because cardamom is meant to aid all sorts of digestive disorders, like nausea, bloating, gas, and lots more.

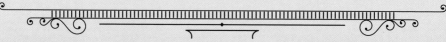

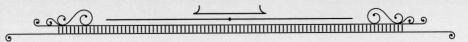

PROFESSOR MEIKLEJOHN'S PINKY

Named for a professor made famous for his relationship with the writer Robert Louis Stevenson, this rye whiskey–based cold-weather cocktail is sure to restore and inspire. And the best part: It's really easy to prepare. Whip up a batch of the Best Hot Chocolate so it can play host to organic root tea liqueur, rye, and—since this drink really has a flair for the dramatic—a pinch of cayenne pepper. It's a very grown-up version of every kid's favorite wintertime treat. Serve after dinner alongside a plateful of simple, buttery cookies, like homemade madeleines. Oh, and be sure to preheat your mug with boiling water beforehand to ensure that your Pinky stays toasty warm.

INGREDIENTS

- 1 OUNCE (30 ML) RYE WHISKEY
- 1/2 OUNCE (15 ML) ORGANIC ROOT TEA LIQUEUR
- 3 OUNCES (90 ML) BEST HOT CHOCOLATE (SEE PAGE 313)
- TINY PINCH CAYENNE PEPPER
- 1 OUNCE (30 ML) SIMPLE SYRUP (SEE PAGE 311)
- 1 DASH ORANGE BITTERS

DIRECTIONS

Preheat your favorite ceramic mug by filling it with boiling water, and then pour the water out. Add the rye whiskey, root tea liqueur, and then top them with the Best Hot Chocolate. Now add the Simple Syrup—about 1 ounce (30 ml), or to taste—and the cayenne pepper. Finish with a dash or two of orange bitters. Lift your mug in a toast to the Professor.

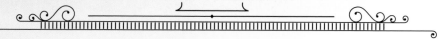

THE CRAFT COCKTAIL COMPENDIUM

"CRANBERRY SAUCE" SHRUB

When you sit down to Thanksgiving dinner, do you lunge for the big cut-glass bowl of tart, textured, homemade cranberry sauce? If your answer is yes, then this easy-to-make shrub's right up your alley. It's a distilled version of that classic New England dish, and it's redolent of cinnamon, citrus, and wintery baking spices that smell just like Christmas.

INGREDIENTS

_ 1 CUP (110 G) CRANBERRIES, LIGHTLY CRUSHED

_ 1 CUP (200 G) DEMERARA SUGAR

_ 1 CINNAMON STICK

_ ZEST OF 1/2 AN ORANGE

_ 1/2 TEASPOON FRESHLY GRATED NUTMEG

_ 1/2 TEASPOON GROUND CLOVES

_ 1 CUP (235 ML) RED WINE VINEGAR

DIRECTIONS

Time: 2 weeks. *Combine the cranberries and spices with the sugar in a nonreactive bowl, and stir well to combine. Cover tightly, and let the mixture sit at cellar or fridge temperature for at least 2 days, mixing several times per day to combine the flavors. Then, pour the vinegar over the cranberry mixture and let it sit for 1 week at cellar or fridge temperature. Now, place a sieve over another nonreactive bowl, and transfer the mixture to the sieve. Use a wooden spoon to press as much of the rich liquid through the sieve as possible. Discard the fruit pulp. Funnel the mixture into sterilized bottles or jars, and age the shrub at fridge or cellar temperature for another week or so before you use it. Use your shrub in my Cocktail Whisperer's twist on the classic Rob Roy.*

SIDENOTE

⇒ **Cranberries: a seventeenth-century superfood.** There's a reason pharmacists of yore would have gone to great lengths to preserve cranberries—also known as "bearberries" back in the day—in their medicinal shrubs. (And it's not because they're such a great match for turkey.) Cranberries are one of the original American superfoods, and early settlers knew it. Jam-packed with vitamin C, they'd have helped to prevent scurvy; plus, they have plenty of antioxidants, dietary fiber, and a hefty helping of manganese, a valuable dietary mineral. They're also said to help boost the immune system, lower blood pressure, and treat urinary tract infections, and they may even promote dental health since they prevent plaque from adhering to teeth. And cranberries weren't just useful in the kitchen, either: Thanks to their trademark scarlet hue, colonial settlers also used them to dye clothing.

PAGE | 126 |

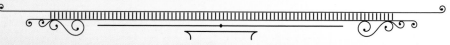

ROB'S SONNY, ROY

My grandfather was very fond of Rob Roys. He'd make them with Dewar's White Label Scotch—and that's how I knew he thought of them as a special treat, since the only spirit I'd ever seen in his house was bourbon whiskey. I'm not a big Scotch drinker myself, but even I have to admit that the Rob Roy is a woefully underrated cocktail. It's very similar to a Manhattan, only it's made with Scotch whisky instead of bourbon or rye—and it's got all the stuffing to stimulate your appetite, which makes it both a powerful aperitif and an effective digestif. So what's my Cocktail Whisperer's twist on the classic recipe? Well, I've added a portion of my fragrant Cranberry Sauce Shrub to the mix, since Scotch and the perky, crisp shrub are a naturally delicious pair. Try one before Christmas dinner.

INGREDIENTS

_ 2 OUNCES (60 ML) SCOTCH WHISKY

_ 1 OUNCE (30 ML) CRANBERRY SAUCE SHRUB (SEE PAGE 126-127)

_ 1/4 OUNCE (7 ML) SWEET VERMOUTH, SUCH AS CARPANO ANTICA

_ 4 DROPS ORANGE BITTERS

DIRECTIONS

Fill a cocktail mixing glass half full with ice. Add the Scotch, the Cranberry Sauce Shrub, and the Carpano Antica. Stir gently, and then strain the mixture into a coupe glass. Dot the orange bitters over the top to finish—and lift your hat to Roy as you sip.

CENTERBA AND CHOCOLATE CHAUD

The spicy, potent liqueur Centerba, distilled from over a hundred wild, aromatic (but top-secret) botanicals, hails from northern Italy, a region with a rich history of creating and enjoying herbal Alpine elixirs. It's got a slightly acerbic edge, but never fear: This hot, boozy chill-chaser made with classic hot chocolate—*chaud* means "hot" in French—takes the edge off its bite.

INGREDIENTS

_ 3 OUNCES (90 ML) CENTERBA

_ 5 TO 6 OUNCES (150 TO 175 ML) HOT CHOCOLATE (COMBINE 3/4 CUP (175 ML) OF WHOLE MILK WITH 1/4 CUP (60 ML) OF HEAVY CREAM. ADD 1/4 POUND (115 G) OF GRATED BITTERSWEET CHOCOLATE: HEAT SLOWLY, DO NOT BOIL, AND WHISK CONSTANTLY UNTIL SMOOTH.)

_ SUGAR OR HONEY, TO TASTE (OPTIONAL)

_ FRESHLY MADE WHIPPED CREAM (SEE SIDENOTE)

DIRECTIONS

Preheat two mugs by filling them with boiling water; discard the water after a few seconds. Add 11/2 ounces (45 ml) Centerba to each mug; pour half the hot chocolate over the Centerba in each mug. (Add a little sugar or honey to taste, if necessary.) Spoon the fresh whipped cream over the top—then relax, indulge, and sip until you're thoroughly thawed. Serves 2.

SIDENOTE

⇒ **Homemade whipped cream in minutes.** Put down that aerosol can right now. You don't need to buy pre-made, processed, preservative-laden whipped cream from the supermarket! It's ridiculously easy to make your own, and it tastes so much better than the store-bought stuff. Just add 1 cup heavy whipping cream and 2 tablespoons sugar (or more or less, to taste), plus 1/2-1 teaspoon vanilla extract, if you like, to a medium bowl, then use an electric mixer to whip the mixture until soft peaks form (about 4-5 minutes). Do not overwhip, or the mixture may become lumpy. Use it to top your Centerba and Chocolate Chaud—or a round of Irish coffees!—then store leftovers in an airtight container in the refrigerator for 1-2 days.

PACKING THE OLD PICKUP TRUCK

This memorable, white whiskey–laden cocktail was inspired by the quince fruit grown on my family's farm. A late-season fruit that's usually ripe by November, quince looks like the offspring of an apple and a pear, and it's a bright lemon yellow. When roasted, it's absolutely sublime: It has a faint citrus flavor, and it's tinged with the restrained elegance of light stone fruits. After spending some time in a hot oven, the natural sugars in the quince ooze out, and it becomes a wonderful addition to cocktails like the Old Pickup Truck. You can find quince in specialty food shops or, in season, at your local farmer's market—but feel free to use store-bought quince paste instead. Combined with raki (a strong Turkish aniseed liqueur), club soda, and a hint of orange flower water, this cocktail is sophisticated and exotic, all at once.

INGREDIENTS

_ 3 OUNCES (90 ML) WHITE WHISKEY

_ 1 OUNCE (30 ML) RAKI

_ 3 OUNCES (85 G) QUINCE PUREE (SEE PAGE 312), OR STORE-BOUGHT QUINCE PASTE

_ 2 OUNCES (60 ML) RAW HONEY SIMPLE SYRUP

_ 1 OUNCE (30 ML) CLUB SODA

_ VERY SMALL DASH OF ORANGE FLOWER WATER

_ HAND-CUT ICE

DIRECTIONS

Add the first four ingredients to a Boston shaker filled three-quarters full with ice. Shake hard for about 15 seconds. Place a chunk of hand-cut ice into a rocks glass, and strain the mixture into the glass. Top with the club soda and the orange flower water, and, if you like, garnish with an orange pinwheel. Serves 2 quinceheads.

GENERAL JACK'S CRISP APPLE FIZZ

This cocktail celebrates those late September days when the sunlight becomes syrupy and mellow, the air takes on that bracing, autumnal crackle, and apple trees yield their generous bounty. Out here in western New Jersey, we're blessed with trees that produce gorgeous cider apples, and cider—and all things that smack of apple, really—is a great match for the smoky flavor inherent to Tennessee sipping whiskey. Here, whiskey, apple brandy, and apple cider are rounded out with a homemade honey simple syrup and doused with seltzer water just prior to serving for a drink that's the essence of fall. Plus, when you mix Tennessee sipping whiskey with apple cider, magical things happen: The world takes on a lovely golden hue, and troubles seem just a bit further away.

INGREDIENTS

- _ 2 OUNCES (60 ML) TENNESSEE SIPPING WHISKEY
- _ 1/2 OUNCE (15 ML) 100 PROOF APPLE BRANDY (LIKE LAIRD'S)
- _ 1/2 OUNCE (15 ML) UNFILTERED APPLE CIDER
- _ 1/2 OUNCE (15 ML) RAW HONEY SIMPLE SYRUP (SEE PAGE 312-313)
- _ 1 OUNCE (30 ML) SELTZER WATER
- _ EXTRA-LONG TWIST OF GRAPEFRUIT ZEST

DIRECTIONS

Fill a Boston shaker three-quarters full with ice. Add the Tennessee sipping whiskey, the apple brandy, the apple cider, and the Honey Simple Syrup. Shake like crazy for about 20 seconds. Pour over hand-cut ice in a tall Collins glass. Top with the seltzer, garnish with the grapefruit zest twist, and serve.

SIDENOTE

⇒ **Tennessee sipping whiskey** lives up to its name. It's whiskey that's produced in the state of Tennessee, and was traditionally made to be sipped slowly (instead of thrown back as a shot or diluted with mixers). Jack Daniel's is probably the best-known producer of Tennessee sipping whiskey. Their distinctive, black-labeled bottles appear in bars (and in private homes) all over the world, even in the smallest of villages. The Jack Daniel's proprietary method of distillation involves deep charcoal filtration: Towards the end of the production process, the whiskey is filtered through charcoal in wooden vats. This charred-wood filtration creates JD's trademark smoky flavor, and balances the naturally sweet flavor of corn, its main ingredient. It's a flavor that's unique to Tennessee whiskeys; bourbon whiskeys produced elsewhere in the United States don't possess this smokiness because they're not filtered through charcoal. If you enjoy Scotch whiskey, try a Tennessee sipping whiskey: Stylistically, they're very similar due to their smoky flavor. That said, traditional distillation laws in the state are changing, and not all Tennessee whiskey is as smoky in the nose and mouth as Jack Daniel's is (whose Black Label, in particular, is not for the faint of heart!). Craft liquor producers are now seeking new licenses that'll permit them to produce their own versions of Tennessee sipping whiskey, using the state's locally drawn, fragrant, mineral-packed water.

QUICK BALSAMIC-FIG SHRUB

Here's another sumptuous quick shrub for those of you who crave instant gratification—and it's a combination that works so well in autumnal cocktails. My Quick Balsamic-Fig Shrub calls upon flavors you already know and love: Who hasn't enjoyed a salad of figs (and, perhaps, arugula) drizzled with good-quality balsamic? There's a reason it's such a good match: Fresh figs, with their sweet funkiness, are a great foil for tart, viscous balsamic vinegar. And capturing their essences in a shrub means instant success when it comes to making cocktails. This shrub would be wonderful in bourbon- or rye whiskey-based cocktails, but using booze is completely optional: You could also skip the liquor completely, and mix it with nothing more than a little soda water and a dash of simple syrup, as in the sublimely named Lady Frazier's Harried Excuse (see page 136–137).

INGREDIENTS

_ 4–5 PLUMP FRESH FIGS, QUARTERED

_ 1 CUP (200 G) DEMERARA SUGAR

_ 1 CUP (235 ML) BALSAMIC VINEGAR

DIRECTIONS

Place the fig quarters in a nonreactive bowl, and cover them with the sugar. Add the vinegar immediately, and mix well. Cover tightly, and let the mixture sit on the countertop for 2–3 days. Then, uncover the fig mixture, and mash it up a bit with a fork. Place a strainer over another nonreactive bowl, and transfer the mixture to the strainer. Press down on the fruit mixture with a wooden spoon to squeeze out as much liquid as possible. Voila: a shrub is born. Store the mixture in a sterilized bottle or jar, and use in your mock-or cocktails immediately.

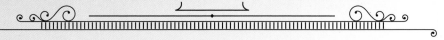

LADY FRAZER'S HARRIED EXCUSE

Cultivated by humans for thousands of years, the fig figures heavily in world mythologies. Take, for instance, an anecdote mentioned in that famous study of religion and mythology, James Frazer's *The Golden Bough*: Members of Aboriginal tribes in northern Australia believed the fig-tree was the conduit by which sun fertilized the earth. This innovative mocktail honors Frazer's wife, who, like her husband, must have been well versed in fig-related lore—but I bet she'd never tried drinking them. She should have, since this tipple is wonderful: A brown-sugar simple syrup loosens my lush, dark, tart Quick Balsamic-Fig Shrub before it's diffused in refreshing soda water and topped with a bright-yellow lemon twist. And it makes a great early-autumn aperitif. Serve a few rounds at your next party; it's sure to delight seasoned drinkers and teetotalers alike.

INGREDIENTS

_ 2 OUNCES (60 ML) QUICK BALSAMIC-FIG
SHRUB (SEE PAGE 134–135)

_ 1 OUNCE (30 ML) DEMERARA SUGAR
SIMPLE SYRUP (SEE PAGE 311)

_ 5 OUNCES (150 ML) SODA WATER

_ LEMON ZEST TWIST

DIRECTIONS

Pour the Balsamic-Fig Shrub into a Collins glass, then add the Demerara Sugar Simple Syrup. Add a spear of hand-cut ice. Top with soda water and garnish with a twist of lemon. (Adjust the sweetness to taste by adding a little more Demerara Sugar Simple Syrup, if necessary.)

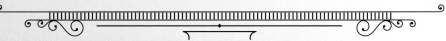

A QUARTER APIECE COCKTAIL

Thanks to the natural astringency of the quince fruit, rye whiskey and quince is a delicious (and highly effective) pairing. The only way to improve upon it is to smoke fresh sage into your Boston shaker: It gently perfumes the Quarter Apiece with an inimitable, savory-charred scent.

INGREDIENTS

_ 1 SMALL BUNCH OF FRESH SAGE

_ 2 OUNCES (60 ML) RYE WHISKEY

_ 1/2 OUNCE (15 ML) BOTANICAL GIN

_ 1 OUNCE (30 ML) APPLE JUICE

_ 2 OUNCES (60 ML) QUINCE
  PUREE (SEE PAGE 312), OR
  STORE-BOUGHT QUINCE PASTE

_ 1/2 OUNCE (15 ML) CLUB SODA

_ SEVERAL DASHES RHUBARB BITTERS

DIRECTIONS

Pre-chill a martini glass by filling it with crushed ice and cold water, and then pour the ice water out. Place the sage in a fireproof metal or ceramic bowl. Using a match or lighter, carefully set the sage on fire so that it smokes and smolders. Take a Boston shaker and hold it upside down over the burning sage, so that the shaker's interior is filled with the sweet, sticky smoke. Turn the shaker right-side up, and add the rye whiskey, the gin, and the apple juice. Then, fill the shaker three-quarters full with ice, add the quince puree, and shake for about 20 seconds. Pour the mixture into the martini glass, top with the club soda, and finish with a few dashes of rhubarb bitters.

SIDENOTE

⇒ **Smoking permitted.** But only in the name of mixology, of course. Smoking your fresh herbs before using them—or just their smoke, as in the Quarter Apiece—in cocktails can add a toasty, earthy, mysterious note to your handmade drinks. And you don't need any specialized equipment to do it, either. The Quarter Apiece calls for sage, but you can smoke or char other woody herbs, too. Apply the same method to capture the smoke from, say, rosemary, thyme, or even a cinnamon stick, and use it in your cocktails—especially ones with spirits like rum, whiskey, tequila, or mezcal. Just don't forget to use a fireproof bowl!

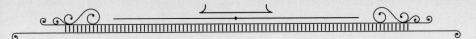

NAVY GROG

Today, we know how important vitamin C is to a healthy immune system, especially during the winter months when colds and flu run rampant. During the seventeenth and eighteenth centuries, sailors and ship doctors discovered that citrus fruits could combat scurvy, a disease that afflicted many sailors due to the lack of vitamin C in their diets. Soon afterwards, citrus juices and extracts were added to sailors' daily rations of rum and water—a combination called "grog." If a sailor took ill, a hot, restorative tea might have been added to his regimen of rum, citrus juice, and water. Rum—or "kill-devil," as it was called—has been used as a curative for centuries, and the triumvirate of tea, lemon, and rum was said to relieve fevers and stomach maladies. Easy-to-make and satisfying, hot grog is still delicious today—for "medicinal" uses only, of course.

INGREDIENTS

_ 10 OUNCES (285 ML) HOT, STRONG BLACK TEA

_ 6 OUNCES (175 ML) NAVY-STRENGTH (OVER 90-PROOF) RUM

_ 6 OUNCES (175 ML) FRESHLY SQUEEZED LEMON JUICE

DIRECTIONS

Prepare the tea in a teapot. Add 3 (90 ml) ounces each of rum and lemon juice to two mugs, then fill the mugs with the hot tea. Administer in piping-hot doses to two tired sailors until rosy-cheeked and refreshed.

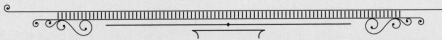

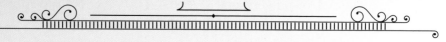

HOT APPLE PIE OLD-FASHIONED

Traditionally, an Old-Fashioned involves muddling sugar and bitters in the bottom of a glass, then adding a citrus twist and blended whiskey. Minimalist, delicious, and very *Mad Men!* But my Cocktail Whisperer's take on this classic transforms it into a warming winter drink that's a lovechild of the Old-Fashioned and a hot toddy. It replaces the sugar with grilled fruit, the citrus with grilled orange, and the regular ol' whiskey with Tennessee sipping whiskey. And hot tea, steaming apple cider, and raw honey make it just the thing for kicking back by the fire. I recommend grilling both the apples and oranges, since it gives the drink a toastiness that can't be beat. The Hot Apple Pie Old-Fashioned will warm your hands—and the cockles of your heart—on even the wintriest of days.

INGREDIENTS

_ 1/2 OUNCE (15 ML) ABSINTHE

_ GRILLED, MUDDLED FRUIT (GRILL ORANGE SLICES AND APPLE SLICES IN A CAST-IRON PAN, OR OVER CHARCOAL UNTIL GRILL MARKS APPEAR ON THEM—THEN CHOP INTO SMALL PIECES AND MUDDLE)

_ 3 OUNCES (90 ML) (NON-ALCOHOLIC) APPLE CIDER, WARMED THROUGH

_ 4 OUNCES (120 ML) TENNESSEE SIPPING WHISKEY

_ 4 OUNCES (120 ML) HOT ENGLISH BREAKFAST TEA

_ 2 OUNCES (57 G) RAW HONEY (OR TO TASTE)

_ EASY HOME-CURED COCKTAIL CHERRIES (SEE PAGE 311) FOR GARNISH

DIRECTIONS

Pre-heat two mugs by filling them with boiling water, and then pour the water out. Wash each mug with 1/4 ounce (7 ml) of absinthe, and then pour that out too (into your mouth, if you like!) Split the charred fruit between the mugs, then muddle them with the back of a bar spoon or the end of a wooden spoon. Pour the hot tea over the fruits, and then pour the whiskey over the hot tea. Top with the hot cider, add the raw honey to taste, and mix gently. Garnish with apple and orange slices, and an Easy Home-Cured Cocktail Cherries (throw out those red things in a jar: the homemade ones are so much better!) Serves two chilly drinkers.

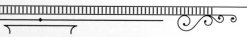

"CORRECTED" SCOTCH BROTH

One of my favorite winter warmers hails from Scotland, where the Scots "correct" a steaming mug of rich lamb broth with a famous barley-based digestive called—you guessed it—Scotch whisky. Piping-hot Scotch broth is practically a full meal, being packed with lamb, carrots, celery, and onions, and interwoven with lashings of smoky Scotch whisky. (Try to make your own lamb stock for your Scotch broth, since it's so much better than the store-bought stuff.) Like its distant cousin borscht, this fine corrective warms the body, calms the mind, and soothes the spirit—even on the icy winter months when the cold seems to seep into your bones. Can it cure cold-weather maladies? Well, as the Scottish proverb goes, "Whiskey may not cure the common cold, but it fails more agreeably than most things."

INGREDIENTS

_ 8 OUNCES (235 ML) LAMB STOCK, EITHER HOMEMADE OR STORE-BOUGHT, SIMMERED WITH VEGETABLES OF YOUR CHOICE, SUCH AS ONIONS, CARROTS, CELERY, AND POTATOES—BEST SIMMERED IN A CAST IRON POT ON A WOOD-FIRED STOVE!

_ 3 OUNCES (90 ML) VERY SMOKY SCOTCH WHISKY

DIRECTIONS

Pour the steaming lamb stock with vegetables into a bowl. Add the Scotch whisky, and mix gently. Grab a spoon, and get ready: This curative broth will warm you from the inside out for hours.

PARSNIP, CARROT, AND FENNEL SHRUB

This savory, root-vegetable-based shrub is the very essence of autumn. Lightly seasoned with fresh sage and tarragon, its flavors are subtle and delicate, and patience is one of its main ingredients. Don't try to rush things here: The vegetables in my Parsnip, Carrot, and Fennel Shrub need to be chopped finely, and once *in situ* in their sugar-vinegar bath they do take several weeks to ferment—but it's all worth it in the end. Once it's ready to use, you can partner it with lightly sweetened lemonade. Or, if you feel like adding something a little stronger, know that this shrub is marvelous with gin, or even with a healthy hit of aquavit, the infamous Norwegian caraway seed–based liquor.

INGREDIENTS

_ 3–4 CUPS (435–580 G) PARSNIPS, CARROTS, AND FENNEL BULB CUT INTO SMALL COINS OR CHUNKS

_ 2 CUPS (400 G) DEMERARA SUGAR

_ 2 CUPS (475 ML) RED WINE VINEGAR

_ 4 LEAVES FRESH TARRAGON

_ 4 LEAVES FRESH SAGE

_ 1 TEASPOON FRESHLY GRATED NUTMEG

DIRECTIONS

Time: 2-3 weeks. *Place the chopped vegetables in a wide glass bowl, cover them with the sugar, and mix well. Cover the mixture, and let it sit at cellar temperature for 2–3 days. Now add the red wine vinegar, the herbs, and the nutmeg, and mix again. Continue to let the mixture ferment at cellar temperature, stirring each day until the sugar is dissolved, and adding a little more vinegar if necessary. After 2–3 weeks, place a strainer over a nonreactive bowl, and transfer the mixture to the strainer. Use a wooden spoon to press as much of the vegetable mixture through the strainer as possible. Funnel into sterilized bottles or jars and store them in the fridge for several more weeks, shaking the bottles daily to combine and mellow the flavors.*

THE THEODORE ALLEN MOCKTAIL

Named for a larger-than-life rabble-rouser, saloon owner, and criminal (Tony Soprano had nothing on him), this intriguing libation doesn't include hooch—and that's because it doesn't need any. (Unlike Allen himself, of course, who was partial to the stuff.) There's plenty of flavor in this booze-free cocktail, thanks to my Parsnip, Carrot, and Fennel Shrub: After aging for a few weeks, the parsnips' sweetness becomes more pronounced, and aromatic herbs like tarragon and sage, combined with the licorice-tinged fennel root, imbue it with subtle layers of flavor. A little lemonade and a pinch of sea salt add flavor and texture—and act as a melancholy tip-of-the-hat to the fading summer. If you ask me, mocktails made with root-vegetable-based shrubs are especially beguiling on late fall afternoons, when dusk falls early over bare trees. Go ahead and add gin here if you want to kick it Theodore Allen–style—but it's just as good *sans* liquor, if not better.

INGREDIENTS

_ 1 OUNCE (30 ML) PARSNIP, CARROT, AND FENNEL SHRUB (SEE PAGE 144–145)

_ 2 OUNCES (60 ML) COOL SPRING WATER

_ 1/4 OUNCE (7 ML) LEMONADE (SWEETENED WITH A LITTLE RAW HONEY SIMPLE SYRUP: SEE PAGE 312–313)

_ PINCH OF SEA SALT

DIRECTIONS

Add the shrub to a 4 ounce (120-ml) cordial glass. Top with cool water, a drop of sweetened lemonade, and a pinch of sea salt. Sip to your heart's content, and don't be afraid to pour yourself a second round.

MAPLE SMOKE FIZZ

And now for something completely different. See, I lived in southern Maine after college, and I have delicious memories of the scent of maple wood smoke, which seemed to infiltrate everything during the long winters. Same with sticky-sweet maple syrup: No matter what I do, I just can't forget the deep, caramelized aromatics of boiled sap. What if those woody, maply scents could be turned into a cocktail? Like the Quarter Apiece Cocktail on page 138, this drink involves some minor pyrotechnics: It asks you to make your own smoke by lighting up a few splinters of maple wood, and then to "wash" a cocktail shaker with a few wisps of that enchanting fragrance. (Proceed carefully.) That, plus the mysterious qualities of both absinthe and Tennessee sipping whiskey, makes this unique take on the classic Sazerac truly captivating.

INGREDIENTS

_ A FEW SPLINTERS OF MAPLE WOOD, PLACED INSIDE AN ASHTRAY OR A FLAMEPROOF METAL OR CERAMIC BOWL

_ 2 OUNCES (60 ML) TENNESSEE SIPPING WHISKEY

_ 1/2 OUNCE (15 ML) HERBSAINT OR ABSINTHE

_ 1 OUNCE (30 ML) MAPLE SYRUP

_ SEVERAL DASHES PEYCHAUD'S BITTERS

_ 1 OUNCE (30 ML) CLUB SODA

_ ORANGE PEEL ZEST TWIST

DIRECTIONS

Pre-chill your cocktail glass by filling it with ice, cold water, and the Herbsaint or absinthe. Then pour the mixture out (consider drinking it—why waste fine spirits?) Using matches or a lighter, carefully light the pieces of maple wood so that they kindle and smolder, producing smoke. Hold a Boston shaker over the miniature fire, letting the sweet wood smoke gather inside. Then, fill the Boston shaker three-quarters full with ice. Add the Tennessee sipping whiskey, then the maple syrup. To the cocktail glass, now chilled and tinged by Herbsaint or absinthe, add several dashes of Peychaud's bitters. Finally, strain the maple smoke Sazerac into the cocktail glass, top with the club soda, and garnish with the orange peel zest, twisting it slightly to release the fragrant orange oils from the skin. Sip—and start making another immediately.

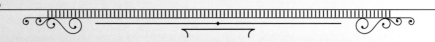

TO MR. W. E. HENLEY

Named after the author of the famously rousing poem "Invictus," this is a riff on the classic, perfect-for-daytime-drinking hot chocolate toddy, and it's a first cousin of the Irish coffee. It's an excellent vehicle for spelt whiskey—and those orange bitters that make up the finale? They provide much-needed balance in your cup that runneth over with the sweetness of hot chocolate, simple syrup, and whipped cream.

INGREDIENTS

_ 2 OUNCES (60 ML) SPELT WHISKEY

_ 3 OUNCES (90 ML) THE BEST HOT CHOCOLATE (SEE PAGE 312)

_ 2 OUNCES (60 ML) ESPRESSO COFFEE (MADE FRESH OR FROM ESPRESSO POWDER, IN A PINCH)

_ 1/2 OUNCE (15 ML) BASIC SIMPLE SYRUP, OR TO TASTE (SEE PAGE 311)

_ HOMEMADE WHIPPED CREAM (SEE PAGE 312)

_ ORANGE BITTERS

DIRECTIONS

Preheat a mug by filling it with boiling water, and then pour it out. Add the spelt whiskey, and top with the hot chocolate and espresso coffee. Sweeten with the Simple Syrup, spoon the whipped cream over the top, and dot with orange bitters. Bliss!

A PLEASANT LITTLE GENTLEMAN

A Pleasant Little Gentleman makes an excellent companion. This warming, tummy-taming toddy is a lovely way to finish a long day. Try one just before bedtime: I can't think of a better way to relax than with a steaming Gentleman and a good book. This cocktail combines that famous *digestif*, Fernet Branca, with a dose of rye whiskey, and then sweetens the deal with a simple syrup made from raw honey. In conjunction with the rye and Fernet, raw honey's naturally salubrious enzymes do wonderful things for your uneasy belly—and for your flagging spirits. Sip it from a vintage teacup: That way, the Pleasant Little Gentleman will look just like a regular old cup of tea to the casual observer. The only person who'll know that you're actually taking a healthy sup of something much stronger is you.

INGREDIENTS

_ 2 OUNCES (60 ML) FERNET BRANCA

_ 1 OUNCE (30 ML) RYE WHISKEY

_ 1 OUNCE (30 ML) RAW HONEY SIMPLE
SYRUP (SEE PAGE 312-313)

_ 2 TO 3 SHAKES WHISKEY
BARREL-AGED BITTERS

_ BOILING WATER OR VERY HOT
BLACK TEA (OPTIONAL)

DIRECTIONS

Preheat a teacup by filling it with boiling water, and then pour the water out. Add the rye, the Fernet Branca, and the Raw Honey Simple Syrup. Stir gently. Add a couple dashes of the whiskey barrel bitters. The Pleasant Little Gentleman is now ready to serve—but I recommend topping it up with a dose of either boiling water or strong black tea.

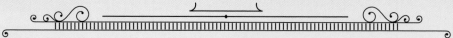

MOORS AT NIGHT PUNCH

Scotch is the essential ingredient in many hot punches, and with good reason: There's really no better restorative for both body and soul. Scotch works its healing magic not only through its soothing-yet-stimulating smoky taste, but also through its scent; a mere sniff of a hot, Scotch-based cocktail is enough to calm the nerves and warm the bones. If you've been roaming England's chilly moors with a heavy tread (or if you just feel like you have), rest assured that this savory potion will help you beat the "brrr." Combining steaming-hot, herb-infused beef bouillon with a hearty dose of Scotch and a whack of fresh lemon juice, the Moors at Night Punch was inspired by a couple of particularly cold winters I spent on mid-coast Maine during the 1980s.

INGREDIENTS

_ 1 CUP (235 ML) VERY HOT, STRONG BEEF BOUILLON (SEE BELOW)

_ ASSORTED HERBS FROM THE GARDEN, SUCH AS THYME, ROSEMARY, SAGE, AND LAVENDER

_ 1 CHEESECLOTH BAG FOR STEEPING THE HERBS

_ 3 OUNCES (90 ML) SMOKY SCOTCH WHISKY

_ 2 TABLESPOONS (30 ML) RAW HONEY SIMPLE SYRUP (SEE PAGE 312-313)

_ 1 OUNCE (30 ML) FRESHLY SQUEEZED LEMON JUICE (NO SCURVY ABOARD THIS SHIP!)

DIRECTIONS

Place the pre-made bouillon in a small saucepan. Place the herbs in a cheesecloth bag, and steep them in the hot bouillon for about five minutes. Preheat a ceramic mug by pouring boiling water into it, and then pour the water out. Add the whisky and Raw Honey Simple Syrup to the mug, and then pour the herb-steeped bouillon over the mixture. Finally, stir in the fresh lemon juice. Serves 2 frozen souls.

SIDENOTE

⇒ **Homemade beef bouillon** is an all-day event, but it's so worth the effort. Here's my family's recipe: Preheat the oven to 400 degrees. Sear 3 pounds beef bones, 3 pounds oxtail, and 3 pounds shin- and "osso-buco"-style beef cuts in the oven in a very large sautoir or Dutch Oven. After 1 hour, or when the meat is very brown, add 1 pound washed, peeled, and chopped root vegetables, like carrots, parsnips, celery, and onion, plus 5-6 halved, peeled shallots and 3-4 whole, unpeeled cloves garlic. Turn the heat down if it starts to smoke. Scrape up any browned bits, then add a pinch of star anise and 1 cup dry white wine. Reduce the heat to medium-low and simmer for 30 minutes. Season with salt and pepper, then add 1 stalk lemongrass and 2 gallons spring water. Cover and cook in the oven at 275 degrees (or simmer on the stovetop) for at least 4 hours. Strain out the meat, and reserve for another recipe. Reduce the stock to the desired thickness, then cool and use in recipes or freeze for up to several months.

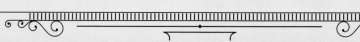

MOUNTAIN BODY WARMER

That world-famous herbal (or sometimes fruit-laced) German concentrate of distilled spirits called *schnapps* delivers rapid inner heating that can counteract the effects of cold and snowy weather. Schnapps—which has been around for centuries, and was originally only available from apothecaries—can also offer much-needed relief from the winter colds and coughs that can ravage the throat and respiratory system. (As the Russian proverb goes, "Drink a glass of schnapps after your soup and you steal a ruble from the doctor.") Germans mix it with hot tea, honey, and lemon; pour it into flasks; and use it to warm both body and mind when outdoors during the chilly months. Mix up a pot of this soothing tea before or after heading outdoors in wintertime; you'll feel refreshed by the crisp peppermint aroma, and you'll stay toasty warm from the inside out.

INGREDIENTS

_ 16 OUNCES (475 ML) HOT HERBAL TEA
  (SUCH AS PEPPERMINT OR SPEARMINT)

_ 4 OUNCES (120 ML)
  PEPPERMINT SCHNAPPS

_ 4 OUNCES (120 ML) APRICOT SCHNAPPS

_ 4 TABLESPOONS (80 G)
  WILDFLOWER HONEY

_ JUICE OF 3 LEMONS

DIRECTIONS

Make the pot of herbal tea in a teapot. Add the peppermint schnapps and the apricot schnapps, and mix well. Then add the honey and lemon juice (feel free to use a bit more or less, to taste). Serve immediately, or pour into individual flasks and bring them with you into the cold weather for serious warming that'll last for hours. Serves 2 chilly drinkers.

AQUAVIT WITH HEALING BITTER HERBS AND HOT TEA

Caraway seeds, which were traditionally used in topical medicinal preparations such salves or balms, made their way into the potent Norwegian tipple *aquavit*, a marvelous caraway- and anise-scented elixir made from potatoes. Taking its name from the Latin phrase *aqua vitae*, or "water of life," aquavit is also very popular in northern European countries such as Sweden and Denmark, regions in which below-zero weather is status quo during the winter months. Originally invented in the sixteenth century as a digestive aid, in the era of the pharmacist and the apothecary, aquavit might have been prepared with other medicinal herbs and sweet spices in addition to caraway, in order to stave off other cold-weather-induced maladies. It's especially delicious when served on its own alongside platters of smoked fish—or in this healing concoction of aquavit, herb-infused simple syrup, and good old-fashioned hot tea.

INGREDIENTS

_ 1 CUP (235 ML) (OR MORE, TO TASTE) HOT BLACK TEA

_ 2 OUNCES (60 ML) HEALING HERB SIMPLE SYRUP (SEE PAGE 312)

_ 3 OUNCES (90 ML) AQUAVIT

_ GROUND CLOVES FOR DUSTING

DIRECTIONS

Make a pot of strong, hot, black tea, and pour a cup into a large mug. Add the healing herb simple syrup and the aquavit, mixing well after each addition. Dust the top of the drink with the ground cloves. Warm yourself to the bone. Repeat if necessary.

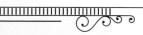

HONEY HEALER

In Germany, certain herb-based liqueurs are produced with enzyme-rich honey from the Yucatan Peninsula in Mexico in order to offset the liqueurs' acerbic bitters. This rich, darkly colored honey is a great healer: Raw honey has been said to alleviate the symptoms of seasonal allergies when consumed regularly, and may be good for digestive ailments like colitis. In Ayurvedic medicine, too, honey is highly valued—it's reputed to be one of the most powerful substances for promoting good health in general. And honey can sweeten the spirit as well as the body:

Suspending it in alcohol and combining it with black or herbal tea and plenty of ice makes it a highly refreshing mood enhancer. The honey, rum, and German herbal spirits in this tall cocktail weave an enchanting spell—one that never fails to relax, re-animate, and restore.

INGREDIENTS

_ 12 OUNCES (355 ML) COOL BLACK TEA

_ 4 TABLESPOONS (80 G) RAW HONEY

_ 6 OUNCES (175 ML) NAVY-STRENGTH (OVER 90-PROOF) RUM

_ 3 OUNCES (90 ML) GERMAN HERBAL LIQUEUR

DIRECTIONS

Prepare the tea; stir in the honey; and let the mixture cool. Pack two glasses with crushed ice, and divide the rum and the herbal liqueur between them. Top each glass with the honey-sweetened tea. Stir, taste, adjust the sweetness if necessary, and say guten Morgen to a great mood.

GINGER-LIME SHRUBB COCKTAIL

Okay, so the Ginger-Lime Shrubb Cocktail isn't a hot drink, but it'll warm the cockles of your heart nonetheless. Shrubb cocktails are derived from historic maritime cocktail ingredients that include vinegar for the preservation of easily spoiled—and valuable—citrus fruits. Without preservatives, citrus fruits would have quickly rotted under the hot sun. In traditional Shrubb cocktails, lime and ginger supplement honey, vinegar, and cider, packing powerful health benefits. They take their inspiration from the concentrated citrus syrups once used to stave off tropical diseases that plagued seafarers, such as scurvy. The intense flavors of lime and ginger can act as an antidote to seasickness on their own, but they're especially delicious alongside rum and hydrating, refreshing seltzer water—particularly soothing when fighting a body-ravaging cold.

INGREDIENTS

_ 3 OUNCES (90 ML) RHUM AGRICOLE

_ 3 TO 4 TABLESPOONS (45 TO 60 ML) GINGER-LIME SHRUB (SEE PAGE 82)

_ SELTZER WATER

_ SEVERAL DASHES OF ANGOSTURA BITTERS

_ ICE

DIRECTIONS

Toss a handful of ice cubes into a short rocks glass. Add the Rhum Agricole and stir in the ginger-lime Shrubb syrup. Top with the seltzer water and a dash or two of stomach-healing Angostura bitters, to taste. Sip slowly, letting the bracing ginger-lime combination nurse you back to health.

BELLE ISLE COCKTAIL

Brewing up a strong hot toddy is one of my favorite ways to get rid of a headache, or to put the kibosh on a pesky cold. And Scotch makes a top-notch toddy: Combining Scotch with hot water or strong black tea enhances its peaty flavor. (I prefer tea, to be honest, since watery toddies aren't up my alley; but if you're avoiding caffeine, hot water really does work just as well. Or, you might try decaffeinated black tea instead.) Scotch, fresh lemon juice, hot black tea, and simple syrup combine in the Belle Isle Cocktail for a hot punch that really packs a punch. This gorgeous little glug comprises no more than four simple ingredients, but it's certain to help you shake that woolly-headedness that accompanies winter colds and other bugs. Apply as needed.

INGREDIENTS

_ 2 OUNCES (60 ML) SCOTCH WHISKY

_ 1 OUNCE (30 ML) FRESHLY
SQUEEZED LEMON JUICE

_ 3 OUNCES (90 ML) FRESHLY
BREWED STRONG BLACK TEA

_ 1 OUNCE (30 ML) BASIC SIMPLE
SYRUP (SEE PAGE 311)

DIRECTIONS

Preheat your favorite ceramic mug by filling it with boiling water, and then pour the water out. Add the simple syrup and the Scotch to the mug, followed by the tea and the fresh lemon juice. Stir gently. Serve and sip, preferably under a warm quilt.

⇒ **Start your love affair with Scotch.** Scotch whisky (note that missing "e"!) certainly looms large in the collective memory of drinkers around the world, and whether you're an expert or a neophyte when it comes to Scotch, I'll wager you're familiar with the tipple, if only in theory. So, what is the stuff, anyway? Basically, "Scotch" refers to malt whisky or grain whisky (note the spelling: There's no "I" in "team," but in Scotland, there's no "e" in "whisky," either) that's made in Scotland. (By law, whiskies labeled as "Scotch" must be made in Scotland, so don't bother looking: You won't find American-made Scotch.) It's often made from barley, which has been malted. That is, the grains have been placed in water and allowed to germinate, and are then removed from the water and dried in hot air to stop the germination process. Scotch whisky usually clocks in at between forty percent and forty-six percent alcohol by volume, and it must be aged for at least three years (and it's often aged for much longer than that). Part of the aging process often takes place in wooden casks that were formerly used to store port, sherry, or even bourbon.

When it comes to the flavor, character, and aromatics of this venerable spirit, each version is unique: Part of the wonder inherent in experimenting with Scotch is that each expression of the spirit will be different to the last one that you tried. Some Scotch whiskies are sweet and delicate; some are lightly smoky and fruity; and some are dark, heavily smoky, peaty, and earthy. Not every variety of Scotch whisky will appeal to you, and that's fine. A good rule of thumb is simply to experiment with an open mind—you're sure to find at least one, if not many, that you enjoy. As in love, so in spirits: Just like the best relationships, knowing and loving Scotch is a quest that can and should become a lifelong endeavor.

POTENT PAINKILLERS:

POTABLE BALM FOR ACHES
AND PAINS

◆ · ◆ · ◆

SO FAR, YOUR DAY'S BEEN JUST FINE. THERE'S NO TRAFFIC ON YOUR MORNING COMMUTE; YOUR BOSS IS ON VACATION AND YOU'VE BEEN SUPER-PRODUCTIVE ALL MORNING; AND YOU GOT YOUR FAVORITE CHINESE TAKEOUT FOR LUNCH. THEN: WHAM. PAIN STRIKES. NOW YOU'VE GOT THE HEADACHE FROM HELL; A BACKACHE THAT MAKES YOU WANT TO GO STRAIGHT BACK TO BED; OR JOINT PAIN THAT JUST WON'T QUIT. AND YOU'RE NOT SURE HOW YOU'RE GOING TO MAKE IT THROUGH THE REST OF THE DAY IN ONE PIECE. *OY VEY*. ACHES AND PAINS LIKE THESE CAN BE VERY FRUSTRATING, AND EVEN DEBILITATING. SO WHAT'S A BODY TO DO?

Ask your ancestors. For hundreds of years, sufferers have been visiting apothecaries seeking solutions for pain of all sorts. Some early analgesics contained powerful concentrations of highly addictive, narcotic drugs, including heroin, morphine, and cocaine. Sometimes the cure truly was worse than the disease: Users of drugs like these ran a significant risk of becoming addicted to them, replacing illness with dependence. Happily, though, there were far less risky—and, arguably, more effective—curatives at the apothecary's disposal. Many herbs, spices, fruits, and vegetables contain natural properties that can easy bodily pain and calm the sufferer's uneasy, stressed-out mind. But these delicate botanicals had to be preserved: Without refrigeration, many of them would have rotted, ruining their restorative properties—especially in warmer climates. That's where alcohol comes in. Suspending fragile botanicals in alcohol prevents rotting, and can release their potential healing benefits. Blackberries, for example, have been used as analgesics for centuries—but how to preserve their painkilling power for months at a time? The answer is simple: Combine them with high-proof spirits into delicious infusions that'll last well into winter.

Of course, there are hundreds of natural remedies for easing pain. Celery juice has been used as an analgesic since Roman times, and today, it may be effective in reducing arthritis-related joint pain. Lavender, peppermint, and clary sage have offered relief from stress-induced headaches for centuries, while chamomile calms the entire body and, some say, quickly relieves menstrual pain. The herb lemon balm, a relative of peppermint, is also said to relieve stubborn body aches. Nutmeg is said to restore a wilting appetite, which can help ease the headaches and fatigue brought on by hunger. Turmeric, garlic, ginger, chiles, poppy seeds, and anise also have venerable reputations as painkillers.

And when it comes to cocktails, there are plenty of easy-to-make drinks that are surprisingly effective at banishing pain, since they feature ingredients that old-time pharmacists would have had at their fingertips. For instance, my Lemon Balm Gin and Tonic sports a dose of lemon balm-enhanced simple syrup, which may ease digestive disorders and help mitigate bodily pain in general. Then there's the whiskey- and coffee-laced Revenge of the Painkiller, a luscious concoction that'll chill you out and get rid of that pesky caffeine-withdrawal headache. Nineteeth-century tipplers would have recommended the Green Fairy to fight pain, so you might want to reach for that bottle of absinthe and make a Soft Grey Lace, a winning combination of quinoa whiskey, absinthe, ginger beer, and a dusting of cayenne pepper—or an icy, mint-laden Absinthe Frappé, since cool, refreshing liquids never do any harm when it comes to easing pain. (Remember that it's important to stay hydrated, especially when you're drinking alcohol: in fact, sometimes simply drinking a fizzy glass of seltzer water can be a quick way to keep pain at bay.)

If you haven't got time for the pain—and who does?—whip up a couple of the craft cocktails in this chapter. Relief is just a few pages away!

LEMON BALM GIN AND TONIC

When headaches strike, they can be distracting and even debilitating. Instead of reaching for synthetic painkillers, try a restorative cocktail made with lemon balm, a popular herbal cure that old-time pharmacists would've sworn by. Its lemon-scented leaves boast a long history of treating tension and stress, promoting refreshing sleep, sharpening concentration, improving mental performance, and easing nervous conditions that may lead to headaches and even migraines. Here, it's infused in simple syrup and served up on ice with a generous dose of gin for a prescriptive take on the classic gin and tonic.

INGREDIENTS

_ 3 OUNCES (90 ML) BOTANICAL GIN

_ 2 TABLESPOONS (30 ML) LEMON BALM
SIMPLE SYRUP (SEE PAGE 312)

_ 1/4 FRESH LIME, CUT INTO CHUNKS

DIRECTIONS

Pack a tall glass with ice; then slowly pour the gin over the ice so it's well chilled. Add the lemon balm simple syrup, and mix well. Top it with the tonic water and garnish with a lime chunk or two for an extra spritz of citrus. It's sure to clear the head and chase pesky headaches away.

BLACKBERRY ELIXIR →

Berries are truly one of nature's superfoods. Today, we know that they're high in antioxidants, jam-packed (no pun intended!) with vitamin C, folic acid, and potassium, and may play a role in cancer prevention. But that wouldn't have surprised German apothecaries of days gone by: In Germany, blackberries and elderberries have been prized for their painkilling properties for hundreds of years. Blackberries contain salicylic acid—a compound that's also present in aspirin while elderberries are said to combat pain resulting from rheumatism or traumatic injuries. Blackberry brandy, which apothecaries once prescribed as an able painkiller, is at the heart of this luscious elixir.

INGREDIENTS

_ 1 EGG WHITE

_ 1 OUNCE (25 ML) LIME JUICE

_ 3 TABLESPOONS (45 ML) BERRY
VODKA INFUSION (SEE PAGE 311)

_ 3 OUNCES (90 ML) BOTANICAL GIN

DIRECTIONS

Combine the egg white and lime juice in a Boston shaker, and shake without ice—a technique known as dry shaking—for one minute until the egg white stands up in fluffy peaks. Add 2 tablespoons (30 ml) of the berry infusion and the gin; then fill the shaker three-quarters full with ice, and shake for twenty seconds until well-combined. Place the remaining tablespoon of the berry puree into a coupé glass, and pour the mixture over it.

COCKTAIL WHISPERER'S PAINKILLING SYSTEM # 200

Sailors of the eighteenth and nineteenth centuries were well aware of rum's power as a painkiller. These days, rum is still an effective anodyne—when taken in small doses, of course! Here, fresh citrus juices balance out two types of rum, while orgeat syrup and coconut milk add sweetness and richness. The final flourish? A scraping of fresh nutmeg.

INGREDIENTS

_ 3 OUNCES (90 ML) DARK RUM

_ 1 OUNCE (25 ML) 140-PROOF RUM

_ 1 TABLESPOON (15 ML)
ORGEAT SYRUP

_ 1/2 OUNCE (15 ML) SWEETENED
COCONUT MILK

_ 2 OUNCES (60 ML) FRESH
PINEAPPLE JUICE

_ 2 OUNCES (60 ML) FRESHLY
SQUEEZED ORANGE JUICE

_ 2 OUNCES (60 ML) FRESHLY
SQUEEZED GRAPEFRUIT JUICE

_ COCONUT ICE CUBES (FILL AN
ICE CUBE TRAY WITH A MIXTURE
OF 1 PART WATER TO 1 PART
SWEETENED COCONUT WATER
AND FREEZE OVERNIGHT)

_ 4 DASHES ORANGE BITTERS

_ FRESHLY GRATED NUTMEG

DIRECTIONS

Fill a Boston shaker three-quarters full with ice. Combine all the liquid ingredients over the ice, and shake vigorously for twenty seconds. Fill a tall glass half full with crushed ice made from the coconut ice cubes, and strain the mixture into the glass. Garnish with a pineapple spear and a dusting of fresh nutmeg. Sip until pain free.

SIDENOTE

⇒ **Nutmeg** has been highly prized by apothecaries, cooks, and diners alike since at least the early medieval period. (In fact, when Christopher Columbus set out in search of the East Indies, nutmeg was one of the valuable spices he was seeking, along with mustard seed, peppercorns, turmeric, ginger root, and many others.) It's widely used in cuisines around the world, and early pharmacists would have known that a dash of nutmeg could act as an appetite stimulant and an antibacterial, and could ease certain psychological conditions, such as those which cause insomnia. And its essential oil has been said to alleviate joint pain. Don't start chomping down whole nutmeg seeds, though: in large quantities, nutmeg can be psychoactive, and even toxic.

REVENGE OF THE PAINKILLER

Rye whiskey is fabulous in drinks that are traditionally made with rum, including my Cocktail Whisperer's riff on the classic Painkiller. A famously dangerous drink that hails from the British islands in the Caribbean, your average, everyday Painkiller consists of rum, pineapple juice, orange juice, and cream of coconut. But, if you ask me, the ingredients in my version are far more interesting. Here, rye binds espresso, rum, coffee liqueur, and chocolate liqueur together in a lip-smacking concoction that's very effective when sipped just before lunch in the hot sun, on the prow of a yacht, or beside a swimming pool. (Do pre-chill your glassware with crushed ice before serving: Revenge is a drink best served iced.) This lush cocktail is built for two, so share it with someone special. Otherwise, the Painkiller has a tendency to bite back.

INGREDIENTS

_ 2 SHOTS FRESHLY-PULLED, COOLED ESPRESSO COFFEE

_ 1/2 OUNCE (15 ML) COFFEE LIQUEUR

_ 1 OUNCE (30 ML) CHOCOLATE LIQUEUR

_ 1/2 OUNCE (15 ML) DARK RUM

_ 1 OUNCE (30 ML) RYE WHISKEY

_ 2 OUNCES (60 ML) SIMPLE SYRUP (SEE PAGE 311)

_ 4 DROPS AZTEC BITTERS

_ CRUSHED ICE

_ FRESHLY SCRAPED NUTMEG

_ EASY HOME-CURED COCKTAIL CHERRIES (SEE PAGE 311)

DIRECTIONS

Add all the liquid ingredients and the crushed ice to a blender, and pulse until smooth. Pour the mixture into pre-chilled pint glasses, and scrape some fresh nutmeg over the top. (Avoid the pre-ground stuff—fresh nutmeg is so much better!) Garnish each drink with an Easy Home-Cured Cocktail Cherry, and serve with straws.

SOFT GREY LACE

This cocktail doesn't do what it says on the label. There's nothing soft or grey about it—although it is "laced" with lime and cayenne pepper for a riff on the famous (or infamous?) Moscow Mule. I like to make it with quinoa whiskey, which starts off dry on the palate, and then mellows into sweetness and a pillow-soft finish. That said, I think quinoa whiskey benefits from a fizzy mixer, hence the addition of cane-sugar beer. While the traditional Moscow Mule is little more than vodka and ginger beer served up in a mug, using quinoa whiskey and washing the pre-chilled mugs with absinthe really makes this drink shine. Plus, it's a great hangover cure: It's cold and refreshing, but a judicious dash of cayenne will help you sweat out the effects of the night before.

INGREDIENTS

_ 2 OUNCES (60 ML) QUINOA WHISKEY

_ 1/2 OUNCE (15 ML) ABSINTHE

_ 2 OUNCES (60 ML) CANE SUGAR-BASED GINGER BEER

_ VERY LIGHT DUSTING OF CAYENNE PEPPER

DIRECTIONS

Pre-chill a mug by filling it with ice water and the absinthe, and then pour the icy mixture out (into your mouth, that is: No wasting good liquor, remember?) Pack your chilled mug with crushed ice, and then add the quinoa whiskey. Mix very gently with a long spoon. Dust the mixture with the cayenne pepper, then the ginger beer, and stir gently again. Sip cautiously, armed with cold towels for your soon-to-be sweaty brow!

WATERMELON "MARTINI" →

Watermelon packs an especially substantial wallop of antioxidants. Cocktails that include watermelon, like this refreshing Watermelon Martini, may help to relieve headaches and back pain. Inspired by apothecaries of yesteryear, who would have preserved concoctions of fruits and spices in preservative spirits, it combines freshly crushed watermelon with aromatic, curative vermouth and citrus-tinged, botanical gin. It's a deeply delicious curative that helps assuage aches gently and quickly.

INGREDIENTS

_ 1/2 OUNCE (15 ML) DRY VERMOUTH

_ 3 OUNCES (90 ML) BOTANICAL GIN

_ 2 OUNCES (60 ML) PUREED WATERMELON

_ LEMON ZEST TWIST

DIRECTIONS

Wash a cocktail shaker with the vermouth; then pour it out (into your mouth, if you like!). Fill the shaker one-quarter full with ice; then add the gin and pureed watermelon. Stir, strain into a coupé glass, and garnish with a lemon zest twist. Prost!

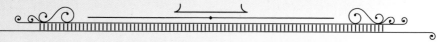

THE OLD OAK TREE COCKTAIL

Like the classic Manhattan, The Old Oak Tree Cocktail combines vermouth with spirits and bitters, but this curative libation is rum-based, and it calls for a hit of fresh lime juice, which is a great complement to the rum. If you ask me, this restorative, analgesic cocktail can relieve the pain of just about any minor injury—from the inside out.

INGREDIENTS

_ 3 OUNCES (30 ML) RHUM
VIEUX AGRICOLE

_ 11/2 OUNCES (45 ML)
CANE SUGAR SYRUP

_ 1/2 OUNCE (15 ML)
SWEET VERMOUTH

_ 3 TO 4 DASHES ANGOSTURA BITTERS

_ 11/2 OUNCES (45 ML)
FRESH LIME JUICE

_ SPRIG OF FRESH THYME

_ ICE

DIRECTIONS

Combine the liquid ingredients in a Boston shaker. Fill the shaker three-quarters full with ice; then shake for twenty seconds. Strain the mixture into a rocks glass with one ice cube, and garnish with a sprig of thyme. Relax, sip, repeat, and let tension and body aches melt away.

SIDENOTE

⇒ **Thyme as a tonic.** Since time immemorial, the herb thyme has been prized for its stimulating, balancing, and purifying properties. In healing preparations of old, pharmacists may have used it in a number of ways: as an antispasmodic, an antifungal, a digestive aid, a remedy for respiratory infections—"It is a noble strengthener of the lungs, as notable a one as grows," wrote Nicholas Culpeper in his *Complete Herbal* (1652)—and to promote healthy circulation and overall good health. Because it's highly antiseptic, early pharmacists would also have used thyme in a number of topical preparations, including salves and liniments. And the ancient Greeks and Romans used it as incense, believing that it would imbue soldiers with courage before battle. Just another reason to mix yourself a bracing, stimulating Old Oak Tree!

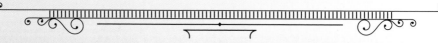

ABSINTHE FRAPPE

These days, when we think of frappés, we usually imagine high-octane, sugar-laden, iced-coffee drinks. Traditionally, though, a frappé is simply a liqueur poured over shaved ice—and it can be a delicious, refreshing treat. This take on the frappé privileges absinthe, which has a reputation for alleviating aches of all sorts due to its high alcohol level. Known as the Green Fairy because of the high chlorophyll levels of the botanicals originally used in its production—and because the psychoactive substances that were also present in them could make heavy drinkers hallucinate—absinthe is said to ease headaches and general malaise, and to soothe stomachs made ornery from exposure to spoiled food. Absinthe frappés have their roots in hot, humid New Orleans, where they were considered to be elegant, cooling potions that could be enjoyed all year.

INGREDIENTS

_ 2 OUNCES (60 ML) ABSINTHE

_ 1/2 OUNCE (15 ML) SIMPLE SYRUP

_ 3 OUNCES (90 ML) SELTZER WATER

_ 10 FRESH MINT LEAVES (PLUS EXTRA FOR GARNISH)

_ CRUSHED, PEBBLE-SIZED ICE

DIRECTIONS

Combine the absinthe, simple syrup, and mint leaves in a large martini glass. Add the ice a spoonful at a time as you stir the absinthe mixture gently with a bar spoon, so that the glass becomes frosty. When the glass is nearly full, top with the seltzer water and stir gently. Tear a few mint leaves and strew them over the top of the drink. When nothing else will shift that truly dogged headache, this icy concoction can help.

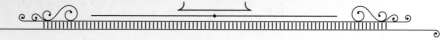
THE TWO MILE COCKTAIL

This thermos-friendly cocktail for two was inspired by a halcyon trip I took one summer, out the Two-Mile Hollow Lane on the east end of New York State's Long Island. It's an easily transportable slurp, and it's simply made, with only a handful of healing ingredients, including white whiskey, absinthe, peach nectar, and cooled jasmine tea. (According to the seventeenth-century *Culpeper's Complete Herbal*, peach-kernels were meant to "wonderfully ease the pains and wringings of the belly through wind or sharp humours.") Make a batch, then pour it into an insulated flask or thermos, and head for the beach: the fresh sea air will clear your head as the Two-Mile sweeps your ache and pains out to sea. Forget the sugar-laden, frat-boy cocktail most bars call the Long Island Iced Tea; this Long-Island-inspired tipple is the real deal.

INGREDIENTS

_ 4 OUNCES (120 ML) WHITE WHISKEY

_ 1/2 OUNCE (15 ML) ABSINTHE

_ 8 OUNCES (235 ML) BREWED JASMINE TEA, COOLED (NOT JASMINE GREEN TEA—THAT'S A DIFFERENT BEAST)

_ 3 SHAKES PEYCHAUD'S BITTERS

_ 3 OUNCES (90 ML) PEACH NECTAR, PREFERABLY ORGANIC

DIRECTIONS

Add all the ingredients to a Boston shaker filled three-quarters full with ice, and shake like crazy for about 15 seconds. (You may have to do this in two batches.) Strain into your insulated flask, and you're ready to go. Head out into the sun with a friend—and be sure to bring straws!

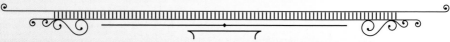

GREEN TEA TONIC

Genever, the botanical gin that hails from Holland and Belgium, has been used as a curative for centuries, and it's packed with healing ingredients like nutmeg, angelica, thistle, and grains of paradise. This tonic unites citrus, fresh ginger, green tea, and mineral-rich Brazil nuts, which are meant to reduce inflammation and relieve pain, into a warming prescription that eases all sorts of aches.

INGREDIENTS

_ 3 OUNCES (90 ML) GENEVER

_ 1 OUNCE (25 ML) FRESHLY
SQUEEZED LEMON JUICE

_ 1 OUNCE (25 ML) FRESHLY
SQUEEZED ORANGE JUICE

_ 1 TABLESPOON GRATED
FRESH GINGER

_ 1 TABLESPOON (15 G)
POWDERED BRAZIL NUTS

_ WARM GREEN TEA

DIRECTIONS

Combine all ingredients in a small saucepan and warm over low heat until the ginger releases its perfume (about 10 minutes). Pour into teacups and serve: Relief is just a few minutes away.

SIDENOTE

⇒ **Green around the gills? Go for green tea.** There are plenty of reasons to sneak a little extra green tea into your diet. While moderate consumption of black tea has been shown to be a healthy habit, green tea, which has been drunk in China for thousands of years, boasts an even wider range of health benefits. Drinking just one cup per day can significantly increase the body's antioxidant levels; lower cholesterol; may help to reduce the risk of liver and cardiovascular diseases; and may be able to aid in weight loss. Since it may help to stabilize blood sugar, it might even have positive effects on type 2 diabetes, and it's said to improve cognitive function as well, reducing the risk of Alzheimer's disease. It's an all-round winner.

CHAMOIS CLOTH SHAKE

No matter how sophisticated you might be, you're never too cool for a milkshake. Especially when that milkshake is, in essence, a Creamsicle for grownups. As soft and smooth as its eponymous chamois cloth, this chilled-out cocktail spikes orange sorbet with white whiskey and a soupçon of rosemary-infused simple syrup, which lends it a woody, elegant edge. Blitz up a batch of Chamois Cloth Shakes to cleanse your guests' palates after a leisurely weekend lunch. (It's a good idea to serve them as quickly as possible after blending for brightness of flavour, so don't make them ahead of time.) If you're a glutton for punishment, go ahead and make your own gelato, but you really don't need to—the store-bought stuff works perfectly. The result is a soothing, cooling libation that literally takes seconds to whip up.

INGREDIENTS

_ 2 OUNCES (60 ML) WHITE WHISKEY

_ 2 SMALL SCOOPS ORANGE GELATO

_ 4 OUNCES (120 ML) WHOLE MILK

_ 2 TO 3 ICE CUBES

_ 1 TABLESPOON (15 ML) ROSEMARY SIMPLE SYRUP (SEE PAGE 313)

DIRECTIONS

Add all the ingredients to a blender, and blend until well combined. Serve the Chamois in a Collins glass with a long straw—for slurping up every last drop.

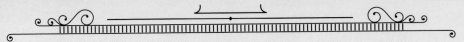

PAIN-PROOF GARDEN ELIXIR

If you're suffering from joint pain due to arthritis, natural remedies may help—and one particularly powerful remedy comes straight from the garden. Fresh vegetables can assist in the treatment of arthritis, especially those with vibrant colors: think spinach, broccoli, tomatoes, and carrots. The antioxidants in these vegetables help reduce joint swelling and inflammation, and the more you eat of them, the better. Here, a variety of veggies are lightly steamed, then pureed into a concentrated "soup" that's packed with pain-fighting nutrients. Adding vodka turns the healthy mixture into a miniature cocktail that can be served Russian-style: that is, well chilled, and doled out in shot glasses. (Talk about literally drinking to your health.) If you enjoy a classic Bloody Mary, you'll love this savory, nutritious libation.

INGREDIENTS

_ 10 CUPS FRESH VEGETABLES, SUCH AS LIGHTLY-STEAMED BROCCOLI, ASPARAGUS, TOMATOES, CABBAGE, AND CAULIFLOWER, LIGHTLY STEAMED AND PUREED IN A BLENDER

_ 2 CUPS (475 ML) VODKA

DIRECTIONS

Combine the pureed vegetables and the vodka in the blender, and continue to puree until the mixture is smooth. Chill in the fridge; then administer in shot glasses (or other small glasses). Raise your glass high: Here's to pain-free joints!

SLEEPY TIME DOWN SOUTH OF BROAD

I'm more than a little obsessed with the mint julep in all of its incarnations. That's because my very first mint julep looms so large in my memory: it was made with care in an antique silver cup in Charleston, South Carolina. The sensation of that drink's icy, refreshing chill against the steamy Charleston night has stayed with me to this day—and it's what's inspired the Sleepy Time Down South of Broad cocktail. This tipple reads like your traditional mint julep—but it takes a sharp right turn off Tradd Street and heads down South of Broad, since it calls for white whiskey instead of the traditional bourbon. And if you haven't slapped your fresh mint before, you should start now: Remove mint leaves from their bitter stem, place them in one hand, and slap your other hand against it. This releases mint's aromatic oils, without chopping or tearing it. Get slapping, and start mixing!

INGREDIENTS

_ 2 TABLESPOONS (30 G) "SLAPPED" FRESH MINT

_ 1 TABLESPOON (15 G) RAW SUGAR

_ 3 OUNCES (90 ML) WHITE WHISKEY

_ CRUSHED ICE

_ STERLING SILVER JULEP CUP, FRESHLY POLISHED

DIRECTIONS

Muddle 1 tablespoon (15 ml) of the slapped mint with half of the sugar in the bottom of the silver cup to release the mint's fragrant oils (with a non-metal utensil, preferably; never use stainless metal against sterling silver, ever!). Add about half of the white whiskey and some crushed ice to the cup, and mix. Then add more ice, the rest of the sugar, the rest of the white whiskey, and the rest of the mint; stir gently until your cup is frosty and glistening. True Southern hospitality dictates that you serve one to a friend before serving yourself. That's one thing Charleston herself taught me.

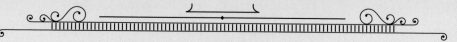

SWEET SHERRY ELIXIR

The essential oil of the herb oregano is another powerful ally when it comes to fighting pain. It's said to alleviate arthritis pain as well as headaches of all sorts and descriptions, and in some cultures, is even used to relieve sore throats. But you don't need to use very much of this intensely flavored herb to heal deeply: Just a drop or two will do the trick. And, curiously, oregano's flavor is a good complement to sweet sherry. Happily, sherry isn't just for medicinal purposes: It's an important ingredient in cocktails, and, of course, it's delicious on its own. When the two are combined, the result is a sweet earthiness that's intensely relaxing. (In the past, the pharmacist might even have prepared a batch of oregano-based bitters especially for this curative tipple.) Today, this simple cocktail is still a winner.

INGREDIENTS

_ 3 OUNCES (90 ML) SWEET SHERRY

_ 1 DROP (AND NO MORE THAN 1 DROP!) OIL OF OREGANO

DIRECTIONS

Pour the sherry into a brandy snifter (or small juice glass). Then, using a medicine dropper (or just extreme care), add a single drop of oil of oregano to the sherry. Sniff deeply, inhaling the potent, earthy aroma. Then pick up your glass and put the aspirin away!

SIDENOTE

⇒ **Sherry's delicious history.** Does the word "sherry" conjure up black-and-white images of men in stiff suits circa 1950 clutching tiny glasses? Well, far from being passé, sherry is very much back in fashion these days, and it's turning up in craft cocktail bars all over the place: It's now gracing Bloody Marys, martinis, and lots more. But what is sherry, and where does it come from? Here's a quick rundown. The resin-colored tipple is a fortified wine with its origins in the town of Jerez in the Andalusia region of Spain, where wines and fortified wines have been produced for centuries, but these days it's made all over the world. There are four main types of sherry: *fino* sherry is dry, delicately flavored, pale in color, and is usually served chilled; *manzanilla*—which means "chamomile" in Spanish—is slightly salty, and is also served at cooler temperatures; *amontillado* sherries are sweeter still, and may taste nutty; and oloroso, or "cream" sherries are quite sweet and are usually enjoyed as digestifs. If you're enjoying them on their own, drier sherries make great aperitifs alongside salty snacks—think bacon-wrapped dates, salted nuts, or grilled, skewered seafood—while sweeter sherries are a fabulous way to finish off a meal.

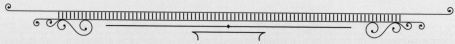

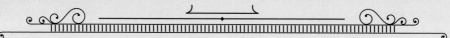

ABRUZZO-STYLE *CAFFÈ CORRETTO*

When I travel abroad, I pay close attention to what the locals are drinking. On a recent trip to Italy, I saw lots of people take small cups of caffè corretto at coffee bars in the mornings. And the actions of the barman who was preparing them were so simple and precise: He just pulled an espresso into a preheated ceramic cup, added about half an ounce of Jack Daniels from a bottle he grabbed from behind the coffee bar, and served it up. There was a perfect, measured cadence to his movements: Take order, preheat cup, pull espresso, correct, serve, and drink (well, it was the customer who was doing the drinking, actually, but still). The whole process was so elegant that I just had to include it here—not least because a prudent amount of liquor combined with a buzz of caffeine can wipe away even the most pernicious pain: There's nothing better for banishing jetlag!

INGREDIENTS

_ 1 OUNCE (30 ML) FRESHLY
PULLED ESPRESSO COFFEE

_ 1/2 OUNCE (15 ML) TENNESSEE
SIPPING WHISKEY

_ 1/2 TEASPOON SUGAR, OR TO TASTE
(PLUS A SMALL COFFEE OR ESPRESSO
SPOON FOR DELICATE STIRRING)

DIRECTIONS

Preheat your espresso cup by filling it with boiling water, and then pour out the boiling water. Pull a single espresso into the cup (it should be no more than one ounce [30 ml]). Now, add the medicine: "Correct" it by adding the Tennessee sipping whiskey, and stir in a bit of sugar. Sip down in one gulp, look around, and have another. It's the Italian way!

THE COCKTAIL WHISPERER'S TWISTED BUSHWACKAH

Down in the Caribbean islands, there are dozens of coffee- and cacao-flavored cocktails. The Bushwacker is one of them, and it matches a dark, aged rum with Tennessee sipping whiskey. It's a perfect marriage, helped along by a hit of freshly brewed, cooled espresso coffee and a dollop of coffee ice cream for sweetness.

INGREDIENTS

_ 2 OUNCES (60 ML) DARK, PREFERABLY
TWELVE-YEAR-OLD, RUM

_ 2 OUNCES (60 ML) TENNESSEE
SIPPING WHISKEY

_ 3 OUNCES (90 ML) ESPRESSO
COFFEE, COOLED

_ HOMEMADE CRUSHED ICE, MADE
FROM COCONUT WATER

_ 3 OUNCES (90 ML) SWEET
CRÈME OF COCONUT

_ 1 SMALL SCOOP COFFEE ICE CREAM

_ 4 DROPS MEXICAN-STYLE SPICY BITTERS

DIRECTIONS

Add all the ingredients to a blender and process until smooth. Pour into a tall parfait glass, garnish with a scraping of fresh nutmeg, and serve. Try not to have more than two—if you do, don't say I didn't warn you.

SIDENOTE

⇒ **Craft your own coconut water ice.** After you've spent time (and money) creating the perfect handmade cocktail, there's nothing worse than watching it get all watered down as you sip it slowly. True, it's nothing less than a tragedy—but it's not inevitable. Since you're making your own ice anyway (never use the store-bought stuff if you can help it!), make your Bushwackah with coconut water ice in place of regular water. Just fill ice cube trays with coconut water and freeze before crushing your ice in a Lewis bag. That way the tropical taste of the coconut cream won't get diluted. Plus, coconut water can help replace the valuable electrolytes you're sweating out while sitting in the hot sun. No hot-weather headaches here!

THE HARTLEY DODGE COCKTAIL →

Bourbon or rye whiskey combined with sweet vermouth laced with healing bitters can act as a powerful painkiller. Although this prescriptive resembles the classic Manhattan, adding muddled peach slices to the mix adds a sweet, fresh, seasonal flavor thanks to the summery stone fruit. And it's a fine balance: The key to this healing cocktail lies in the right proportions of sweet, savory, and blatantly powerful. When combined with the bottled-in-bond bourbon whiskey, the flavor of the peaches becomes even more intense. "Bottled in bond," means the bourbon has been produced according to strict regulations, and it makes for a tastier—and more effective—cocktail. Give it a try: The Hartley Dodge has been known to conquer even the most tenacious aches and pains.

INGREDIENTS

- 3 SLICES FRESH PEACH, PLUS EXTRA SLICES FOR GARNISH
- 3 OUNCES (90 ML) BONDED 100-PROOF BOURBON WHISKEY
- 1 OUNCE (25 ML) SWEET VERMOUTH
- 4 DASHES BITTERS
- ICE CUBES

DIRECTIONS

Place the peach slices in a Boston shaker, and muddle them. Add the bourbon and vermouth, continue to muddle so that the flavors are well combined. Add the bitters and a handful of ice cubes, and stir well. Strain into a Collins glass over a large chunk of ice (larger pieces of ice are less likely to dilute the drink). Garnish with an extra slice or two of fresh peach. It's an analgesic that can't help but take the edge off what ails you.

COFFEE SOYMILK SHAKE

Vegans, rejoice! Although there have been a lot of mixed messages about the health benefits of soy, it's been a staple of Asian diets for thousands of years, and today, soy milk is still a great source of protein: It may help restore and repair damaged muscle tissue and contains pain-alleviating compounds. Thus there's no reason why you shouldn't enjoy a soymilk shake after a long workout, or if you're simply feeling achy. A soymilk shake like this one, made with coffee liqueur and overproof rum, can help fight pain, especially pain in the extremities, such as fingers and toes. (Is that due to the healing powers of soy, or to the rum? Try one and find out.)

INGREDIENTS

_ 6 OUNCES (175 ML) SOY MILK

_ 1 OUNCE (25 ML) COFFEE LIQUEUR

_ 2 OUNCES (60 ML) OVERPROOF RUM

_ ICE

DIRECTIONS

Combine the soy milk, coffee liqueur, rum, and ice in a blender. Process until smooth; pour into a tall glass; and serve with a straw or two. Remember to sip slowly, or you'll bring on another kind of pain: the dreaded ice-cream headache.

CAMPARI AND SODA WATER QUICK FIX

Campari, that ultra-powerful Italian digestive, has an incredible red hue due to its unique mixture of citrus, herbs, and spices. The medicinal tipple is often mixed with a dose of freshly squeezed lemon juice to ward off the scourge of vitamin C deficiencies and other nutrition-related maladies. It's often taken neat, but with the addition of a few ounces of carbonated water, Campari becomes more than just an after-dinner treat: It's transformed into a prescriptive that can affect the spirit as well as the body. Sparkling water delivers the scent of the aromatic, therapeutic herbs straight into the patient's nose, relieving his stomachache, headache, and grumpy mood all at once. Aperol, another bright-red, Italian-made herbal liqueur, can be substituted for the Campari in this easy recipe: It's used to liven up diners' moods and whet their appetites before big meals.

INGREDIENTS

_ 4 OUNCES (120 ML) CAMPARI

_ 3 OUNCES (90 ML) CLUB SODA
  (WITH AN ADDED PINCH OF SALT)

_ ORANGE ZEST TWIST

DIRECTIONS

Add a handful of ice cubes to a Collins glass. Pour the bright-red Campari over the ice and top with the club soda. Garnish with a flamed orange zest twist (pinch the zest firmly and hold it behind a lit match to release the citrusy oils). Breathe deeply: The scent will perk you up before you've even taken a sip.

THE PAINKILLER PRESCRIPTIVE →

The Painkiller Prescriptive has its origins at a beach bar known as the Soggy Dollar, on the island of Jost Van Dyke in the British Virgin Islands. Medicinal preparations were available at this apothecary-cum-bar nearly every day during the winter and spring sailing seasons. If a sailor had spent the night in the grip of that demon, the "old black rum," a dose of this fruity prescriptive would be sure to cure him of the affliction—and fast. A distant cousin of the pina colada, the Painkiller both refreshes and heals: The citrus juices offer a wallop of immunity-boosting vitamin C, while the coconut provides potassium and adds creaminess and heft. Nutmeg, which has long been used to rouse the appetite, tops off the Painkiller—and, of course, the rum warms and soothes the sufferer's mind and body.

INGREDIENTS

_ 3 OUNCES (90 ML) NAVY-STRENGTH
   (OVER 90-PROOF) RUM

_ 1 OUNCE (25 ML) PINEAPPLE JUICE

_ 1 OUNCE (25 ML) ORANGE JUICE

_ 1 OUNCE (25 ML) CREAM OF COCONUT

_ FRESHLY GRATED NUTMEG

DIRECTIONS

Combine the rum, fruit juices, and cream of coconut in a Boston shaker. Then fill the shaker three-quarters full with ice, and shake for thirty seconds or until the outside of the shaker becomes frosty. Resist the urge to slurp down immediately. Strain into a parfait glass filled with crushed ice, and top with freshly grated nutmeg. (Freshly grated nutmeg really is immeasurably better than pre-ground.) Serve with a straw, if desired. Anchors aweigh!

Digestives & After-Dinner Drinks:

BELLY-FRIENDLY COCKTAILS

◆ ◆ ◆

SYMPATHIZE, FOR A MOMENT, WITH THE HUMBLE STOMACH. A MULTI-COURSE MEAL CAN FLIP IT OUT; A DOSE OF THE FLU CAN THROW IT INTO SERIOUS DISTRESS; AND A CASE OF JITTERY NERVES SENDS IT STRAIGHT INTO SOS MODE. AND IF YOU THINK THAT'S ROUGH ENOUGH, GET THIS: OUR FOREFATHERS HAD IT EVEN WORSE.

Here's why: Before the twentieth century, home refrigerators were futuristic dreams, so it was tough to prevent food from spoiling. Plus, kitchen hygiene wasn't what it is nowadays, and antibiotics and flu shots had yet to be discovered. This means indigestion, bellyaches, and food poisoning ran rampant, and apothecaries had to be well-versed in remedies to soothe the tumultuous tummy. With the help of local botanicals, pharmacists would mix herbal tinctures and tonics that could alleviate nausea and stomach pain, and suspend the mixtures in doses of alcohol to keep them fresh. These curatives were available only at the apothecary's shop. Their recipes were usually closely guarded, and they're the ancestors of digestifs that are still enjoyed around the world today, such as Chartreuse, Fernet Branca, amaro, and Bénédictine. Usually taken after dinner to ease bellies that might be suffering from too much good food and drink, these liqueurs often have a bracingly bitter flavor from the wide variety of herbs used to produce them.

Other liquors, too, were created to relieve digestive disorders and make massive meals go down a bit more smoothly. Brandy, for example, was thought to be a powerful laxative and purgative. Apothecaries prescribed it in the hopes that it would quickly eliminate harmful toxins in cases of poisoning. (It was even used to treat recovering opium addicts after an initial purge using vinegar and water. Yikes.) Aromatic bitters, which are related to herbal liquors like Italian amari, would have been used liberally in curatives, or taken on their own with a dash of fizzy water in order to calm edgy stomachs.

Potent liquors and bitter herbs weren't the only belly-friendly ingredients an apothecary would have had on hand, either. Garden vegetables like rhubarb and fennel could also help relieve stomach ailments. Rhubarb is an effective laxative, and has been used to promote good digestion for centuries. And crunchy, anise-flavored fennel, too, is good for the belly: eaten raw or taken as an herbal tea, apothecaries would've recommended it to folks who had overindulged in their victuals (and their cups!).

Pharmacists of yesteryear would also have worked household staples into their curatives. Sparkling waters such as club soda, seltzer water, and quinine-rich tonic water, for example, often top off stomach-soothing libations, and can even bring relief on their own. Like ginger beer, their effervescence can refresh tired palates, and seems to make all the difference when it comes to indigestion. (Bubbles make everything better, don't they?) This chapter shows you how to craft bellyache-banishing concoctions, like digestives, fizzes, liquor-laced coffees, and gastriques. Where to start? For a speedy cure, go for a Habsburg Stomach Healer, which combines the Hungarian liqueur Zwack with tonic water and curried bitters—or, to prevent tummy upsets at a morning-after brunch, make my Blackberry-Fennel Shrub, then use it in a round of As We Approached St-Denis (here, the bubbles come from champagne!). You can take curative shrubs to the table, too: my Red Berry Gastrique is, in essence, a digestive-shrub-turned-sauce, and it's a great accompaniment to just about any dessert. And that's just the beginning. Read on for more delicious ways to relax recalcitrant bellies.

HABSBURG STOMACH HEALER

In 1790, Dr. József Zwack, the royal physician to the Habsburg Court, developed a medicinal blend of forty herbs and spices intended to soothe the stomach and prevent illnesses of all sorts. This tonic-based apothecary liqueur is still produced today according to the same recipe. It calls for macerated and distilled herbs to be aged in specially sourced oak casks, which add color, flavor, and depth to this bitter Hungarian health tonic. Said to be a powerful detoxifier, Zwack is enjoyed both as an *aperitif* and a *digestif*, and it's usually administered straight up and well chilled (according to some, adding ice would only dilute and weaken the effects of the potent liqueur). For the faint of heart, though, it can be mixed with ice and seltzer or tonic water: hence, the Habsburg Stomach Healer. Try to find a tonic water made with cane sugar; it's far superior to the run-of-the-mill stuff.

INGREDIENTS

_ 2 OUNCES (60 ML) ZWACK

_ 3 OUNCES (90 ML) CANE
  SUGAR TONIC WATER

_ ICE

_ FOUR DROPS OF CURRIED BITTERS

DIRECTIONS

Fill a Collins glass with ice. Pour the Zwack over the ice, and top with tonic water. Add the bitters, and mix gently. Sip slowly, and let the Zwack work its medicinal magic.

BLACKBERRY-FENNEL SHRUB

Made from produce that would have grown wild in America's early days, this very special classic shrub is delicious during the summer, when plump blackberries are at their ripest. The boldly flavored, fragile fruits favor fennel, which has a lightly licoricey scent and taste—and grilling fennel really brings out that subtle aniseed flavor. And both fennel and blackberries can boast health-boosting properties: The former is great for digestion, while the latter is packed with vitamins C and K. A bonus: this shrub is relatively quick to make and is ready to use in just two weeks, so you won't have to wait long to enjoy it.

INGREDIENTS

_ 1 CUP (455 G) FRESH
   BLACKBERRIES, HALVED

_ 1 CUP (200 G) DEMERARA SUGAR

_ 1 CUP (235 ML) SHERRY VINEGAR

_ 1 TABLESPOON (15 G) GRILLED
   FENNEL, (BULB ONLY, OF COURSE,
   NO FRONDS), FINELY CHOPPED

_ 1 TABLESPOON (15 G)
   PINK PEPPERCORNS

DIRECTIONS

Time: 2 weeks. *Place the blackberries in a nonreactive bowl, and add the sugar. Mash the fruit and sugar together, then stir well and cover tightly. Leave to sit for 24 hours at room temperature. Then add the vinegar, fennel, and pink peppercorns. Stir well, cover tightly, and leave the mixture either in the fridge or at cellar temperature for 3–4 days. Then, place a strainer over another nonreactive bowl and transfer the mixture to the strainer. Press down on the fruit-vinegar mixture with the back of a wooden spoon to release as much liquid from the blackberries as possible. Discard the fruit pulp. Funnel the liquid into a sterilized bottle or jar. Store in the refrigerator for another week or two, shaking the jar daily to combine the flavors and mellow the vinegar.*

AS WE APPROACHED SAINT-DENIS

My twisted version of the French 75 riffs on the original by skipping the lemon juice, and bolstering the gin-champagne combination with a portion of my delectable, summery Blackberry-Fennel Shrub instead. As We Approached Saint-Denis tips its hat to the bushes full of sumptuous fruit that line the roadways near the French town of the same name.

INGREDIENTS

_ BROWN SUGAR CUBE

_ 2 DROPS COCKTAIL WHISPERER'S RAW HONEY AROMATIC BITTERS (SEE PAGE 311)

_ 1 OUNCE (30 ML) GIN

_ 1 OUNCE (30 ML) BLACKBERRY-FENNEL SHRUB (SEE PAGE 195)

_ 2 OUNCES (60 ML) CHAMPAGNE

_ 1 PLUMP BLACKBERRY, FOR GARNISH

_ SPRIG OF MINT

DIRECTIONS

Place the brown sugar cube into a champagne flute. Moisten with a few drops of my Raw Honey Aromatic Bitters. Then add the gin, the blackberry-fennel shrub, and top with some darned good champagne. Garnish with a single blackberry and a sprig of mint. Avoid having more than four of these little darlings at one go. You'll thank me later.

- -

SIDENOTE

⇒ **The classic French 75.** As We Approached Saint-Denis is a delicious, elegant cocktail—try serving a round of them to a bunch of thirsty (and slightly bleary-eyed?) folks right before a leisurely warm-weather lunch—but even I have to confess that it's pretty hard to improve upon the traditional version. To highlight the drink's powerful kick, it's named for the 75-millimeter M1897, a French gun used in the First World War. Like its namesake, the original French 75 is hardly light fare: It involves combining gin or brandy, simple syrup, lemon juice, and champagne over a whack of cracked ice. If you have more than two—well, don't say that I didn't warn you. Enough said.

RHUBARB SLUSHY

Rhubarb has been used in folk medicine for thousands of years, and, legend has it, first arrived in the United States when Benjamin Franklin brought rhubarb seeds from Europe in the late eighteenth century. Famed for its powerful purgative qualities, rhubarb has been known to ease blockages of the digestive tract that may stem from poor diet. (And it's rich in vitamin C and potassium, too.) In its incarnation as a liqueur, it's a delicious way to relax stomachs on the fritz. Sure to summon up memories of late summers long past, this grown-up slushy puts rhubarb liqueur into the limelight, combining it with a delicately fragrant simple syrup infused with rose. A dash of bitters tops off this restorative cocktail.

INGREDIENTS

_ 3 OUNCES (90 ML) RHUBARB
TEA LIQUEUR

_ CRUSHED ICE

_ 2 TABLESPOONS (30 ML) ROSE-INFUSED
SIMPLE SYRUP (SEE PAGE 313)

_ FOUR DROPS THAI BITTERS

DIRECTIONS

Pack a Collins glass with the crushed ice. Pour the rhubarb tea liqueur and rose-infused simple syrup over it. Mix well with a bar spoon until combined. Add the Thai bitters. The result will be a fantastically icy, slushy concoction—hence the name—that's best served with a spoon and a straw.

CHARTREUSE CURATIVE

This mood-lifting prescriptive combines top-quality chartreuse with vermouth and egg white for a colorful, frothy little cocktail that'll brighten up even the greyest day. Try one after lunch, and top it off with a thread or two of saffron as a nod to Chartreuse's luscious color.

INGREDIENTS

_ 3 OUNCES (90 ML) CHARTREUSE VEP

_ 1 OUNCE (25 ML) DRY VERMOUTH

_ 1 EGG WHITE

_ 2 TO 3 SAFFRON THREADS

DIRECTIONS

Add the chartreuse, vermouth, and egg white to a Boston Shaker; then fill the shaker three-quarters full with ice. Shake vigorously for twenty seconds until frothy. Strain the mixture into a coupé glass, and garnish with the saffron. Then sit back and watch sinking spirits rise.

SIDENOTE

⇉ **Saffron's strengths.** Chartreuse has saffron to thank for its trademark bright-yellow hue. Derived from the crocus flower, this precious spice has long been praised for its healing qualities: It's reputed to be an antiseptic, antidepressant, antioxidant, a digestive aid, and an anti-convulsion restorative. It was probably used in Ayurvedic medicine and Asian and Mediterranean cooking for thousands of years before it made its way to France, where it's showcased in the production of herbal liqueurs like Chartreuse, which French imbibers enjoy as an after-dinner drink. (If you'd like to use saffron in your cooking, don't be put off by the price. Yes, it's astronomically expensive, but never fear: As with most good things, a little goes a very long way.)

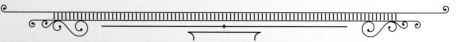

UNDERBERG SETTLER

Underberg is a powerfully healing herbal tonic that hails from Germany. Buy a bottle and you'll see that the slogan on the label reads, "After a good meal." True to its word, Underberg is a highly effective cure after overindulging in both food and drink. Serious imbibers keep a bottle or three handy for medicinal purposes—you never know when you might need it. Underberg can be enjoyed neat or mixed with tomato juice for a German take on the Bloody Mary. The Underberg Settler, created by world-famous Seattle mixologist Rocky Yeh, also features aromatic bitters, which were as commonplace on the shelves of early apothecaries as aspirin is today. Like Underberg itself, aromatic bitters add a punch to the dark rum that helps settle the belly and perk up the brain.

INGREDIENTS

_ 3/4 OUNCES (20 ML) AROMATIC BITTERS

_ 1 OUNCE (25 ML) DARK RUM

_ 3 OUNCES (90 ML) SARSAPARILLA
(OR ORGANIC ROOT BEER)

_ ICE CUBES (OPTIONAL)

DIRECTIONS

Combine all liquid ingredients in a mixing glass and stir. Add ice if desired, and strain into highball glasses. Rinse and repeat if necessary until that hangover disappears.

SMALL WHITE BLOSSOM

The Small White Blossom is my Cocktail Whisperer's take on the classic New Orleans–style Kentucky Whiskey cocktail, which calls for only two ingredients: bourbon and pineapple juice. As usual, I take things a bit further. My version uses craft whiskey made from millet, not bourbon. Its toasted-almond and caramel flavors are a great match for fresh fruit juices. Here, grilled pineapple juice combined with freshly squeezed orange juice gives the Blossom an extra layer of flavor, while a splash of club soda and the tiniest pinch of sea salt add a refreshing, palate-tickling lift. If you can find it, make your simple syrup with gum arabic (also spelled "gomme arabic"), which yields a lush, creamy mouth feel. The result: A cocktail that's small, but perfectly formed.

INGREDIENTS

_ 2 OUNCES (60 ML) MILLET WHISKEY

_ 1 OUNCE (30 ML) GRILLED
PINEAPPLE JUICE (SEE PAGE 312)

_ 1 OUNCE (30 ML) FRESHLY
SQUEEZED ORANGE JUICE

_ 1/2 OUNCE (15 ML) BASIC SIMPLE
SYRUP (SEE PAGE 311) (THIS VERSION
OF THE SIMPLE SYRUP IS MADE WITH 2
TABLESPOONS (30 ML) GOMME ARABIC
FOR EXTRA THICKNESS (ADD 1 TABLE-
SPOON [15 ML] OF GUM ARABIC TO YOUR
PLAIN SIMPLE SYRUP AND HEAT TO
THE DESIRED COLOR AND THICKNESS)

_ PINCH OF SEA SALT

_ DASH OF CLUB SODA

DIRECTIONS

Fill a mixing glass three-quarters full with ice. Add the millet whiskey, fruit juices, and simple syrup. Stir gently, pour into a coupe glass, top with the club soda, and garnish with a narrow spear of grilled pineapple. Add the pinch of sea salt over the top to finish.

SIDENOTE

⇒ **Alternative-grain whiskeys.** Thanks to the rising popularity of distilling with alternative, artisan grains, whiskeymakers have more raw materials to work with than ever before. (And, even more importantly, the arcane laws forbidding any kind of distilling at all have been changed in many states, so that distillers can actually get on with the job.) Sure, producers both large and small are still creating excellent spirits from corn, wheat, or barley—those venerable whiskey-friendly grains. But alternative grains offer craft distillers new ways to shine. This is great news for the discerning drinker, for it means that she has a whole new world of whiskeys at her fingertips, including millet whiskey, quinoa whiskey, oat whiskey, hopped whiskey, and spelt whiskey.

Gluten- and wheat-free foods like these grains are all the rage these days: They're not just for celiacs anymore. Quinoa, for example, has enjoyed a huge spike in popularity. It's a good source of complete protein, and it's super-versatile (try replacing couscous with quinoa in just about any recipe—it's delicious). Indigenous to South America, it has a toasty, deeply earthy flavor when distilled. And oats aren't just for breakfast: They're being transformed into whiskeys that are full of rich, creamy, caramel-vanilla flavors. Then there's spelt: In the kitchen, it's often made into celiac-friendly baked goods, but in the distillery, it becomes a whiskey that can be redolent of yummy things like apples, warm brown sugar, or shortbread. But some craft distillers think millet makes the best whiskey of all, producing a spirit with a sweet, nutty taste. While whiskeys made from alternative grains don't come cheap due to the expense of using artisan ingredients, they're worth the extra money, since they make truly memorable cocktails.

THE BOSPHORUS COCKTAIL

This prescriptive delivers a healthy wallop of turmeric suspended in nutrient-rich carrot juice laced with the Turkish liqueur *raki*, and it's a great way to calm cranky bellies. Rose-infused simple syrup adds a hint of sweetness to take the bitter edge off the raki, and a splash of soda water makes the Bosphorus Cocktail remarkably refreshing and stimulating.

INGREDIENTS

_ 2 OUNCES (60 ML) *RAKI*

_ 4 OUNCES (120 ML) CARROT JUICE

_ 1 TEASPOON TURMERIC

_ 2 TABLESPOONS (30 ML) ROSE-IN-
 FUSED SIMPLE SYRUP (SEE PAGE 313)

_ 3 OUNCES (90 ML) SODA WATER

DIRECTIONS

Add the raki, carrot juice, turmeric, and rose-infused simple syrup to a Boston Shaker. Shake well until combined (about twenty seconds). Place one large ice cube in a rocks glass, and strain the mixture into the glass over the ice. Then top with soda water, and sip for a much-needed lift to both body and mind.

SHERRY–CHERRY COBBLER

Sherry has been suspected of curative powers for centuries. In days of yore, pharmacists often prescribed it as a nerve tonic, or as an antidote to insomnia. Sherry was also used as a suspension for herbal tinctures, powders, and fresh herbs and fruits. Sherry "punches" made with stone fruits are a delicious way to nip that bad mood in the bud, especially if it was brought on by a touch of indigestion. And here's another reason to treat yourself to a Sherry–Cherry Cobbler: Stone fruits like cherries are antioxidant-rich, while sherry may have some of the same heart-healthy properties that red wine does.

INGREDIENTS

_ 2 OUNCES (60 ML) FINO (DRY) SHERRY

_ 2 OUNCES (60 ML) SWEET SHERRY

_ 1/4 CUP (60 ML) RUM-CURED
 CHERRIES (STORE-BOUGHT, IF YOU
 CAN FIND THEM: ALTERNATIVELY,
 CHOP 1 CUP (155 G) FRESH, PITTED
 CHERRIES, AND STEEP IN 1 CUP (235
 ML) RUM IN A STAINLESS-STEEL
 BOWL FOR ONE WEEK BEFORE USE.
 STORE IN THE REFRIGERATOR.)

_ 1 TEASPOON PEYCHAUD'S BITTERS

_ 4 OUNCES (120 ML) SELTZER WATER

DIRECTIONS

Place the cherries in a Boston shaker, and add the sherries. Muddle the cherries, then add the bitters and fill the cocktail shaker three-quarters full with ice. Shake for twenty seconds; then strain the mixture into a coupé glass, and top with the seltzer water. (Grab a spoon and eat the muddled cherries that remain in the cocktail shaker, if you like!) Serve, sip, and float away on a cherry-flavored cloud.

DOCTOR LIVESEY'S COCKTAIL

In the heyday of apothecaries, medicines usually tasted terrible, and weren't often prettied up through the addition of sweeteners or coloring, as they are today. So, as the song goes, a spoonful of ginger could truly help the medicine go down. Alternatively, ginger itself could be used as medicine, since it's said to be an effective cure for a variety of ailments, including headaches, motion sickness, fatigue, and pregnancy-related nausea. Ginger, a close relative of turmeric and cardamom, appears in many forms, including powders, syrups, suspensions, tonics, salves, and infusions, and traditional Chinese medicine is rife with the healing root. Combining ginger with hot punches or beer is a classic way to use the root as a curative, as sailors of yesteryear would have known. Named after the honorable doctor in Robert Louis Stevenson's classic, *Treasure Island,* this cocktail matches ginger beer with its natural partner, rum, into a tipple that rouses the mood and washes the doldrums away.

INGREDIENTS

_ 3 OUNCES (90 ML) DARK RUM

_ 4 OUNCES (120 ML) GINGER BEER (NON-ALCOHOLIC)

_ LIME WEDGE FOR GARNISH

DIRECTIONS

Fill a Collins glass with ice cubes. Pour the ginger beer over the ice; then float the dark rum on top. Garnish with a lime wedge to keep scurvy at bay.

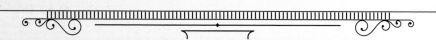

COLONIAL SOUR CHERRY SHRUB

George Washington himself would have agreed that cherries are treasured ingredients when it comes to shrubs. Alas, the growing season is quite short, so if you miss the all-too-brief sour cherry season at your local farm market, never fear: all is not lost. It's easy to make a sour cherry shrub in a hurry if you have a jar of sour cherry preserves on hand. (And you don't have to tell a soul that you cut corners.) Using preserves means you won't have to reduce the fruits over heat; that's already been done for you. This shrub is ready to use in just 36 hours. Or, you can continue to age it in the fridge for up to a month.

INGREDIENTS

_ 1 8 OUNCE (235-ML) JAR OF
SOUR CHERRY PRESERVES

_ 1 CUP (200 G) DEMERARA SUGAR

_ 1 CUP (235 ML) APPLE CIDER VINEGAR

DIRECTIONS

Time: 36 hours. *Place the sour cherry preserves in a nonreactive bowl, and cover with the sugar. Let them steep together for at least overnight (or for a few days) at room temperature. Then strain the cherry mixture through a nonreactive sieve, crushing the tender fruits with a wooden spoon to extract as much flavor and sweet juice as possible. Combine with the vinegar; let the mixture sit for a few hours, and then strain and bottle in sterilized bottles. Use the shrub right away, or let it sit in the fridge for three weeks to a month.*

THE BENJAMIN GUNN MYSTERY COCKTAIL

Named for a former crewman of pirate captain J. Flint in Robert Louis Stevenson's classic novel *Treasure Island*, this cocktail is an homage to Ben Gunn, a sailor who finds himself marooned on Treasure Island for several years. In the end, though, he discovers Captain Flint's treasure—and you'll feel as lucky as Gunn did when you treat yourself to one of these ambrosial tipples. Rich, jammy Colonial Sour Cherry Shrub marries well with oak-aged dark rum: then, a splash of maple syrup sweetens the deal. Finish with a little seltzer water plus a few dabs of medicinal bitters for a cocktail that's sure to soothe even the touchiest of tummies.

INGREDIENTS

_ 2 TABLESPOONS (60 ML) COLONIAL
  SOUR CHERRY SHRUB (SEE PAGE 210)

_ 2 OUNCES (60 ML) DARK RUM (A
  MOLASSES-BASED RUM THAT'S BEEN
  AGED IN EX-BOURBON OAK IS IDEAL)

_ 1/4 OUNCE (7 ML) DARK AMBER
  (COOKING) MAPLE SYRUP

_ SPLASH OF SELTZER WATER

_ DASH OF CHERRY BITTERS

_ LEMON ZEST TWIST

_ HAND-CUT ICE CUBE

DIRECTIONS

Place the ice cube in a rocks glass, and add 2 tablespoons (60 ml) of the Sour Cherry Shrub. (Try making your own maple ice cubes: Combine 1 part maple syrup with 4 parts spring water, and then freeze overnight and hand-cut each cube to order.) Add the dark rum and the maple syrup, and then top with a splash of fizzy seltzer water. Garnish with a lemon zest twist, and dot with cherry bitters.

THE JIMMY GILLESPIE FIZZ

It's easy to showcase the depth of flavor inherent in bitters. The key? Simplicity. When you add a dash of your favorite bitters to a glass of spirits mixed with seltzer water, you'll find that all the heavy lifting has been done for you. Take, for example, the Jimmy Gillespie Fizz, named after a dear friend of mine from Swan's Island, Maine. He was one-of-a kind: an old codger from another generation. Jimmy loved his Scotch, and he inducted me into the pleasures of drinking fine, single-malt Scotch whisky with as few embellishments as possible: except, perhaps, a tiny bit of his brackish-tasting well water alongside the whisky, or maybe a few dashes of bitters. Bitters, he claimed, healed the belly, although I suspect he was more partial to their astringent taste—and their alcohol content.

That was Jimmy for you.

INGREDIENTS

_ 2 OUNCES (60 ML) SCOTCH WHISKY

_ 6 SHAKES OF AROMATIC BITTERS

_ SMALL SPLASH OF SELTZER WATER

_ LEMON ZEST TWIST

DIRECTIONS

Add the Scotch whiskey to a cocktail glass. Top with a few shakes of the aromatic bitters, and then finish with a dribble of seltzer, and a lemon zest twist. Nothing more to do except lift a glass to Jimmy.

A CIGAR DIVAN ON RUPERT STREET →

Back in the day, New York City's far Upper West Side was elegance itself. This cocktail takes its name from an imaginary shop that could have made its home there, since the cigar divan itself was a symbol of moneyed leisure. Drinkers would have whiled the hours away in such an establishment on a low chair (or divan), cigar and cocktail in hand and the world at their feet. These days, mixing yourself a Cigar Divan on Rupert Street is an artful, refreshing way to pep up the appetite and prep your belly for a leisurely evening meal. It combines Tennessee whiskey's inimitable smokiness with a dash of fresh citrus juice, handcrafted bitters, and cane-sugar cola for a tipple that's for grown-ups only. (Try not to resort to big-name colas made with corn syrup—the quality of the ingredients makes all the difference.)

INGREDIENTS

_ 2 OUNCES (60 ML) TENNESSEE
SIPPING WHISKEY, SUCH
AS JACK DANIEL'S

_ 2 OUNCES (60 ML) MEXICAN COLA (OR
ANY GOOD HANDCRAFTED COLA—IDE-
ALLY MADE WITH PURE CANE SUGAR)

_ 1/4 OUNCE (7 ML) EACH OF
LIME AND LEMON JUICES,
STRAINED TO REMOVE PULP

_ 3 DROPS MEXICAN MOLE BITTERS
(OR ANGOSTURA BITTERS)

_ HAND-CUT ICE CUBES

DIRECTIONS

Drip the bitters down the inside of the glass, so as to coat it lightly. Then add the hand-cut ice cubes (the rougher the cut, the better; this'll keep the ice from diluting your drink). Add the whiskey, then the cola of your choice, and finally, pour in the juices. Stir the drink gently, and sip carefully. Cigar divans are optional.

OLDE HOMESTEADER'S SURFEIT COCKTAIL

After a successful late-summer harvest, some lucky farmers might have had more cherries than they knew what to do with. That's where shrub-making would have come in: A farmer's wife would have "put up" plenty of a cherry-based shrub to preserve the essence of summery cherries for the long winter months ahead. A speedily-made cherry shrub is great in cocktails. It practically demands attention from whiskey in all its forms: Think bourbon, Scotch, or rye. The Olde Homesteader's Surfeit—which calls for only a few simple ingredients—is the perfect early-autumn cocktail: Just toss together bourbon, a quick cherry shrub, and aromatic bitters—then zap the mixture with a little seltzer water, and sit back and sip. Best of all, vinegar, seltzer, and bitters are all tried-and-true remedies for maladies of the belly, which means this little drink is as healing as it is delicious.

INGREDIENTS

_ 2 OUNCES (60 ML) BOURBON (OR WHISKEY OF YOUR CHOICE)

_ 1 OUNCE (30 ML) QUICK CHERRY SHRUB: MIX 1 TABLESPOON (15 G) CHERRY PRESERVES WITH 1 TABLESPOON (15 ML) BALSAMIC VINEGAR

_ 1 OUNCE (30 ML) SELTZER WATER

_ 2-3 SHAKES OF MY COCKTAIL WHISPERER'S RAW HONEY AROMATIC BITTERS (SEE PAGE 311)

DIRECTIONS

Fill a Boston shaker three-quarters full with ice, and pour the bourbon and the quick cherry shrub over it. Cap and shake hard. Strain the mixture into a coupe glass, and top with a splash of seltzer water. Finish with a couple drops of my Raw Honey Aromatic Bitters.

LE JAMES BROWN COCKTAIL

There's no better way to finish off a great dinner party than with a round of Le James Browns. It's an elegant riff on the Irish coffee, and since it's served chilled, it's perfect for summer evenings when you're dying for a *digestif*, but can't stand the thought of hot liquids. In it, French whisky meets chilled espresso, black walnut bitters, a dash of club soda, and a dollop of easy-to-make, cognac-spiked whipped cream—along with a little freshly grated nutmeg for good measure. (Feel free to prepare the espresso well in advance—even the day before is fine.) Serve it alongside (or after) a simple, light dessert, like fresh berries over cognac-laced vanilla ice cream—or, with a few good shortbread cookies.

INGREDIENTS

_ 4 OUNCES (120 ML) CHILLED
   ESPRESSO COFFEE

_ 2 OUNCES (60 ML) FRENCH WHISKY

_ SPLASH OF CLUB SODA

_ 1/2 CUP (115 G) COGNAC WHIPPED
   CREAM (SEE PAGE 312)

_ SCRAPING OF FRESH NUTMEG

_ 8 DROPS BLACK WALNUT BITTERS

DIRECTIONS

Brew your espresso and let it cool either in an ice bath or overnight in the fridge.

Add several large cubes of ice to each of two Collins glasses. Top each with 1 ounce (30 ml) of the chilled espresso in each glass, followed by the French whisky. Splash a bit of club soda on top of each drink, then spoon the sweetened, thick cream over the mixture. Scrape a little fresh nutmeg over the top of each glass, and finish each with 4 drops of bitters. Serves 2 thirsty heads. In the immortal words of Brown himself: You'll feel good!

RED BERRY DESSERT GASTRIQUE

This fruit-laden gastrique is so simple to make that you can hardly call it a recipe—but I just had to include it here, since it's one of my favorite ways to pull dessert together in an instant. My Red Berry Dessert Gastrique is a foolproof way to gussy up just about anything sweet, from flourless chocolate cake to fresh fruit to plain old vanilla ice cream. Even though it's made from pureed red berries, I like to drizzle it over more fresh, whole red berries—strawberries, raspberries, whatever's in season—for a healthy finish to a warm-weather meal, like sautéed salmon filets with a simple green salad. And, in case you're having trouble finding it, pomegranate vinegar is available in most Middle Eastern or Asian markets.

INGREDIENTS

_ 1 CUP (200 G) RAW CANE SUGAR

_ 1/2 CUP (120 ML) POMEGRANATE VINEGAR

_ 1 CUP (150 G) PUREED RED FRUITS, SUCH AS STRAWBERRIES, RASPBERRIES, AND/OR CHERRIES

DIRECTIONS

Combine all the ingredients in a small saucepan. Bring to a boil, then reduce the heat and simmer for 10–20 minutes, or until the mixture has reached the desired thickness. Strain the fruit mixture, and let cool. To serve, place a couple handfuls of fresh, assorted red berries into a small glass bowl or martini glass. Drizzle the gastrique over the berries, and serve to your very, very happy guests. If you're a chocoholic—and who isn't? —you can serve it alongside homemade brownies. Or, melt a couple tablespoons of good-quality dark chocolate, and spoon it over the berries. Simple!

SIDENOTE

⇒ **What's a gastrique?** You've used shrubs in your craft cocktails: now it's time to bring them into the kitchen. Allow me to introduce to you to the classic French sauce known as a gastrique. Its very name may sound ultra-elegant and sophisticated, but at the end of the day, a gastrique is simply a shrub that's produced in the kitchen over heat, and the process isn't a difficult one. Like shrubs, gastriques are combinations of vinegar, sugar, fruit, vegetables (or other flavorings), and they're usually combined in a saucepan and slowly reduced over heat until they become thick, concentrated, intensely flavored, sweet-tart syrups. (Unlike shrubs, you won't have to wait days or weeks for them to mature: about an hour is all it takes.) Then, the luscious syrup that comprises a gastrique is added to a dish as a finishing sauce—often to complement the simple, delicate, understated flavors of fresh food. It adds texture, fragrance, acidity, and intensity to everything from pan-sautéed chicken or pork to grilled fish to fresh berries, French toast, and vanilla ice cream. Adding a few drops of a well-made gastrique to just about any dish can excite your palate in a big way.

Over the years, I've experimented with all sorts of ingredients when I'm making gastriques—including peaches, apples, espresso coffee, curry powder, baking spices, plums, leeks, fresh peas, and tomatoes. But they all have one thing in common: their simplicity. Gastriques, like my Red Berry Dessert Gastrique and my Coffee Gastrique for Vanilla Gelato, really are a snap to make, and you don't have to be a culinary genius to put them together. Honestly, if you can boil water, you can make a gastrique. The main ingredient? A little patience, since it takes about an hour for the sauce to reduce down to a nice, viscous thickness. Welcome to your new favorite condiment!

COFFEE GASTRIQUE FOR VANILLA GELATO

Good news for the sweet-toothed: Gastriques can take the form of a luscious, dessert-friendly sauce that'll have your guests coming back for second—and even third, or, heaven help us, fourth!—helpings. Given the chance, gelato is a most welcome recipient for the concentrated flavors inherent in a gastrique, and for its trademark sweet-and-tangy finish. My Coffee Gastrique combines strong, cold coffee with a dose of maple sugar and a hint of apple cider vinegar. After letting the mixture reduce slowly, you'll have an intensely flavored finishing sauce that'll charm the socks off coffee-lovers everywhere. Serve it over the best-quality vanilla ice cream or gelato you can get your hands on for a simple but stunning finale to just about any meal.

INGREDIENTS

_ 1 CUP (235 ML) COLD, EXTRA-STRONG COFFEE

_ 1 CUP (200 G) MAPLE SUGAR

_ 1/4 CUP (60 ML) "MAPLE VINEGAR" (EQUAL PROPORTIONS OF APPLE CIDER VINEGAR AND MAPLE SYRUP)

_ VANILLA GELATO OR GOOD-QUALITY VANILLA ICE CREAM

DIRECTIONS

Add all the ingredients to a saucepan, and place over a medium-low heat. Reduce slowly for about an hour, or until the liquid has reduced in volume by three-quarters. Keep warm. Place two scoops of vanilla gelato or ice cream into a dish or martini glass, and spoon the Coffee Gastrique liberally over the ice cream. Tangy and delicious!

THE VENDETTA COCKTAIL

The inspiration for the Vendetta Cocktail comes from a walk I took through Brooklyn recently. So many of Brooklyn's turn-of-the-century buildings have been demolished, and so many visible memories of the borough's past have been erased during its transformation into the hipster paradise it is today. And it's a huge loss. In order to honor Brooklyn's past, I wanted to combine ingredients from the old neighborhood delis such as Manhattan Special Espresso Coffee Soda and vanilla *gelato* to create this boozy take on the traditional Italian dessert *affogato*, which involves pouring freshly pulled espresso over vanilla ice cream. I like to muddle a few home-cured cocktail cherries into my Vendetta; they help to smooth the smoked whiskey's bold taste. A very grown-up after-dinner drink, indeed.

INGREDIENTS

_ 3 TO 4 EASY HOME-CURED COCKTAIL CHERRIES (SEE PAGE 311)

_ 2 OUNCES (60 ML) SMOKED AMERICAN WHISKEY

_ 4 OUNCES (120 ML) COFFEE SODA, SUCH AS MANHATTAN SPECIAL ESPRESSO COFFEE SODA

_ 1 SCOOP VANILLA GELATO (OR TOP-QUALITY VANILLA ICE CREAM)

DIRECTIONS

With the back of a bar spoon or the end of a wooden spoon, muddle a couple home-cured cocktail cherries to a pulp in the bottom of a mixing glass. Then add the smoked whiskey, followed by the coffee soda and the gelato. Mix gently with a long spoon, and portion between two coupe glasses. Sprinkle a bit of espresso powder over the top of each drink, if you like. Serves two persone.

RHUBARB AND STRAWBERRY SWIZZLE

Strawberry and rhubarb, that classic combination of sweet and tart, are winners when it comes to summery desserts—and what's more, rhubarb has been prescribed as a curative for hundreds of years thanks to its purgative, diuretic effects. That's why this cocktail makes an especially luscious *digestif.* Try it after a long, lazy summer lunch.

INGREDIENTS

_ 3 TABLESPOONS (45 ML) STRAWBERRY-RHUBARB COMPOTE (ROUGHLY CHOP FOUR STALKS OF RHUBARB. IN A MEDIUM SAUCEPAN, COMBINE ONE PINT (360 G) OF STRAWBERRIES AND THE RHUBARB, AND PLACE OVER A MEDIUM HEAT UNTIL SOFTENED. USING A FOOD PROCESSOR OR MORTAR AND PESTLE, PUREE THE MIXTURE UNTIL IT BECOMES A THICK LIQUID. SET ASIDE TO COOL.)

_ 6 OUNCES (175 ML) RHUM AGRICOLE (OR ANOTHER GOOD-QUALITY SPICED RUM)

_ 1 ROCK CANDY SWIZZLE STICK

_ 12 OUNCES (355 ML) CLUB SODA

_ ICE CUBES

DIRECTIONS

Add the strawberry and rhubarb mixture, rum, and ice to a glass beaker, and mix well with the swizzle stick. (The faster you swizzle, the better! Moving the swizzle stick quickly ensures that the liquids and solids in the drink are thoroughly combined.) Strain the mixture into two coupé glasses, top with club soda, and use the swizzle stick as garnish, if desired. Then kick back and let the tart, refreshing fizz chill you out. **Serves 2.**

SIDENOTE

⇒ **The story of the swizzle.** It's hardly used in common parlance these days, but back in the day, a "swizzle" could refer to any drink made with rum, topped up with water or other mixers and flavored with a range of botanicals, and served over ice. According to legend, such drinks were mixed or stirred with roots or twigs—history's very first "swizzle sticks." (If you ask me, though, the rock candy swizzle stick in my recipe tastes just a little bit nicer, and adds the perfect amount of sweetness to the mix!) Some say that the ancestral home of swizzles is the Caribbean islands, so to keep things authentic, see if you can search out Rhum Agricole, a type of rum distilled from sugar cane in the West Indian island of Martinique. There, "kill-devil" was used in traditional curatives—but don't worry, if you can't find Rhum Agricole, any good quality spiced rum will do.

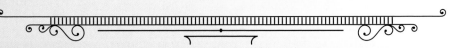

CAFÉ IRLANDÉS

This exotic hot drink is a layered cocktail, based on the pousse-café, a cocktail in which several different kinds of liquor are carefully layered on top of one another. Where the pousse-café is served cold, however, the Café Irlandés is served piping hot. It's a combination of strong, hot coffee; sweet, thick whipped cream; and perky, spicy Irish whiskey. And it's impossible to make without softly made, hand-whipped cream. (Whatever you do, never use that stuff that comes in a can. See page 312 for an easy recipe for whipped cream.) The kind of whipped cream that makes this drink sing is more like a thickly textured emulsion that sticks to the sides of the glass when poured. The result is a magical concoction that's digestif and dessert all in one. Try not to have more than two: Otherwise, you'll be caught in a tug-of-war between the caffeine and the alcohol.

INGREDIENTS

_ 2 TABLESPOONS (30 G) DARK BROWN SUGAR

_ 3 OUNCES (90 ML) ESPRESSO COFFEE

_ 3 OUNCES (90 ML) IRISH WHISKEY

_ 2 OUNCES (60 ML) HOME MADE WHIPPED CREAM (SEE PAGE 312)

_ 1/4 OUNCE (7 ML) ABSINTHE

DIRECTIONS

Preheat a strong wineglass or latte-style coffee glass by filling it with boiling water, and then pour the water out. Add the sugar and about a third of the coffee, and stir with a bar spoon. Then add about a third of the whiskey, by pouring it over the back of a dessert spoon into the glass. Then spoon some cream into the glass, followed by a bit more sugar, and a bit more whiskey. Repeat the process until you've used up all whiskey, sugar, and coffee. (Work slowly; it's an art form, not a race!) Finally, using a medicine dropper (or extreme care), drip the absinthe over the top of the cocktail. Sláinte!

HANGOVER HELPERS:

RESTORATIVE DRINKS FOR THE MORNING AFTER

• • •

LAST NIGHT, YOU WENT OUT FOR A COUPLE OF DRINKS. YOU STARTED ON THE EARLY SIDE, KICKING THINGS OFF WITH A FEW G&TS CIRCA FIVE P.M.—THEN MOVED ON TO DINNER, COMPLETE WITH WINE (RED *AND* WHITE). OF COURSE, DESSERT WAS COMPULSORY, NOT TO MENTION THE IRISH COFFEE YOU ORDERED IN A MOMENT OF OPTIMISM, PLUS THE COMPLIMENTARY COGNAC DELIVERED WITH A FLOURISH BY A SMILING WAITER AT THE END OF THE MEAL. AND AFTER THAT, THE WHOLE GANG DECIDED THAT THE EVENING WOULDN'T BE COMPLETE UNTIL YOU ALL WENT TO THE PUB ACROSS THE STREET FOR A NIGHTCAP.

Oy vey. What you're afflicted with this morning can't really be called a hangover: that's too kind a word. It's more like you've been trampled by a herd of oxen, and spat on by a crowd of angry goats. Your head hurts so badly it's practically hopping off your shoulders; your stomach's a mess; and you're filled with an exhaustion so profound that you're certain you'll Never Ever Drink Again.

That's okay. If you needed a little help lifting your head from your pillow this morning, you've come to the right place. Hangovers are as old as time, which is why a lot of the best cures have their roots in the past. Apothecaries and pharmacists of previous centuries would have been called upon to provide quick, effective remedies for client who were, ahem, feeling poorly after an evening's entertainment—and relief often came in the form of restorative herbs, spices, and citrus fruits that could be combined with a little hair of the dog (or not) in order to perk up the senses and lighten the heart after a late night. These curative cocktails would have taken many forms: fizzes, which cool and refresh the palate as they calm the belly; short, strong drinks that could be sipped quickly, for rapid healing; citrusy concoctions for much-needed rehydration (not to mention a blast of vitamin C); and effervescent cola-based beverages, which offer doses of caffeine, sugar, and spirits all at once, to name but a few. And of course all of the above would be topped off by liberal dashes of medicinal bitters, which have been used to mitigate all manner of maladies for hundreds of years. Most importantly, though, any cocktail meant to lift the spirit after a difficult night out on the town should be enticing both to the nose and the eyes—and it never hurts to serve restorative cocktails in a tall glass with plenty of ice.

So what's your poison? There's a lot to choose from in this chapter. Pharmacists of old often prescribed tonics including lighter spirits such as gin, white rum, or vodka to heal debilitating hangovers, as in my Askew Bloody Mary—or, they may have suggested the simple combination of homemade, healing bitters and soda water, served over ice in a tall glass: Witness my Angostura and Seltzer Restorative, which is still delicious—and effective—today. Then there are herbal liqueurs like Fernet Branca and Branca Menta, which comprise nothing less than divine intervention for hangovers when they're mixed with cane-sugar cola. Extract of milk thistle has been used to heal vehement hangovers for centuries, due to its natural liver-healing qualities, so a Milk Thistle Spritz is a great way to start your detox stat. But if you truly feel like the undead after an evening of debauchery, reach for a cognac-heavy Corpse Reviver: it's sure to bring you back to the land of the living. So read on, and start mixing: Even the most stubborn hangover is no match for these rejuvenating craft cocktails.

FERNET BRANCA AND COLA

When it comes to *mangia e beve,* few cultures can surpass the delights of Italy. And there's little better for healing a truly headbanging hangover than a nip of the Italian herbal liqueur Fernet Branca, which sports an assertive, even bitter flavor that's truly inimitable. This historic cocktail actually hails from Argentina, where Fernet Branca remains popular with the families of Italian immigrants who left their homeland during World War II. I know you're feeling delicate, but don't be afraid of Fernet's bitter edge: When served in a cocktail alongside cane-sugar cola, this deeply engaging elixir goes down remarkably smoothly. The body-warming alcohol levels of the liqueur also play a role in the intense flavor of the naturally sourced herbs and spices. Fernet Branca is delicious when taken ice cold, as is the custom in Argentina and San Francisco—and cool liquids can't help but soothe self-induced aches and pains, like throbbing noggins and parched tongues.

INGREDIENTS

_ 2 OUNCES (60 ML) FERNET BRANCA

_ ICE CUBES

_ 4 OUNCES (120 ML) CANE-SUGAR COLA (OR REGULAR COLA)

_ 1/4 LIME, CUT INTO CHUNKS

DIRECTIONS

Pour the measure of Fernet Branca over a handful of ice cubes in a tall Collins glass. Top with the cane-sugar cola, and add a chunk or two of lime to give the immune system a boost (it rarely hurts to add citrus to curative cocktails). Your stomach—and head—will thank you.

APEROL FIZZ →

Historically, the citrusy Italian *aperitif* Aperol has been enjoyed before, during and after lengthy meals to perk up appetites and ease digestion. Aperol gently raises the spirits as well as the appetite, especially when combined with aromatic bitters and fizzy water. It's just the thing if your spirits need a lift the day after a marathon meal—or a liquid lunch!—with good friends. This historic cocktail was created to get tired bellies back on track, and it's so easy to make. Plus, since it's relatively low in alcohol, the Aperol Fizz is a sensible drink, so you'll be less likely to overindulge (again). It's the quick fix your digestive system needs!

INGREDIENTS

_ 2 OUNCES (60 ML) APEROL

_ 6 OUNCES (175 ML)
  SPARKLING NATURAL MINERAL
  WATER (PREFERABLY ONE WITH
  A STRONG MINERAL FLAVOR)

_ 2 SHAKES ANGOSTURA BITTERS

_ ICE CUBES

_ LEMON ZEST TWIST

DIRECTIONS

*Add the Aperol to a Boston shaker and fill the shaker three-quarters
full with ice cubes. Shake vigorously for twenty seconds. Add
a few cubes of ice to a Collins glass; then strain the mixture
slowly over the ice. Top the chilled Aperol with the sparkling
mineral water; garnish with the lemon zest twist; and prepare
to be transported to an al fresco café in Italy. It's incredibly
light and refreshing, so go ahead and have another!*

ANGOSTURA AND SELTZER WATER RESTORATIVE

All right. The fact is, you're not feeling so well this morning. You had a few drinks with the guys from work last night, usually a tame affair that has you home by nine at the latest. Last night, however, your first drink was a shot of Sambuca—at the shockingly early hour of six-thirty—and things went straight downhill after that. Well, sufferer, meet my simple Angostura and Seltzer Water Restorative, which is the way to mitigate the gruesome effects of a night out on the tiles. It's so easy it can hardly be called a recipe—but I had to include it here for its sheer effectiveness. Both seltzer water and bitters are famous for their ability to subdue unruly bellies. Consuming them both at once is, to use the technical term, a double whammy of a cure. Take two, and call me in the morning.

INGREDIENTS

_ 2 OUNCES (60 ML) FERNET BRANCA

_ 6 OUNCES (175 ML) COOL SELTZER WATER

_ 1 TEASPOON OF ANGOSTURA BITTERS (THINK TWICE BEFORE SUBSTITUTING MY COCKTAIL WHISPERER'S RAW HONEY AROMATIC BITTERS: THEY HAVE QUITE A KICK!)

_ 1 PINCH SEA SALT

DIRECTIONS

Place a spear of hand-cut ice in a Collins glass. Top with the seltzer water, add the bitters, and finish with a quick sprinkle of sea salt.

PEPPERY FENNEL FIZZ →

There's nothing better than a multi-course meal with friends, complete with coffee, dessert, and nightcaps. (Lots of nightcaps.) Of course, your stomach won't always thank you the next day. That's where our friend fennel comes in. It's often used as a diuretic, and is said to remedy digestive malaises of all kinds—plus, it's a powerfully purifying, detoxifying vegetable. Happily, it's simple to whip up a cleansing, refreshing cocktail featuring fennel that peps up your palate as well as your belly. Here, fennel syrup is combined with raki, the anise-based Turkish spirit, along with chile flakes, which jolt taste buds back to life (and if the chile makes you sweat a bit, so much the better.) And the effervescence in a dose of seltzer water helps to settle overworked stomachs, too.

INGREDIENTS

_ 2 OUNCES (60 ML) RAKI OR ABSINTHE

_ 1 OUNCE (25 ML) FENNEL SIMPLE
SYRUP (SEE PAGE 311)

_ 1/4 TEASPOON DRIED CHILE FLAKES

_ 1 TEASPOON ORANGE BITTERS

_ 4 OUNCES (120 ML) SELTZER WATER

DIRECTIONS

Fill a tall Collins glass with crushed ice. Add the fennel simple syrup, raki, chile flakes, and bitters—use the full teaspoon, don't skimp! Stir gently, top with seltzer water, sip, and let the detox begin.

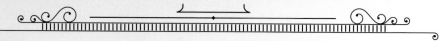

THE IBERVILLE STREET COCKTAIL

The Iberville Cocktail, a tasty variation on the Sazerac theme, is equally as effective as dispersing disorders of the belly—especially ones that are self-induced. (Thank goodness for those healing Peychaud's bitters, which, in days gone by, were even meant to ease the symptoms of more serious diseases such as dysentery and ulcers.) Mix yourself an Iberville, and sip it with the lights off.

INGREDIENTS

_ 2 OUNCES (60 ML) LILLET BLANC

_ 1 OUNCE (25 ML) BRANDY

_ 4-5 DASHES OF PEYCHAUD'S BITTERS

_ 4 OUNCES (120 ML) FRESHLY
   SQUEEZED GRAPEFRUIT JUICE

_ 1/2 OUNCE (15 ML) ABSINTHE

_ LARGE PIECE OF LEMON PEEL

_ 1 ORANGE ZEST TWIST

DIRECTIONS

Add a couple handfuls of ice to a Boston shaker; then add the Lillet Blanc, brandy, bitters, and grapefruit juice, and shake well for twenty seconds.

Wash a short rocks glass with the absinthe by pouring the absinthe into the glass, swirling it around, and pouring it out. Rub the inside of the washed glass thoroughly with the lemon peel. Strain the stomach-healing mixture into the glass, and garnish with a flamed orange zest twist (hold the orange twist firmly behind a lit match, and pinch it to release its natural citrus oils). Sip slowly for quick relief of uneasy stomachs.

SIDENOTE

⇒ **Lillet Blanc** is an aromatized wine—that is, a fortified wine featuring added herbs, spices, or other botanicals—that hails from Pondesac, a small village in the famous French wine region of Bordeaux. It's comprised mostly of white Bordeaux wine with a small amount of added citrus liqueurs—and once upon a time it was also made with quinine (the same stuff that gives tonic water its bitter, refreshing edge), which can be used to treat malaria and fevers. Thanks to strategic advertising, Lillet Blanc became immensely popular in the 1920s and 1930s, especially with upper-class Americans who sampled it on transatlantic liners on their way to and from Europe. These days quinine has disappeared from the recipe, and Lillet has a lighter, fresher taste, but it's still delicious in cocktails like the Iberville Street, or in a Vesper Martini, a potent but terribly tasty combination of gin, vodka, and Lillet.

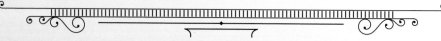

THE FLEMING JENKINS FIZZ

The Fleming Jenkins Fizz is a variation on the ti'punch theme. Ferocious *ti'punch* has its origins in the Caribbean islands like Martinique, Guadeloupe, and Haiti, where *rhum agricole* was traditionally mixed with sugar-cane syrup and fresh lime juice for an aperitif that's so potent, it'd knock more than just your socks off. I think Indian whisky, with its denser mouth feel, is really intriguing when it's mixed with homemade simple syrup, absinthe, and club soda. It makes a smashing aperitif—and, equally, is a gentle way to take the edge off that hot-weather hangover.. It's also a great accompaniment to a light, summery lunch like a salad of baby spinach, fresh mango, grilled chicken, sweet potato crisps, and cashew nuts. Don't wait for warm weather to treat yourself to a Fleming Jenkins, though: All you need on hand is a good bottle of Indian whisky. The rest is easy.

INGREDIENTS

_ 2 OUNCES (60 ML) INDIAN "SCOTCH-STYLE" WHISKY

_ 1 OUNCE (30 ML) CANE-SUGAR SYRUP (OR BASIC SIMPLE SYRUP: SEE PAGE 311)

_ 1/4 OUNCE (7 ML) ABSINTHE

_ SPLASH OF CLUB SODA

_ CURRIED BITTERS

DIRECTIONS

Fill a cocktail shaker three-quarters full with ice. Add the absinthe and the Indian whisky. Shake well for about 20 seconds, and strain over one cube of hand-cut ice into a rocks glass. Add a splash of club soda and three drops of curried bitters, and serve immediately. Then start preparing round two!

SIDENOTE

⇒ **The rise of Indian whiskey.** Since the 1980s, India, like Japan, has been giving Scotland a run for its money when it comes to the whisky making game. And that's a bit of a surprise. Why? First of all, India is part of an equatorial climate zone, and its off-the-chart temperatures can be overwhelming to both humans and the production of distilled spirits. After all, whisky's ancestral homes are Scotland and Ireland, where early producers distilled their liquor in climates far cooler than India's—and for longer periods of time. In India (except, perhaps, in the far northern Himalayan Mountains where logistics make it impossible to distill whisky anyway), the temperature is hot for most of the year. That, coupled with the high humidity, makes the aging of whisky a far faster process than it would be in Europe.

However, the final results are incredibly delicious. Indian distillers are beginning to experiment with whiskies bottled at cask strength—a potent reminder that great whisky certainly doesn't have to come from Scotland. A word of warning, though: Most Indian whisky isn't actually made from grain. Instead, it's often distilled from sugar cane or molasses, and is more of a flavored whisky substitute. The label on its bottle may hint at a fine Scottish heritage, but don't be fooled: Be sure you're buying *grain-based* Indian whisky when you invest in some. (Rum-based "whisky" of the lesser sort possesses all the stuffing to give you one of the most memorable hangovers of your life. Keep a large bottle of Fernet Branca handy for any such experiments into foolhardiness.)

SAMBUCA TWIST

One of my favorite restorative cocktails, this easy-to-make tipple features Sambuca, which can act as a powerful "wake-me-up" for a stressed-out stomach. The freshly squeezed grapefruit juice adds a much-needed dose of vitamin C, while the citrusy, singed orange peel and the licorice-flavored Sambuca—not to mention the bitters—combine to reanimate the spirits of even the most zealous drinker. Do try my Sambuca Twist even if you're not usually a fan of the liqueur's distinctive aniseed scent and taste: You'll be amazed at how healing and refreshing it is after you've spent a long night propping up the bar.

INGREDIENTS

_ 4 OUNCES (120 ML) BOTANICAL GIN

_ 1 OUNCE (25 ML) SAMBUCA

_ 3 OUNCES (90 ML) FRESHLY
   SQUEEZED GRAPEFRUIT JUICE

_ SLICE OF FRESH ORANGE PEEL

_ SEVERAL SHAKES OF AROMATIC
   BITTERS, SUCH AS PEYCHAUD'S

_ GRAPEFRUIT ZEST TWIST

DIRECTIONS

Add the gin, Sambuca and grapefruit juice to a Boston shaker. Shake vigorously for fifteen seconds. Add a handful of ice cubes to a Collins glass, and strain the mixture over the ice. Singe a slice of fresh orange peel, pinching it firmly just behind the match to release its natural citrus oils, and then add it to the glass. Finally, shake the bitters into the drink, and garnish with the grapefruit zest twist. Your stomach will perk up after just a few sips.

SHIP OF FOOLS COCKTAIL

It was later than I thought when I woke up in New Orleans. How many different drinks had I consumed at that Tales of the Cocktail event? My throbbing head told me there were too many to count. I needed something to take the edge off. Fortunately, I knew I had a small bottle of Fernet Branca in my kit bag, along with samples of aromatic bitters from several different producers—and a bottle of aspirin. Whew. My Ship of Fools Cocktail is named for the suffering devils that forgot to pack a bottle of Fernet Branca or aromatic bitters before visiting the Big Easy in high summer. If you're one of them, find a sympathetic bartender to mix you up this restorative combo of Fernet, grilled lemon juice, good-quality cane-sugar cola, finished off with a dash of bitters. Relief is just a few sips away.

INGREDIENTS

_ 2 OUNCES (60 ML) FERNET BRANCA

_ 1 OUNCE (30 ML) GRILLED LEMON JUICE (SIMPLY LIGHTLY SCORE LEMON ROUNDS OVER AN OPEN FLAME, THEN COOL AND JUICE)

_ 3 OUNCES (90 ML) CANE-SUGAR COLA

_ 2–3 DROPS MAPLE SYRUP AND RYE WHISKEY BARREL-AGED BITTERS

_ LEMON ZEST TWIST

DIRECTIONS

Fill a Boston shaker three-quarters full with ice. Add the Fernet Branca and the Grilled Lemon Juice to the shaker, and shake hard for 10 seconds. Rub a lemon zest twist around the rim of an old-fashioned glass, and add 2 large ice cubes; then add the Fernet Branca mixture, and top with the cola. Garnish with the lemon zest twist. Drip the bitters over the top for the win!

ASKEW BLOODY MARY →

A twentieth-century classic, the Bloody Mary is everyone's favorite hangover cure. Originally created as a bracing, hair-raising combination of vodka, tomato juice, lemon juice, Worcestershire sauce, salt, and pepper, it's got the power to revive even the most debauched drinker after a serious session. My Askew Bloody Mary is just as powerful as its predecessor, but it's far more nuanced: lightly spiced, astringent, and terribly healing. It also involves a make-in-the-shaker shrub: Combine a tomato-celery puree with a little white wine vinegar and agave syrup, add to the other ingredients in your cocktail shaker, and bang!—all the flavor of an aged shrub, whipped up in seconds. What's more, my Bloody calls for tequila instead of vodka, as well as a few drops of my Sherry Pepper Infusion for a little palate-cleansing heat. Serve with a protein-rich breakfast, like an omelet stuffed with feta, spinach, and bacon.

INGREDIENTS

_ 4 OUNCES (120 ML) QUICK ROASTED
TOMATO-CELERY PUREE (SEE PAGE 313)

_ 1/2 OUNCE (15 ML) WHITE WINE VINEGAR

_ 1 OUNCE (30 ML) AGAVE SYRUP

_ 11/2 OUNCE (45 ML) BLANCO
TEQUILA, SUCH AS CASA NOBLE

_ 4 DROPS SHERRY PEPPER
INFUSION (SEE PAGE 32-33)

_ 2 DROPS CELERY BITTERS

_ LEMON CHUNKS

DIRECTIONS

Add all the ingredients but the bitters to a Boston shaker filled half-full with ice. Roll the shaker on an angle across the top of the bar to combine the ingredients. (You must not shake a Bloody Mary, ever! Shaking this elegant drink will bruise the delicate tomato fruit, and that'll yield a Bitter Mary instead of a Bloody one.) Pour the mixture over a hand-cut spear of ice into a tall Collins glass. Garnish with lemon chunks, and squeeze a little of the fresh lemon juice directly into the cocktail. Dot the celery bitters over the top to finish.

CORPSE REVIVER

The Corpse Reviver was designed to counteract truly a horrible hangover—the kind that won't let you lift your head off the pillow. (Sound familiar?) True to its name, this potent combination of cognac, gin, apple brandy, vermouth, and falernum soothes the pain of the night before and rejuvenates all five aching senses at once.

INGREDIENTS

_ 3 OUNCES (90 ML) COGNAC

_ 2 OUNCES (60 ML) CALVADOS

_ 1 OUNCE (25 ML) GIN

_ 1 OUNCE (25 ML) SWEET VERMOUTH

_ 1 OUNCE (25 ML) FALERNUM

DIRECTIONS

Fill a Boston shaker three-quarters full with ice. Gently pour the cognac, calvados, gin, vermouth, and falernum over the ice, and shake briskly for thirty seconds. Toss a few ice cubes into a short rocks glass. Strain the mixture into the glass, sit back, and slowly sip that hangover away.

SIDENOTE

⇒ **Falernum fables.** Made in the West Indies, falernum is a liqueur that sports a heady mixture of Caribbean flavors such as almond, ginger, cloves, vanilla, and lime—a fragrant combination that, if you ask me, takes the sting out of even the most heinous of hangovers. Its origins are obscure, but it was probably first made in Barbados sometime in the nineteenth century. These days, "falernum" is a nonalcoholic syrup, but it takes its name from an different source—an ancient Roman wine called *falernian*, which was made from late-harvested grapes, and which, according to legend, was so high in alcohol it could be set on fire. (Modern falernum isn't flammable, so don't try this at home!) You can make a homemade version of it, if you like, but it's also widely available in liquor stores. Use it in your Corpse Revivier, and in tiki-style drinks of all sorts.

RAMOS GIN FIZZ COCKTAIL

Like the Corpse Reviver, this deliciously fizzy cocktail is effective against the most brutal hangovers. Designed to heal the adverse effects of late nights without doing damage to sensitive stomachs, it combines fragrant orange flower water with gin, frothed egg white, half-and-half, sugar, milk, lemon juice, and lots of fizzy soda water. Then it's shaken for several minutes in order to "cook" the egg whites and make for a softly fizzy cocktail that is a powerful emulsifier for maladies of the belly and your aching head (orange flower water has been known to ease headaches and calm jazzy nerves). The creamy quality of the egg whites and the half-and-half soothe the belly in ways totally unappreciated until a hangover actually hits. If you're really feeling rough, get someone else to shake the cocktail for you; remember, no sudden movements.

INGREDIENTS

_ 3 OUNCES (90 ML) GIN

_ 3 DROPS ORANGE FLOWER WATER

_ 3 EGG WHITES

_ 1/2 TEASPOON BAR SUGAR
  (OR POWDERED SUGAR)

_ 1 OUNCE (30 ML) LEMON JUICE

_ 1/4 TEASPOON VANILLA EXTRACT

_ 2 OUNCES (60 ML) CLUB SODA

_ DASH OF SALT

_ 2 OUNCES (60 ML) HALF-AND-HALF

_ 1 OUNCE (25 ML) REGULAR MILK

DIRECTIONS

Fill a Boston shaker three-quarters full of ice. One at a time, add all the ingredients to it, and mix well. Shake well for at least two minutes. (Legend has it that real connoisseurs shake their Ramos Ginn Fizzes for upwards of ten minutes!) You'll be thirsty long before that: When your arm gets tired, strain the mixture into a large glass, and prepare to be healed.

THE AIL AND CURE SWIZZLE

The Ail & Cure, a cousin of Doctor Livesey's Cocktail, was created by cocktail connoisseur Christopher James, head bartender at the four-star Ryland Inn in Whitehouse, New Jersey. Chris says, "I can envision this cocktail being sipped during a beautiful day, on an island, by someone who might have a bit of a bellyache. Ginger beer was used medicinally in the Caribbean in the eighteenth and nineteenth centuries, since ginger was especially good for relieving stomach pain. Angostura bitters were developed by a German army doctor, Dr. Ben Siegert, in Venezuela in order to aid his troops in the digestion of their food. And we all know Caribbean rum can very well cure all the imagined ills that ail you! With the first sip of this drink, as you inhale the soothing scent of the aromatic mint garnish, I'm sure you will be transported to this special place I've imagined—and I'm positive your bellyache or bad mood will subside."

INGREDIENTS

_ 2 OUNCES (60 ML) DARK RUM

_ 3/4 OUNCE (20 ML) ORGEAT

_ 1 OUNCE (25 ML) FRESH LIME JUICE

_ 2 HEALTHY DASHES OF
  ANGOSTURA BITTERS

_ 4 OUNCES (120 ML) GINGER
  BEER (NON-ALCOHOLIC)

_ ROCK CANDY SWIZZLE STICK

_ SPRIG OF FRESH MINT

DIRECTIONS

Fill a tall pilsner glass three-quarters full with crushed ice. Pour the first four ingredients over the ice, and mix well with the rock candy swizzle stick. Top with the ginger beer, and gently swizzle again for a second or two to combine. Top with more crushed ice, and garnish with a sprig of mint. Hangovers will disappear over the horizon.

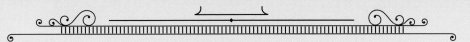

JOSÉ GASPAR COCKTAIL

Each year, Tampa, Florida holds the Gasparilla Pirate Festival. It's named for the Spanish pirate José Gaspar, who was, at first, a perfectly gentlemanly buccaneer, licensed by the Spanish crown to make a living by preying on merchant ships in the Gulf of Mexico and the Caribbean. However, legend has it, José Gaspar went rogue and attacked the city of Tampa. He came to no good end. This fruity, liquor-laden libation, the José Gaspar Cocktail, is an unlikely combination of two rogue spirits: Irish whiskey and rum, and this combination of the two best-known sea-going liquors has been known to transform the living into the living dead—and vice versa. If you fall into the latter category after last night's antics, now's the time to mix up a batch of Gaspars and lift a glass to old José. (Oh, and do consider making your own grenadine: It's so easy, and the store-bought stuff hasn't got a patch on it.)

INGREDIENTS

_ 2 OUNCES (60 ML) IRISH WHISKEY

_ 1 OUNCE (30 ML) DARK RUM

_ 1/2 OUNCE (15 ML) FRESHLY
  SQUEEZED PINEAPPLE JUICE

_ 1/2 OUNCE (15 ML) FRESHLY
  SQUEEZED ORANGE JUICE

_ 1/2 OUNCE (15 ML) FRESHLY
  SQUEEZED GRAPEFRUIT JUICE

_ 1/4 OUNCE (7 ML) CRÈME DE BANANE

_ 1/2 OUNCE (15 ML) HOMEMADE
  GRENADINE SYRUP (SEE PAGE 311)

_ 4 DROPS CURRIED BITTERS (USE
  YOUR FAVORITE BRAND, OR MAKE
  YOUR OWN: SEE PAGE 311)

DIRECTIONS

Fill a mixing glass three-quarters full with ice. Add all the ingredients except the bitters, and mix well to chill. Strain the mixture into a parfait glass half-filled with crushed ice. To finish, drip the curried bitters over the top of each drink. Serves two heavy heads.

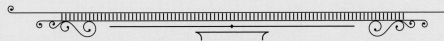

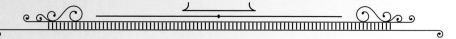

THAI BASIL FIZZ

Just like snowflakes, no two hangovers are alike. Did you get yours by indulging in spicy food, washed down by one (or four) too many cocktails? If that rings a bell, try a Thai Basil Fizz. Each of its ingredients are curatives, right down to the absinthe wash and lemon zest twist, and it's constructed to be heavenly balm to both belly and head.

INGREDIENTS

_ 2 OUNCES (60 ML) BOTANICAL GIN

_ 1/4 OUNCE (7 ML) ABSINTHE

_ 1 SPRIG HOLY BASIL (OR REGULAR BASIL), FINELY CHOPPED

_ 3 TO 4 SHAKES OF PEYCHAUD'S BITTERS

_ 2 TO 3 OUNCES (60 TO 90 ML) GINGER BEER

_ LEMON ZEST TWIST

DIRECTIONS

Toss the chopped basil into a Boston shaker. (Be sure to lean over the shaker for a restorative whiff of its crisp, spicy scent!) Add the gin and absinthe, and fill the shaker three-quarters full of ice. Sprinkle the bitters into the mix, then shake for twenty seconds, strain into a coupé glass, and top with the ginger beer. Garnish with the lemon zest twist. The heady combination of basil, ginger, and lemon is sure to brush the cobwebs away.

- -

SIDENOTE

⇒ **Basil** isn't just for pesto anymore. With its bracing, peppery taste, the "royal herb," as the ancient Greeks called it, has often been used in curatives in a number of ways. It was said to mitigate the symptoms of malaria; was made into a liniment to soothe sunburns, and a nerve tonic against stress and anxiety; and it is even said to promote longevity. One variety of the herb, called holy basil or Thai basil, is used as an ingredient alongside other green herbs in both absinthe and green chartreuse, due to its antiseptic and antibacterial qualities. (In fact, the striking green color of absinthe and chartreuse may pay homage to basil's brilliant green hue.) And if you're feeling poorly thanks to a night on the tiles, you'll be delighted to learn that Thai basil can be very effective when it comes to healing a sour stomach. You're welcome.

SCRIVENER'S CAMP

Featuring a final flourish of luscious, dark chocolate bitters, this bracing cocktail is named for the men (and they usually were men) who, unlike many of their peers, could read and write. These gentlemen could be hired to perform secretarial duties for the population at large—most of whom were illiterate. Beware: After a couple rounds of Scrivener's Camps, you may well need a scrivener to sign your name in your stead. That's because three types of liquor work their potent magic in this cocktail: bourbon, absinthe, and, not least, vermouth, which was originally used as a hair tonic and scalp invigorator because of the exotic herbs, flower essences, and spices contained in each bottle. (My thoughts? Avoid this. Stick to applying vermouth to your mouth only.) But then again, if you were celebrating a little too avidly last night, that may be just what you need.

INGREDIENTS

_ 2 OUNCES (60 ML) BOURBON,
SUCH AS FOUR ROSES

_ 1/2 OUNCE (15 ML) SWEET VERMOUTH,
SUCH AS CARPANO ANTICA

_ 1 OUNCE (30 ML) FRESHLY
SQUEEZED GRAPEFRUIT JUICE

_ 1/2 OUNCE (15 ML) ABSINTHE

_ SEVERAL DROPS OF CHOCOLATE BITTERS

_ EASY HOME-CURED COCKTAIL CHERRIES
(SEE PAGE 311), FOR GARNISH

DIRECTIONS

Fill a cocktail mixing glass half full with ice. Add the bourbon, the Carpano Antica, and the grapefruit juice, and stir about 20 times to combine. Then pour the absinthe into a coupe glass: You can either drink it immediately and leave its residue in the glass as a glass wash, or you can leave the full portion of absinthe in the glass (I prefer the latter). Strain the bourbon mixture over the absinthe into the coupe glass; dot the top of the cocktail with the chocolate bitters, and garnish with an Easy Home-Cured Cocktail Cherry.

ROAMING HOUND DOG COCKTAIL →

White whiskey—also known as "white dog"—is a versatile spirit indeed, and it's especially delicious when paired with that toothsome Asian concoction known as bubble tea. Traditionally meant to accompany Vietnamese cuisine, bubble tea is a blend of coconut milk, ice, tapioca pearls, and sweet fruit or tea, and it's wonderfully refreshing. While you can buy it at most Asian supermarkets, it's easy to make at home. My version calls for pureed tropical fruits, like starfruit, Asian pears, jackfruits, and oranges, plus a dose of white whiskey and a little good-quality dark rum. If you can, use rhum agricole: Its intense sugar-cane flavor is delicious against the icy creaminess of coconut milk and coconut cream. The Roaming Hound Dog has the bite to match its bark, which means it's just the ticket if you're looking for a little hair of the dog.

INGREDIENTS

_ 2 OUNCES (60 ML) WHITE WHISKEY

_ 1/4 OUNCE (7 ML) DARK RUM

_ 2 TABLESPOONS (30 G) LUSCIOUS
  ASIAN FRUIT PUREE (SEE PAGE 312)

_ 1/2 CUP (120 ML) COCONUT MILK

_ 1/4 CUP (60 ML) SWEETENED
  COCONUT CREAM

_ CRUSHED ICE

_ 1/4 CUP (60 ML) BREWED,
  COOLED JASMINE TEA

_ 1 TABLESPOON (15 G) COOKED
  TAPIOCA PEARLS

DIRECTIONS

Pour the white whiskey and dark rum into a blender. Then add the fruit puree, coconut milk, and coconut cream, along with a few handfuls of crushed ice and the jasmine tea. Blend until smooth. Toss the tapioca pearls into a tall glass, and pour a large measure of the Roaming Hound Dog mixture over them. Use a colorful, wide-mouthed straw to suck up each succulent pearl.

THE DEEP HEALER

Like the classic Bloody Mary, the Deep Healer's tomato base is jam-packed with the antioxidant lycopene—and plenty of vodka—but the addition of onions, chiles, and leafy, magnesium-rich green vegetables make it more of a salad in a glass. A Deep Healer or two with a protein-packed brunch such as a veggie omelette will fix that pesky hangover in no time.

INGREDIENTS

_ 1-CUP TOMATO PUREE

_ 1/2 CUP (120 ML) ONION PUREE

_ 1/4 CUP (60 ML) HOT CHILE PASTE

_ 1 OUNCE (28 G) SPINACH, KALE, OR OTHER DARK LEAFY GREEN

_ 5 OUNCES (150 ML) VODKA

DIRECTIONS

Add all ingredients to a blender, and blend on regular speed until thoroughly combined. Serve over ice cubes in two tall glasses, and wait for the pain to evaporate. Serves two suffering souls.

SIDENOTE

⇒ **Chile for the cure.** Chiles may set your heart racing and make you break out in a sweat with their fiery heat, but after eating them, you feel cleansed and purified, in both body and soul. And the same went for your ancestors. Historically, pharmacies might have concocted products combining chile peppers with magnesium. When these ingredients were combined with grain alcohol and used either as an external salve or an internal elixir, they'd have offered sufferers relief from a whole score of painful ailments, such as lower back pain, muscle cramps, and fibromyalgia. And chiles are also rich in vitamins A, C, and E, as well as potassium and magnesium. Today, a chile-laden cocktail such as the Deep Healer is a great way to relieve headaches caused by overindulgence.

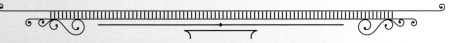

PURGATORIAL BRANDY FIZZ

Next time you find yourself in a purgatory of your own making after a little too much good food and wine, just relax: The Purgatorial Brandy Fizz is nothing short of a miracle worker. Here, spicy rye whiskey meets a measure of strong apple brandy and fizzy pear cider in a long, tall drink that's pure refreshment for flagging spirits. But don't be fooled, for the Fizz is in no way a sweet drink: After all, that's not what atonement for your sins is all about. However, the final flourish is probably the most medicinal: My aromatic bitters will sort out your stomach while the whiskey takes the edge off that headache. While the Purgatorial Fizz is a perfect remedy when you're feeling rough, be forewarned that drinking more than four will send you to Hades and back.

INGREDIENTS

_ 2 OUNCES (60 ML) RYE WHISKEY

_ 3/4 OUNCE (20 ML) 100-PROOF
APPLE BRANDY

_ 3/4 OUNCE (20 ML) HARD PEAR
CIDER (THE CARBONATED KIND)

_ 5 DROPS COCKTAIL WHISPERER'S
RAW HONEY AROMATIC
BITTERS (SEE PAGE 311)

_ HAND-CUT ICE CUBE

DIRECTIONS

Fill a mixing glass three-quarters full with ice. Add the whiskey, apple brandy, and the pear cider, and stir 30 times (the mixture will fizz up: that's to be expected!). Pour the mixture over your hand-cut ice cube into a Collins glass, and dot with the raw honey bitters to finish.

WRINGING OUT HIS FISHERMAN'S CAP

Not every hangover calls for the hair of the dog. Soothe yours with this cool mocktail instead, which features what's probably the best lemonade you'll ever try. It takes a little extra time to prepare, but it's so worth it: Before juicing, you submerge your lemons in a bath of spring water, raw honey, and sea salt—and then you grill them over wood charcoal for a new, unexpected flavor. Lemon and mint, of course, are a time-honored duo, and they taste even better when you slap your mint before using it as a garnish. (Never slapped your herbs before? Start now. Simply wash a piece of spearmint well, then place it into the palm of one hand and slap your other hand against it. This releases the mint's oils and makes it cocktail-glass-ready without bruising the leaves too much.) Named for the salt-drenched headgear of hardy fishermen, this invigorating drink is especially lovely before or after lunch.

INGREDIENTS

_ 4 OUNCES (120 ML) GRILLED
LEMONADE (SEE PAGE 312)

_ 2 OUNCES (60 ML) RAW HONEY
SIMPLE SYRUP (SEE PAGE 311)

_ 1 OUNCE (30 ML) FIZZY WATER

_ PINCH OF SEA SALT, THEN
ANOTHER PINCH ON THE LEMONS
JUST BEFORE GRILLING

_ FEW DROPS COCKTAIL WHISPERER'S
RAW HONEY AROMATIC
BITTERS (SEE PAGE 311)

_ FRESH SPEARMINT, SLAPPED

_ PEBBLED ICE, SMASHED IN A LEWIS BAG

DIRECTIONS

Add a handful of ice to a Collins glass, then add the Grilled Lemonade and the Raw Honey Simple Syrup. (Adjust sweetness to taste, adding more Raw Honey Simple Syrup if necessary.) Add the fizzy water, another scant handful of ice, and a pinch of sea salt. Finish with 3–4 drops of my homemade aromatic bitters, and garnish with a few leaves of the slapped fresh spearmint.

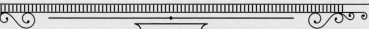

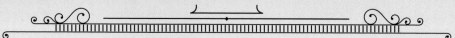

CLEVER LEMONADE FIZZ

I'm a huge fan of Vietnamese salty lemonade, an ultra-refreshing drink that uses *chanh muối*, or lemons preserved in salt, as its base. It's not as weird as it sounds. An Asian home remedy that's as old as the hills, *chanh muối* has been credited with curing everything from head colds to nausea—and it's a surprisingly versatile and delicious creature. (Don't worry about preserving lemons yourself: They're easily found in most Asian supermarkets.) This simple cocktail spikes Vietnamese lemonade with Tennessee sipping whiskey, and the result is more than clever—it's enchanting. The whiskey's tangy, smoky aroma is illuminated by deep citrus flavors enrobed in salt spray, and it's just the ticket when you're craving something salty, citrusy, thirst-quenching, and belly-friendly all at once.

INGREDIENTS

- 2 OR 3 ICE CUBES (OR ONE TALL SPEAR OF HAND-CUT ICE)
- 2 OUNCES (60 ML) TENNESSEE SIPPING WHISKEY
- 4 OUNCES (120 ML) VIETNAMESE FIZZY LEMONADE (SEE PAGE 313)
- SEA SALT AND EASY HOME-CURED COCKTAIL CHERRIES (SEE PAGE 311), FOR GARNISH

DIRECTIONS

Place the ice into a Collins glass, and pour whiskey over it. Top with the fizzy lemonade, then sprinkle a pinch of sea salt over the top of the drink. Garnish with a home-cured cocktail cherry (or a maraschino cherry, if you get desperate—they're not as good, though!) and a long straw.

GIN AND COCONUT ICE WITH SELTZER

Some hangover remedies act as a welcome slap in the face for tired taste buds, and jolt the senses back to life with a bang. If your body and mind feel a bit on the tender side, though, you crave a tipple that'll ease you back to the land of the living as painlessly as possible. This delicious tonic takes the edge off an ornery stomach in a gentle way, combining gin, fizzy seltzer, healing bitters, calming Thai basil, all well chilled by coconut-water ice cubes. (*Nota bene:* Coconut water adds a whack of potassium and hydrates the body as well.) A gin and coconut elixir should always be served as a long drink: that is, in a tall glass, and it should also run heavy on the gin and light on the seltzer and ice for maximum health benefits.

INGREDIENTS

_ COCONUT-WATER ICE CUBES (SIMPLY FREEZE UNSWEETENED COCONUT WATER IN AN ICE-CUBE TRAY OVERNIGHT)

_ 2 OUNCES (60 ML) BOTANICAL GIN

_ 1 OUNCE (25 ML) SIMPLE SYRUP (SEE PAGE 311)

_ 2 DROPS AROMATIC BITTERS (SUCH AS BITTER END THAI BITTERS OR ANGOSTURA BITTERS)

_ 1 1/2 OUNCES (45 ML) SELTZER WATER

_ SPRIG OF THAI BASIL (OR REGULAR BASIL)

DIRECTIONS

Fill a tall glass with the coconut-water ice cubes. Pour the gin over them, followed by the simple syrup. Shake a couple drops of bitters into the glass and top with seltzer water. (Open a fresh bottle for maximum fizz!) Garnish with a single sprig of Thai basil, gently crushed to release its fragrant natural oils. This drink is especially soothing for a hot-weather hangover.

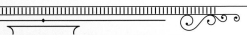

BRANCA MENTA AND COLA

Since time immemorial, potent herbal digestifs such as Branca Menta have been mixed with cool water, ice, and sugar to relieve tired, overheated bodies and to calm and cheer testy moods. Like its Italian cousin Fernet Branca, it's an aromatic, herbal liqueur that contains over forty (top-secret!) herbs, plus an extra dose of menthol and peppermint, both of which cool down the body and mellow out the mind. It also contains anise, which as any apothecary worth his salt would tell you, adds a crisp licorice flavor to the mix, and encourages relaxation. (And after all that wine you had last night, relaxation is just what you need.) This simple, bracing cocktail rounds out the Menta with a hit of cola, which takes the bitter edge off the liqueur's remedial botanicals.

INGREDIENTS

_ 3 OUNCES (90 ML) BRANCA MENTA

_ 6 OUNCES (175 ML) CANE SUGAR
COLA (OR REGULAR COLA)

_ ICE CUBES

DIRECTIONS

Pack a tall glass with ice cubes. Pour the Branca Menta over the ice—you'll feel revitalized after just a whiff of its bracing scent. Add the cola slowly, and sip your way to relief.

MILK THISTLE SPRITZ →

Set firmly in the early ages of the apothecary, this healing spritz derives its benefits from the curative herb milk thistle, and the herbs inherent in the bracing taste of the Italian digestif aperol. Since milk thistle is said to promote liver health, there's nothing better than this fizzy, rejuvenating tipple for cleansing the body and lightening the mind.

INGREDIENTS

_ 1 TABLESPOON (15 ML)
MILK THISTLE POWDER

_ 2 OUNCES (60 ML) APEROL OR CAMPARI

_ 4 OUNCES (120 ML) WHITE RUM

_ 2 OUNCES (60 ML) FRESHLY
SQUEEZED LEMON JUICE

_ 2 OUNCES (30 ML) SIMPLE
SYRUP (SEE PAGE 311)

_ 2 TO 3 OUNCES (60 TO 90
ML) SELTZER WATER

_ 4 DROPS PEYCHAUD'S BITTERS

DIRECTIONS

Combine all the ingredients except the seltzer water and bitters over a few handfuls of ice in a Boston shaker. Shake for a few seconds until well combined. Divide the mixture between two Collins glasses; then top each with the seltzer water, and add two dashes of bitters per glass. Serve, imbibe, and prepare to feel refreshed and renewed. **Serves 2.**

SIDENOTE   ⇒ **Thwart that hangover with milk thistle.** Renowned as a liver
tonic for hundreds of years, milk thistle promotes digestive health and helps
the liver eliminate toxins. (It may be helpful for kidney and gallbladder health,
too.) Practitioners of traditional Chinese medicine prescribe it to help reduce
inflammation and facilitate the growth of new cells: In fact, it may both prevent
and repair liver damage, which is, of course, great for whole-body health. After
all, when the liver is doing its job well, the entire body feels better. Just another
reason to mix up a Milk Thistle Spritz next time a hangover rears its ugly head.

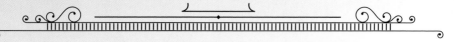

CAPTAIN SWANK'S SANDWICH SIPPAH

This long drink will add a touch of class to just about any casual meal. It's simple: Just ditch the boring corn syrup-based sodas in favor of this kicked-up cousin of the rum 'n' cola. The Captain Swank is definitely on the sweet side—which is no bad thing if you like a little sugar the morning (or afternoon) after—but the maple syrup does add a woody depth of flavor to this cocktail that keeps it from cloying. Ready for lunch? Try a Swank alongside just about any sandwich—like a bacon-laden club sandwich made with good bread and straight-off-the-vine tomatoes, or a blue-cheeseburger laced with caramelized onions and a handful of fries.

INGREDIENTS

_ 2 OUNCES (60 ML) WHITE WHISKEY

_ 4 OUNCES (120 ML) CANE SUGAR–BASED SARSAPARILLA SODA

_ 1 TABLESPOON (15 ML) MAPLE SYRUP

_ EASY HOME-CURED COCKTAIL CHERRY (SEE PAGE 311), FOR GARNISH

_ LIME ZEST TWIST

_ ICE

DIRECTIONS

Place one long spear of hand-cut ice, or 2 ice cubes, in a Collins glass. Pour the white whiskey over the ice, and then add the sarsaparilla soda and the maple syrup. Stir gently. Squeeze a lime chunk into the drink, and garnish with a lime zest twist and an Easy Home-Cured Cocktail Cherry. Serve immediately. Guaranteed to brighten up any lunchtime.

A SENSIBLE THING

With its notes of salt and smoke, Japanese whisky is reminiscent of its namesake, Scotch whisky. And, like Scotch, it can be used with impunity in all sorts of hot toddies. A Sensible Thing, with its whisky and freshly squeezed lemon juice for snap and acidity, is a bit of an oxymoron: a chilled toddy. Like a hot toddy, though, it's still a wonderful way to revive body and soul—and besides, some say cooling drinks are more soothing if you're nursing a bit of a banger. I like to twist my toddy up a bit by adding yuzu syrup (yuzu is a Japanese citrus fruit), and a final float of plum wine. I finish it off with a bit of fizzy water for lift, and I always serve it over a hand-cut-and-polished ice round. A Sensible Thing is fabulously refreshing, but observe the name and sip 'em sensibly—more than a couple, and you might find your faculties seriously compromised.

INGREDIENTS

- 1 OUNCE (28 G) CHOPPED PICKLED GINGER

- 1 OUNCE (30 ML) YUZU SYRUP (STORE-BOUGHT, OR MAKE YOUR OWN ORANGE JUICE SIMPLE SYRUP: SEE PAGE 312)

- 1 OUNCE (30 ML) FRESHLY SQUEEZED LEMON JUICE

- 2 OUNCES (60 ML) JAPANESE WHISKY

- 1/4 OUNCE (7 ML) PLUM WINE

DIRECTIONS

Using a muddler or the end of a wooden spoon, muddle the pickled ginger in the bottom of a mixing glass. Add the yuzu citrus syrup and the lemon juice. Then, fill the mixing glass three-quarters full with ice. Add the whisky, and mix carefully with a bar spoon. Using a Hawthorne strainer, strain the mixture over a single hand-cut ice cube into a coupé glass. Float the plum wine over the top of the drink, and sip—sensibly, of course.

SIDENOTE

⇒ **Japanese whisky: versatile and luxurious.** True, it doesn't sound like a terribly traditional Japanese drink, but whisky (no "e" again, in this case) is hugely popular in Japan. Today, the country's whisky distillers are practically beating the Scots at their own game—the game of distillation, that is. The Japanese are crafting super-premium, luxury whiskys that are being enjoyed all over the world. As with Scotch whisky, every sip of Japanese whisky features that unmistakable scent of peat smoke, then widens into the sweetness and long finish provided by the slowly-cooked grains that lend liquid sophistication to the sup and simply shimmer across the palate. Enjoying Japanese whisky can be every bit as elegant and pricy—if not more so—as some Scottish single-malt whiskys. Plus, it doesn't have to be drunk neat: It's just marvelous with a splash of seltzer water and a teaspoon of one of Japan's other great exports, sake, swirled with green tea. It's also highly expressive in a head-cold-busting hot toddy that combines freshly squeezed yuzu juice, hot cider, and raw honey. And that's just the beginning. Invest in a bottle of Japanese whisky stat, and experiment by using it in your craft cocktails in place of Scotch.

Notable Nightcaps:

HANDCRAFTED REMEDIES FOR RESTLESSNESS

• • •

YOU'VE BEEN LYING IN BED WATCHING THE CLOCK FOR—WELL, IT SEEMS LIKE FOREVER. MINUTES CREEP INTO HOURS: IF ONLY YOU COULD TURN OFF YOUR BRAIN AS EASILY AS YOU TURN OFF THE TELEVISION. SINCE YOU CAN'T, YOUR MIND IS AT ITS OWN MERCY, AND THOUGHTS RATTLE AND CREAK THROUGH YOUR HEAD LIKE RUSTY WHEELS. YOU LOOK AT THE CLOCK AGAIN, AND DO THE MATH: IF I FALL ASLEEP RIGHT NOW, I'LL STILL GET FIVE—NO, FOUR—HOURS IN BEFORE I HAVE TO GET UP. BUT THE SANDMAN IS NOWHERE IN

We've all been there. Sleeplessness seems to strike just when you most need the rest. Terribly unfair, isn't it? But taking some downtime before bed can help ease you into the serene mood that'll help you fall asleep, and stay asleep till morning. And you can rest assured (no pun intended!) that old-time pharmacists and apothecaries would have been plagued by customers complaining of the very same problem. Luckily, they'd have had a few powerful remedies in their alleviative arsenal. For instance, teas made from valerian root or chamomile could (and can still) relieve anxiety and irritation, and could help the patient fall into a restorative sleep that would ease peevishness and help heal illnesses. And the natural oils in herbs like sage and rosemary can promote a sense of calm and content, which might have taken the nervous edge off the stressed, the sick, and the restless. They probably used other botanicals, too, like St. John's wort, which is still used today in supplement form to balance negative moods, thereby promoting healthy sleep patterns.

And, of course, alcohol was recommended as an antidote to insomnia (and besides, it was essential in preserving the healing plant material in apothecary preparations). Today, we know that too much alcohol, especially right before bed, can actually harm restful sleep, but a well-chosen nightcap (one, now, not six) can still be part of the process of relaxing before turning in for the night. And that's where the craft cocktails in this chapter really shine. Traditionally, warm drinks, like toddies, hot milk, or spiked tea, are recommended when it comes to welcoming sleep, and there are some delicious, easy-to-make examples in the pages that follow. Try, for instance, the Sailor's Friend: it's nothing more than a well-crafted combination of hot tea, rum, and a little honey and lemon, but I challenge you to find a better before-bed beverage. Then there's the Mexican Sleep Cure, which is luxuriously rich hot chocolate that's been warmed with a little cayenne pepper and a dose of smoky mezcal: it's dessert and a nightcap all in one.

But what do you do if the weather's warm and sticky, and hot drinks are the last thing you're craving? The good news is that there are plenty of cool, soothing cocktails than can have a soporific effect. My Les Heretiers Curative is a prime example: it's a combination of rum, coconut water, sugar syrup, and aromatic bitters suspended in fizzy water, which is just what you want if the temperature's soared and sleep is elusive. And my Herbal Sleep Punch combines herbal infusions with a little botanical gin for an evening sedative that's as tasty as is relaxing. Or, if you want a more traditional (read: short, whiskey-based) nightcap, make yourself a Thomas Riley Marshall Cocktail: it's nothing more than Scotch, peach brandy, and curried bitters over ice. Then simply sip it slowly and meditatively, and let sleep steal over you.

There's plenty more where those came from. The handmade cocktails in this chapter are sure to help you unwind and de-stress after a long day. Which one will be your favorite?

SAILOR'S FRIEND

This toddy is built with simple, honest materials that haven't changed much over the years: hot water, a large dose of spiced rum, and lemon—a trinity that can't help but hasten the old closed-eye relaxation. And we have the seamen of yore to thank for its popularity: Sailors whose watch was scheduled for the middle of the night would have to force themselves to sleep during the day, whether they liked it or not. This historically accurate toddy would have been a sailor's best friend when cold, misty weather made it difficult to get some shut-eye. Plus, honey has been used as an expectorant since Roman times. Today, it's still a powerful ally against scratchy sore throats and those pesky, chesty coughs that can keep you tossing and turning at night. Enjoy one an hour before bedtime.

INGREDIENTS

_ BOILING WATER

_ 3 OUNCES (90 ML) DARK SPICED RUM

_ HONEY, TO TASTE

_ LEMON WHEEL

DIRECTIONS

Preheat a mug by filling it with boiling water; discard the water after a few seconds. Add the rum to the mug and top with boiling water. Stir in honey to taste, and sip until sleep approaches off the ship's starboard side. Oh, and don't forget to float the lemon wheel on top of the toddy to stave off your chances of contracting scurvy.

SIDENOTE

⇒ **A rum deal?** The Sailor's Friend calls for dark spiced rum, since it's especially lovely in a toddy. But wait a minute: What's the difference between light rum and dark rum? The answer is more complex than you'd think. It might sound counterintuitive, but light rum isn't necessarily young, and dark rum isn't necessarily old.

Here's why. All rum is made from fermented sugar cane extract, and most is distilled from fermented sugarcane molasses (except Rhum Agricole, which is made from sugar cane juice, not molasses). Light rum is aged in stainless-steel or uncharred oak barrels, which means it's pretty much colorless. Medium-bodied or "golden" rums are darker and more deeply-flavored, but don't be fooled: Unfortunately, most golden and dark rums have artificial flavoring and coloring added to them in order to trick the buyer into thinking they've been resting in oak barrels for years. (The truth is that rum, like whiskey, can actually get lighter in color over time. Some of the finest rum I've ever enjoyed was twenty-three years old and light in color—not stained the color of Admiral Nelson's blood!) Because of this, color is by no means an indication of age or quality. (Regardless of color, rums that have been aged for longer earn the designation *anejo*, which means "old" in Spanish.)

That said, there are rums on the market that do not use caramel coloring or artificial flavouring. So do your research before you buy. Visit distillers' websites (or the actual premises, if you can!) and don't be afraid to contact them with any questions. Alternatively, you can ask an expert at your local wine and spirits store for guidance. Respect your craft cocktails by using the best-quality rum you can afford!

MEXICAN SLEEP CURE

Hot, bittersweet, chile-laden concoctions hailing from Mexico are said to enhance repose and restfulness. Here, *mezcal* tops up a cup of spicy Mexican hot chocolate; it's not only delicious, it's also very effective when it comes to chasing the sandman. Skip the sleeping pills, and indulge in a cupful this evening.

INGREDIENTS

_ 3 OUNCES (90 ML) MEZCAL

_ 1 CUP (235 ML) MEXICAN "SPICY" HOT
CHOCOLATE (COMBINE 3/4 CUP (175
ML) OF WHOLE MILK WITH A 1/4 CUP
(60 ML) OF HEAVY CREAM. ADD 1/4
POUND (115 G) GRATED BITTERSWEET
CHOCOLATE. HEAT SLOWLY, DO NOT BOIL,
AND WHISK CONSTANTLY UNTIL SMOOTH.
ADD 1/2 TEASPOON OF CAYENNE
PEPPER, AND SUGAR TO TASTE)

_ 1/2 TEASPOON VANILLA EXTRACT

_ DARK BROWN SUGAR, TO TASTE

DIRECTIONS

Prepare the hot chocolate. Preheat a mug by pouring boiling water into it; discard the water after a few seconds. Add the mezcal to the mug, followed by the hot chocolate, and then doctor it with the vanilla extract and sugar. Sip, and sleep is sure to follow.

SIDENOTE

⇒ **Meet mezcal.** Let me introduce you to the Mexican spirit mescal, which sure is a potent beast. It's made from the agave plant, which grows in many parts of Mexico, and is said to be sacred in Mexican culture; it's certainly played a large part in the country's history and mythology since well before the Spanish conquest in the sixteenth century. Mezcal is a pale-yellow color, sports a distinctively smoky aroma, and is usually served neat. These days it graces the shelves of cocktail bars around the world, but apothecaries of old might have suggested a slug of this *aguardiente*, or firewater, to those whose love lives were drooping, since it's reputed to lift the libido—and the spirits.

GERMAN RELAXATION

We all know that restful sleep doesn't come easy, especially when you really need it. So it's no surprise that nearly every country in the world has developed its own remedies for wakefulness. In Germany, a teaspoon of distilled Alpine herbs suspended in a tonic made with wildflower honey and then added to a cup of hot water or tea is known to ease stress and to set tired eyelids fluttering. Made with dozens of herbs and spices— don't bother asking which ones, since the recipes for these tonics are usually guarded like state secrets—it's likely that these tonics were originally designed as cough remedies or digestives. Today, many of these liqueurs are widely available outside of *Deutschland*, so they should be relatively easy to find. This simple recipe is just the ticket when it comes to combating restlessness and inducing relaxation.

INGREDIENTS

- 3 OUNCES (90 ML) ALPINE HERBAL ELIXIR (SUCH AS JÄGERMEISTER)
- 6 OUNCES (175 ML) BOILING WATER
- 1 OUNCE (25 ML) RAW HONEY SIMPLE SYRUP (SEE PAGE 312-313)

DIRECTIONS

Preheat a mug by filling it with boiling water; discard the water after a few seconds. Add the Alpine herbal elixir to the mug, and top with more boiling water. Sweeten with the honey simple syrup and you'll drift off to sleep dreaming of little goats frolicking on Alpine mountaintops.

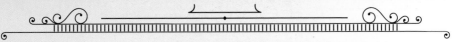

COLD CURE #1001

Colds can strike year-round, and when they do, they can keep you up at night—all night. It'd take magical powers beyond even the Cocktail Whisperer's understanding to actually *cure* a cold—but it's certainly possible to relieve its symptoms. For starters, peppermint has analgesic qualities, which means it's known to ease cold-related pain like headaches, and peppermint infusions can also relieve ailments of the stomach, such as nausea, indigestion, and seasickness. It's also used in Bénédictine, one of the main ingredients in this insomnia-banishing drink. Be sure to crown your Cold Cure #1001 with Jamaican bitters, which are said to contain ingredients widely used in folk healing, such as allspice, ginger, and black pepper. Breathe deeply before taking a sip of this curative: If that stubborn cold makes breathing feel like snorkeling with a drinking straw, a few whiffs of these aromas will alleviate congestion and speed snoozing.

INGREDIENTS

_ 12-OUNCE (355-ML) POT OF
HOT PEPPERMINT TEA

_ 5 TO 6 OUNCES (150 TO 175
ML) BÉNÉDICTINE

_ 3 TO 4 OUNCES (90 TO 120
ML) SWEET VERMOUTH

_ 10 DROPS JAMAICAN BITTERS

DIRECTIONS

Prepare the pot of peppermint tea; then remove the teabags. Preheat two large mugs by filling them with boiling water; discard the water after a few seconds. Add the Bénédictine, followed by the vermouth, to the pot. Mix gently, and let the mixture sit for a few minutes. Add the bitters, pour into the mugs, and serve immediately. Inhale, soothing those grumpy sinuses. Serves two sniffling, sleepless sufferers.

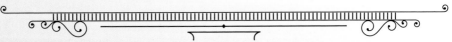

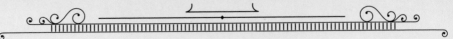

LES HÉRITIERS CURATIVE

Back in the day, apothecaries in the Caribbean knew just what to do if a patient complained of feeling heavyhearted, glum, or irritable. They'd prescribe a hearty dose of their favorite curative, Rhum Agricole. Made from cane sugar, this overproof rum would've acted as a preservative for delicate herbs and spices, and it might have given the patient something to look forward to at the end of an interminable (and possibly expensive) curative session. Rum takes pride of place in the Les Héritiers Cocktail, alongside healing bitters and fizzy water: a wonderfully simple combination that's sure to help you unwind—especially in warm weather, when you need a soothing nightcap but can't stand the thought of hot liquids. *Les héretiers* means "the princes" in French, and you're sure to feel like one after a dose of this delicious prescriptive.

INGREDIENTS

- 3 OUNCES (90 ML) RHUM AGRICOLE
- 1 OUNCE (25 ML) CANE-SUGAR SYRUP
- 1 OUNCE (25 ML) COCONUT WATER
- 2 OUNCES (60 ML) SELTZER WATER
- 2 DASHES AROMATIC BITTERS

DIRECTIONS

Combine all the liquid ingredients except the bitters in a cocktail shaker. Add a few handfuls of ice, then the bitters. Taste, and add another dash or two of bitters to taste, if you like. Strain the mixture into a coupé glass, and serve. Relax, sip, and repeat, and let that cranky mood drift away.

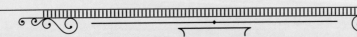

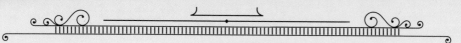

SCOTCHMAN'S SLUMBER

Warm drinks made with Scotch whisky are tried-and-true ways for courting that elusive gnome named Sleep. That's because Scotch is such a versatile healer: It's said to be effective against tension, restlessness, and even sleepwalking. Back in the heyday of apothecaries, high levels of stress probably contributed to insomnia: If the pharmacist could treat the stress, his patient would be more likely to get some shut-eye. And some things never change: Unfortunately, anxiety can still make bedtime an ordeal, but it'll ebb away after a few sips of this robust curative. Of course, Scotch is delicious—and remedial—when taken neat or on the rocks, but its unique, smoky flavor is also a great complement to savory beef broth. And this toddy is naturally caffeine-free, making it especially good at dimming the internal lights.

INGREDIENTS

_ 3 OUNCES (90 ML) SCOTCH WHISKY

_ 6 OUNCES (175 ML) STRONG
  BEEF BOUILLON

_ JUICE OF A 1/2 LEMON

DIRECTIONS

Preheat a mug by filling it with boiling water; discard the water after a few seconds. Add the Scotch whisky to the mug and top it with the beef bouillon. Add a squeeze of lemon to the mixture, stir gently, and sip. As the Irish say, a good laugh and a long sleep are truly the best cures.

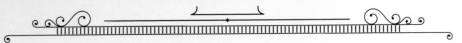

HERBAL SLEEP PUNCH

Hot drinks aren't the only answer when it comes to curatives that enhance restful sleep. In fact, I'm especially fond of cool liquids when sleep seems miles away. That's where this recipe comes in: A punch made from herbal teas and botanical gin can relieve sleeplessness, even when it feels as if nothing could possibly bring you a single step closer to the land of Nod. This cocktail combines infusions of herbs known to relax the sleep-deprived, and traditional apothecaries would have been well versed in their benefits. Chamomile, an anti-inflammatory, has been used as an antidote to anxiety for centuries; lavender is said to gently ease irritating sleep disturbances; and fennel helps to keep digestion on track. A dose of botanical gin and lime juice bind the infusions together into a gentle tipple that will help turn off the lights for even the most dedicated insomniac.

INGREDIENTS

_ 1 TEABAG EACH CHAMOMILE TEA, LAVENDER TEA, AND FENNEL TEA

_ JUICE OF 1 LIME

_ RAW HONEY SIMPLE SYRUP (SEE PAGE 312-313), TO TASTE

_ 3 OUNCES (90 ML) BOTANICAL GIN

DIRECTIONS

Infuse the teabags in hot water for at least an hour. When cool, pack a tall glass with ice. Pour the tea over the ice; add the lime juice, and sweeten to taste with the honey simple syrup. Finally, add the gin, and mix gently. Sleep tight!

CABIN IN THE PINES COCKTAIL

Here's another cooling cocktail that's great for relaxing both body and mind. If you need more than a little help winding down in the evenings, stage a retreat from the real world, and mix yourself a Cabin in the Pines. Here, stone fruits like peaches and plums become extra-luscious when slow-roasted in the oven: They assume otherworldly shapes and colors, their sweet, summery flavors become concentrated and intensified, and viscous juices flow from deep within their shriveled flesh. (Roast and cool your fruit well before bedtime; you won't want to wait that long for your Cabin.) When muddled and mixed with white whiskey, they become magical stuff. Add a bit of club soda and a splash of Fernet Branca for health—just in case overindulgence is the cause of your insomnia!—and you've got a chilled-out restorative of the highest order.

INGREDIENTS

_ 2 HEAPING TABLESPOONS (30 G) ROASTED STONE FRUITS (SEE PAGE 313)

_ 2 OUNCES (60 ML) WHITE WHISKEY

_ 1/2 OUNCE (15 ML) FERNET BRANCA

_ 2 OUNCES (60 ML) RAW HONEY SIMPLE SYRUP (SEE PAGE 312-313)

_ 1 OUNCE (30 ML) CLUB SODA

_ 2 TO 3 DROPS AROMATIC BITTERS

DIRECTIONS

Add the roasted stone fruits to a Boston shaker, and using the back of a bar spoon or the end of a wooden spoon, muddle them to release their juices. Then, add the white whiskey, the Fernet Branca, and the Raw Honey Simple Syrup. Fill the shaker three-quarters full with ice and shake for about 15 seconds. Strain into a coupe glass, and top with a splash of the club soda. Finish with a couple drops of aromatic bitters of your choice.

SAKE RACER →

Suffering from wakeful nights? Enjoying *sake*—that is, Japanese rice wine —may encourage sleep to come knocking. Sake has a higher alcohol content than table wine, typically around 18 to 20 percent, but it's said to be gentler on the stomach than other forms of alcohol—and that's good to know if typical table wine doesn't agree with you. Since it's packed with amino acids, it's even said to promote healthy skin when applied topically. (In creams and cosmetics, that is. Don't wash your face with it.) In addition to the warm sake—which shouldn't be heated over 140 degrees, by the way—the Sake Racer includes an infusion of healing, soothing herbs, along with a bit of botanical gin and a final touch of rich plum wine for sweetness. Combined, these ingredients can offer asylum even from the most obstinate insomnia. Sayonara, sleeplessness!

INGREDIENTS

_ 6 OUNCES (175 ML) WARM SAKE

_ 3 OUNCES (90 ML) WARM PLUM WINE

_ 2 OUNCES (60 ML) BOTANICAL GIN

_ 2 TEASPOONS HEALING HERBS, SUCH
AS GINSENG, HOPS, CAFFEINE-FREE
GREEN TEA, OR PASSION FLOWER
(ADD ABOUT 1/2 TEASPOON OF
EACH TO A MESH TEA BALL)

DIRECTIONS

*Preheat a mug by filling it with boiling water; discard the
water after a few seconds. Pour the sake, plum wine, and gin
in a large mug and stir gently; then let the tea ball steep in
the mixture for at least five minutes. Remove the tea bag, and
sip until sleep arrives like the moon over Mount Fuji.*

NIEUWPOORT ELIXIR

Rosemary marries so well with lime juice and genever, a juniper-flavored, herb- and spice-laden medicinal curative with roots in the Netherlands. This cocktail calls for fresh rosemary—whatever you do, don't substitute the dried version—suspended in ice cubes: As the cubes melt, the rosemary-infused water seeps into the drink, clearing pain-fogged heads before bedtime.

INGREDIENTS

_ ROSEMARY WATER ICE CUBES
(PLACE CRUSHED ROSEMARY LEAVES
IN AN ICE-CUBE TRAY AND FILL
WITH FILTERED WATER AND A FEW
DROPS OF SIMPLE SYRUP (SEE
PAGE 311). FREEZE OVERNIGHT.

_ 3 OUNCES (90 ML) GENEVER

_ 4 OUNCES (120 ML) CLUB SODA

_ LEMON AND ORANGE TWISTS

_ SEVERAL DROPS OF ANGOSTURA BITTERS

DIRECTIONS

Add several rosemary ice cubes to a Collins glass; then pour the genever and club soda over it. Mix gently, and finish with several drops of Angostura bitters. Garnish with the lemon and orange twists—then take three doses immediately. It's sure to relieve symptoms of malaise, letting you get the forty winks you long for.

SIDENOTE

⇒ **Rosemary for restlessness.** Migraines, colds, and flus can chase sleep away fast, but rosemary may be able to help. This fragrant herb has been cultivated since ancient times, and for centuries it's been renowned for its potent antibacterial properties. (In fact, French hospitals used to burn it, along with juniper berries, to purify the air.) The plant's flowers, wrote botanist Nicholas Culpeper in 1653, "are singularly good to comfort the heart"—that is, it's cheering and relaxing—and it also offers many other health benefits that can speed snoozing: like chamomile, it contains anti-inflammatory properties, and like peppermint, it's said to be good for pain relief. Plus, rosmarinic acid, one of the phytochemicals found in rosemary, can help respiratory illnesses that make it hard to sleep, such as asthma and allergies

THOREAU COCKTAIL WITH WARM CRANBERRY, BLUEBERRY, AND SCOTCH

The original Thoreau Cocktail calls for botanical gin, but I find that Scotch, due to its depth of flavor, is an even better pairing for cranberries and blueberries. If at all possible, use wild Maine blueberries to mix up my Cocktail Whisperer's twisted take on the Thoreau, a fruity, caffeine-free libation that's so warming and soothing. Wild Maine blueberries are tiny—about the size of your fingernail, or even smaller—with an intense taste and great acidity, and I think they're an excellent match for tart New England cranberries. Go ahead and use an inexpensive Scotch here: The crushed fruit and fresh citrus juice would mask the advantages of a pricey one. (Not that you need another excuse to use blueberries in your cocktails, but just in case: Blueberries are reputed to be "superfoods," packed with disease-fighting antioxidants.)

INGREDIENTS

- 1/4 CUP (35 G) EACH CRUSHED CRANBERRIES AND BLUEBERRIES
- 1/3 CUP (85 G) UNSWEETENED, SMOOTH CRANBERRY SAUCE (WITH A BIT OF SUGAR ADDED FOR TASTE)
- 4 OUNCES (120 ML) BLENDED SCOTCH WHISKY (NO SINGLE MALTS IN THIS ONE!)
- 1/3 CUP (80 ML) WATER
- 1 CUP (235 ML) CRANBERRY JUICE
- 1/4 CUP (60 ML) FRESHLY SQUEEZED LIME JUICE
- 1 TABLESPOON (15 ML) MAPLE SYRUP (OPTIONAL)
- SEVERAL THICKLY CUT ORANGE SLICES
- 2 SPRIGS OF FRESH THYME

DIRECTIONS

Using a muddler or the end of a wooden spoon, muddle the crushed cranberries with the blueberries in the bottom of a heatproof mixing glass to make a slurry, and then add the cranberry sauce to the mix. Add the Scotch, and let sit for a few minutes so the flavors combine. In a small saucepan, bring the water to the boil, and then add the cranberry and lime juices. Pour this heated cranberry juice over the muddled cranberry-blueberry mixture, and stir together. Divide between 2 preheated ceramic mugs, straining the cooked fruit out first, if you like. Sweeten with the maple syrup (if using), and garnish each mug with the orange slices and a sprig of thyme.

SIDENOTE

⇒ **Blended whiskey: What's in a name?** There are so many different types of whiskeys (or whiskys: For reasons mostly lost to history, the Scottish still spell the world without the "e," while in the United States, "whiskey" retains that missing "e." Meanwhile, tipplers in Japan, India, and Canada spell the word *sans* "e," while the Irish spelling, like the American one, favors it. However you spell it, it's still delicious!) on the market that it can be hard to make sense of their labels. Straight whiskey, single malt, blended: Aren't they pretty much the same? Nope. Blended whiskey is a combination of two or more 100-proof straight whiskeys blended with neutral grain spirits plus flavorings and colorings. It's much cheaper than single-malt or straight whiskeys, and is often used in cocktails where mixers tend to mask its taste. Single malt whiskeys are simply malt whiskeys made by a single distillery, while straight whiskey may be made from different barrels in different distilleries (although, in order to be called "straight whiskey" in the United States, the distilleries must all be located within the same state). Ultimately, single malt and straight whiskies are best if you're planning on enjoying them neat or on the rocks, but it's fine to use blended whiskey in cocktails with strong flavors, like the Thoreau.

HELP ME, MR. KENTISH!

Comfort food is one of the best ways to nourish both body and soul after a long day. Well, here's the mixological equivalent of mashed potatoes: whiskey-spiked bubble tea. Named for a brisk, efficient ship's officer of the same name in a short story by Robert Louis Stevenson, it's mightily effective when it comes to calming edgy minds and jittery bodies. Curiously, Tennessee sipping whiskey is a beguiling match for Chinese bubble tea, which is a combination of milk or coconut milk and slowly cooked tapioca, which has a sort of soft-to-the-tooth, gummy-bear consistency (minus the tooth-injuring texture, of course). I suggest using coconut-flavored bubble tea here, but feel free to use your own favorite flavor instead. Help yourself to a Help Me, Mr. Kentish! before bed: there's nothing better when it comes to winding down and chilling out.

INGREDIENTS

_ 8 OUNCES (235 ML) COCONUT BUBBLE
TEA (OR YOUR FAVORITE FLAVOR)

_ 2 OUNCES (60 ML) TENNESSEE
SIPPING WHISKEY

_ A VERY WIDE-MOUTHED STRAW!

DIRECTIONS

Fill a parfait glass with the bubble tea, and then add the Tennessee sipping whiskey. Stir gently, and then pop a wide-mouthed straw into the drink so that it's easy to slurp up the tapioca pearls. Slurp your way to sweet dreams.

RUM TODDY FOR RESTLESS NIGHTS

Hot rum cocktails aren't just cold-weather cures. Sure, they're warming and restorative, but they're also well-known curatives for sleeplessness. Rum toddies like this one are simple to make, and deliver powerful healing to body and mind alike. This version calls for liberal dashes of highly alcoholic, aromatic bitters, which are said to relieve anxiety and insomnia by themselves. Here, they're added to a base of tannic black tea that's been topped up with a hearty dose of rum and lemon—a marriage made in heaven—and then sweetened with honey. (If the caffeine in tea keeps you up at night, just substitute with the decaf variety.) Like a warm blanket, the gentle heat and fragrance from this toddy will envelope you slowly, and sleep is sure to catch up with you fast.

INGREDIENTS

_ 3 OUNCES (90 ML) DARK RUM

_ 6 OUNCES (175 ML) HOT BLACK TEA

_ JUICE OF ONE LEMON

_ SEVERAL DASHES OF
HEALING BITTERS

_ ONE TABLESPOON (20 G) OF
HONEY (OR MORE TO TASTE)

DIRECTIONS

Prepare a pot of hot tea. Preheat a mug by filling it with boiling water; discard the water after a few seconds. Add the rum to the mug; then top it with the tea. Mix in the lemon juice, add honey to taste, as well as a dash or two (or three) of bitters. You won't need to count sheep tonight!

KRUPNIKAS AND HOT TEA

Krupnikas, the unique herbal elixir indigenous to Lithuania, can be found in regions of the United States in which Lithuanian immigrants made their homes, such as Cleveland, Ohio, where winters tend to be long and frigid. Combat chills and restlessness with this simple, age-old remedy: Make yourself some steaming-hot black tea, then top with Krupnikas. Instant relaxation.

INGREDIENTS

_ 3 OUNCES (90 ML) KRUPNIKAS

_ 6 OUNCES (175 ML) HOT BLACK TEA

DIRECTIONS

Preheat a large mug by filling it with boiling water; discard the water after a few seconds. Add the Krupnikas to the mug, then fill with the hot tea. Mix gently, enjoy a couple deep lungfuls of the fragrant steam and let the concoction work its warming magic.

SIDENOTE

⇒ **"Correct" your favorite beverage with Krupnikas** Eastern Europe boasts a long tradition of using raw honey and potent, distilled alcohol in medicinal, root-based elixirs, and Krupnikas is just what the apothecary ordered when it comes to curing what ails you. Comprised of herbs, spices, and raw honey combined with alcoholic spirits of nearly 140-proof, Krupnikas can be sipped straight (although I don't recommend it, unless you have an extremely stout constitution!) or enjoyed over ice with soda water and lemon in the summer. But it's particularly conducive to cold weather, since you can use it to "correct" just about any hot liquid—like your favorite teas or infusions, a cup of coffee, or even a hot bowl of thick cabbage soup.

THE THOMAS RILEY MARSHALL COCKTAIL →

Depending on its *terroir*, Scotch whisky can taste richly earthy and spicy, followed by a long, vanilla-flavored finish. And it makes a smashing nightcap when it's paired with peach brandy: its flavors of juicy, freshly crushed peaches bring out Scotch's spicy sweetness. A final touch of curried bitters adds depth and more spice to this short, fragrant curative. Named for the U.S. vice president who said, infamously (and, one hopes, with his tongue firmly in his cheek), "What this country needs is a really good five-cent cigar," The Thomas Riley Marshall features only a few ingredients, but its simplicity belies its depth—you'll be enchanted by its spicy, sweet heat.

INGREDIENTS

_ 2 OUNCES (60 ML) BLENDED
  SCOTCH WHISKEY

_ 1/4 OUNCE (7 ML) PEACH BRANDY

_ SEVERAL DROPS OF CURRIED BITTERS

_ EASY HOME-CURED COCKTAIL
  CHERRIES (SEE PAGE 311)

DIRECTIONS

Pre-chill a rocks glass by filling it with ice water, and then pour the ice water out. Wash the inside of the glass with the peach brandy, and then pour the brandy out (into your mouth, please—what have I told you about wasting good liquor?) Add a single hand-cut ice cube to the glass, followed by the Scotch. Dribble 2 to 4 drops of the curried bitters over the top of the drink, and garnish with an Easy Home-Cured Cocktail Cherry. Then light up that imaginary five-cent cigar, and kick back for the evening.

FLEMINGTON COCKTAIL

There's little better than the delicious trinity of honey, stone fruits, and Scotch whisky when it comes to banishing the blues, and the sweet-tart, sage-strewn Flemington Cocktail puts this luscious preparation to good use. Make yourself one as an after-dinner treat, then kick back and relax until bedtime: You'll slip off to sleep in a flash.

INGREDIENTS

_ 3 TABLESPOONS (45 ML) MUDDLED STONE FRUITS (PEACHES, PLUMS, OR NECTARINES)

_ 1 OUNCE (25 ML) HONEY SIMPLE SYRUP (SEE PAGE 312-313)

_ 3 OUNCES (90 ML) SCOTCH WHISKY

_ 1/2 OUNCE (15 ML) SWEET VERMOUTH

_ FEW DASHES ANGOSTURA BITTERS

_ 1 OUNCE (25 ML) FRESHLY SQUEEZED LEMON JUICE

_ 1 LARGE FRESH SAGE LEAF, CHIFFON-ADED (THAT IS, ROLLED UP LIKE A CIGAR AND FINELY SLICED ACROSS THE GRAIN)

DIRECTIONS

Muddle the stone fruit in the bottom of a Boston shaker. Add the honey simple syrup, Scotch whisky, sweet vermouth, bitters, and lemon juice, and shake for twenty seconds until combined. Strain the mixture into a martini glass, and garnish with the chiffonaded sage leaf. Sip slowly until the dark clouds start to lift.

LEAVES STRAINING AGAINST WIND →

Picture this: it's late autumn. The trees are nearly barren of leaves, and a single leaf hangs onto its branch by sheer willpower, despite the chill winds. You gaze up at the tenacious leaf, and meditate upon the past, the possibilities the future holds, and the truth inherent in the present moment. Then you take a sip of this exquisite slurp—and while you might not reach immediate enlightenment, the stuff in your glass sure tastes good. A drink to be enjoyed oh-so-slowly, Leaves Straining Against Wind comprises no more than four ingredients: Japanese whisky, enriched by a splash of savory *junmai sake*, plus some fizzy, salty club soda and a paper-thin slice of cucumber. No need for ice here: for this cocktail, cool cellar temperatures are best. Serve it in your favorite teacup half an hour before bed.

INGREDIENTS

_ 2 OUNCES (60 ML) HIGH-QUALITY
   JAPANESE WHISKY

_ 1/2 OUNCE (15 ML) HIGH-QUALITY
   JUNMAI SAKE

_ THINLY CUT CUCUMBER SLICES

_ PINCH OF SEA SALT

DIRECTIONS

*Add a pinch of sea salt to a mid-sized ceramic tea cup. Pop a
cube of hand-cut ice into the cup, and then pour the whisky
over it. Float the sake on top of the whiskey, and garnish
with a cucumber slice. Sip slowly and meditatively.*

Tipples for Toasting:

FESTIVE CRAFT COCKTAILS FOR PARTIES AND CELEBRATIONS

◆ ◆ ◆

PARTIES ARE ONE OF LIFE'S GREAT PLEASURES, AND HOSTING ONE IS A GREAT PRIVI-
LEGE—BUT THERE'S A GOOD DEAL OF FORETHOUGHT AND PLANNING INVOLVED, TOO. ARE
YOU HOSTING AN INTIMATE WEEKEND BRUNCH OR LUNCH, SO THAT YOU CAN KICK BACK
AND ENJOY AN AFTERNOON WITH JUST A COUPLE OF CLOSE FRIENDS? PERHAPS YOU WERE
THINKING OF DINNER FOR EIGHT—OR, YOU MIGHT BE BANKING ON A BIGGER EVENT, LIKE
A BARBEQUE, A PRE-THEATER COCKTAIL PARTY, A WEDDING SHOWER, OR A BACHELOR
PARTY. THEN THERE'S THE GUEST LIST, PLUS THE MENU—AND, OF COURSE, YOU'LL WANT
TO CHOOSE DRINKS TO COMPLEMENT WHATEVER YOU'RE SERVING.

S ure, the idea of throwing a party—small or large—can be daunting. But half the fun of a party is prepping for it, and plus, I'll wager you'll find that all your hard work is well worth it when the bash is in full swing: Laughter, conversation, and drinks are flowing, and that's when you get to stand back and admire your handiwork. Everyone's having a great time, and who made it all happen? You did.

And that's where this chapter comes in. Dedicated to craft cocktails that are perfect for celebrations of all sizes, it's full of ideas for your next bash. If it's an occasion that calls for shots (and some events do: Did you submit your Master's dissertation? Get elected to plan your best friend's bachelor party? Decide to move to Scotland for a year?), you can drink to the health of the company without overdoing it: Whip up a batch of my Roasted Beet Borscht and serve it in shotglasses topped with just a nip of vodka. And the next morning? Make a round of Fernet Branca Shots, and let Fernet's secret blend of herbs annihilate that fearsome hangover. If you're looking for a quick after-dinner fix that features a little fizz, serve your guests a Benedictine Twist Elixir each: It's a short, punchy, easy-to-make tipple that delivers instant—and delicious—healing to overstuffed bellies.

If you're expecting quite a crowd and you're hosting solo, don't stress yourself out by trying to be host, bartender, and chef all at once. Instead, check out the recipes for punches in the pages ahead. They're great for groups; they're lovely to look at; and since all of my handmade punches call only for top-quality ingredients, you can be rest assured that they won't skimp on sophistication or subtlety. And for something even more elegant, go for an sparkling, bourbon-laden Assembly Ball Cocktail; a champagne-driven Squire's Shrub Cocktail, a classy riff on the traditional French 75; or Poppa's Got A New Bag, a melange of top-quality rum, broiled citrus juices, and luscious chocolate bitters.

Keep reading: Whether it's an intimate dinner for four, an impromptu cocktail party, or a couple dozen thirsty folks, you'll find plenty of inspiration in this chapter for crowd-friendly drinks that are sure to cheer, refresh, and relax your guests. Let's get this party started!

FERNET BRANCA SHOTS

Since its invention in nineteenth-century Italy, Fernet's qualities as a soothing digestif after a large meal have spread far and wide—but it's also one of the best hangover cures on the books. Made with dozens of herbs from all over the world, the recipe for Fernet Branca is top-secret, but we *do* know it has a great history as a fixer-upper for flagging spirits: A few ice-cold shots of Fernet are known to vanquish pesky hangovers nearly immediately. (Then again, the 80-proof spirits may also have something to do with it.) Either way, if you've got a gang of suffering houseguests on your hands, pour them a round of these neat treats on the morning (or afternoon) after: They're nothing more than Fernet plus a ginger-beer crown, but they'll leave your entourage wide-awake and ready to take on a new day—hangover-free.

INGREDIENTS

_ 1 OUNCE (25 ML) FERNET BRANCA

_ DASH OF GINGER BEER

DIRECTIONS

Simply add one shot of Fernet Branca to a short glass, then top with ginger beer or ginger ale. (Don't add ice.) Pay no attention to your aching head, guys: Lift your glass, down the contents, and repeat if necessary. Salut!

ASSEMBLY BALL SHRUBB COCKTAIL →

As elegant as eveningwear, this simple citrusy cocktail is a celebration in a glass. It takes its name from the Assembly Ball, a debutante ball first held in Philadelphia in 1748. (Assembly Balls are still held in lots of communities around the country today.) I like to imagine our eighteenth-century ancestors drinking a version of this effervescent cocktail at the event of the season—only, our eighteenth-century ancestors might have used English marmalade or another kind of orange preserves in the absence of easily available fresh oranges. Luckily, you have a batch of my Italian Blood Orange and Charred Rosemary Shrub (see page 22) ready and waiting. Combine it with the best bourbon you can get, plus a dash of Rhum Agricole, grapefruit bitters, and garnish with a piney sprig of rosemary. Serve a round of Assembly Balls as aperitifs at an intimate, late-spring dinner party.

INGREDIENTS

_ 2 OUNCES (60 ML)
   GOOD-QUALITY BOURBON

_ 1/2 OUNCE (15 ML) 100-PROOF RHUM
   AGRICOLE (OR OTHER GOOD WHITE RUM)

_ 2 OUNCES (60 ML) ITALIAN BLOOD
   ORANGE AND CHARRED ROSEMARY
   SHRUBB (SEE PAGE 22)

_ SPLASH OF SELTZER WATER

_ 2-3 DROPS GRAPEFRUIT BITTERS

_ ROSEMARY SPRIG, FOR GARNISH

DIRECTIONS

Fill a Boston shaker three-quarters full with ice, and pour over the bourbon, the Rhum Agricole, and the Italian Blood Orange and Charred Rosemary Shrubb. Cover and shake hard for 15 seconds, and then pour into a coupe glass. Top with the seltzer, and drip 2–3 drops of the grapefruit bitters over the top of the drink. Garnish with a small (non-charred!) sprig of rosemary (try to avoid using too much of the tough, bitter stalk).

AN ENGLISH AFTERNOON PUNCH

Tea is an essential ingredient in traditional punches, and my version is built upon a base of strong Chinese tea: I like lapsang souchong's aromatic smokiness, and it's such a good match both for Scotch and for Drambuie (which has a sort of honeyed, smoky flavor itself). Then, equal measures of fresh citrus juices and my Blood Orange Shrub balance things out for a tangy, spirit-lifting elixir that's sure to pep you up before your next game of croquet. A thoroughly modern examination of this quintessentially English beverage, my English Afternoon Punch will make a dozen or so of your closest friends very, very happy on a wet Saturday afternoon.

INGREDIENTS

_ 1 750 ML BOTTLE BLENDED
SCOTCH WHISKY

_ 1/2 750 ML BOTTLE DRAMBUIE

_ 2 CUPS (475 ML) ITALIAN BLOOD
ORANGE AND CHARRED ROSEMARY
SHRUB (SEE PAGE 22)

_ 1/2 CUP (120 ML) FRESHLY
SQUEEZED LEMON JUICE

_ 1/2 CUP (120 ML) FRESHLY
SQUEEZED LIME JUICE

_ 1 QUART (946 ML) SELTZER WATER

_ 1 QUART (946 ML) LAPSANG
SOUCHONG TEA, STRONGLY
BREWED AND THEN COOLED

_ 20 SHAKES OF MY COCKTAIL
WHISPERER'S RAW HONEY AROMATIC
BITTERS (SEE PAGE 311)

DIRECTIONS

*Make a very large ice cube by filling a Tupperware container with spring water, then freeze. Place the ice cube into a very large punch bowl, add all the ingredients and mix well. Ladle into vintage porcelain tea cups—for all your nosy neighbors know, you're simply enjoying an abstemious cup of tea. **Serves 10.***

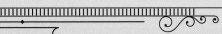

SIDENOTE

⇒ **Punch** as we know it—a fruity, juicy mixture that may or may not contain booze—is, relatively speaking, a newcomer to Western European and American traditions. (And, happily, it bears little to no resemblance to those corn-syrup- and additive-laden potions of the same name, which are usually preceded by the appellation "Hawaiian.") A seventeenth-century import from India, punch in its original form was actually a cooling concoction that consisted of five simple ingredients: Alcohol, sugar, water, lemon, and tea. (In fact, the word "punch" is derived from the Sanskrit word for the number five.) In pre-seventeenth-century Britain, most punch-style drinks were wassails—that is, warmed, sweetened wine or ale, sometimes mixed with spices and fruit. But after Jamaican rum arrived on the scene around 1650, punches became the rum-driven crowd-pleasers we know and love today.

If you haven't had a glass of punch since that particularly raucous party in your freshman year of college, now's the time to reacquaint yourself with it. (In fact, since there are tapas bars in just about every major city these days, you've probably already enjoyed a glass or two of punch's close cousin—sangria.) Punches have a couple special advantages: they tend to be slightly lower in alcohol than traditional cocktails, which means they're lovely aperitifs—and plus, if you're hosting a large group, it's much easier to made a single bowl of punch than it is to make individual cocktails for each guest. So, check out the punch recipes in this chapter next time you're planning a shindig; your guests are sure to love them all.

BÉNÉDICTINE TWIST ELIXIR

This elixir is just the thing when it comes to rousing the digestion after an especially rich meal. With its haunting notes of exotic spices and deeply aromatic Bénédictine, it tastes just medicinal enough to convince you that the liqueur is doing its healing work—and doing it well. Serve a round as a last course at your next dinner party: Your guests are sure to head home with happy bellies.

INGREDIENTS

_ 2 OUNCES (60 ML) BÉNÉDICTINE

_ 2 TO 3 LEMON
ZEST TWISTS

_ ICE CUBE

_ 1 TO 2 OUNCES SELTZER WATER

DIRECTIONS

Add the Bénédictine and the lemon zest twists to a snifter glass.
Pop one large ice cube into the glass, and top with the seltzer water.

SIDENOTE

⇒ **Angelica's alimentary assets.** The herb angelica, which is used in the production of spirits such as Bénédictine, chartreuse, gin, and vermouth, has been used as a natural stimulant for hundreds of years. In traditional Chinese medicine, it's used to improve circulation and moderate blood pressure, while *Culpeper's Herbal* (1652) claims that it can "warm and comfort a cold stomach"—that is, stimulate digestion either before or after a meal. And it has been said to relieve illnesses of the respiratory system like colds, congestion, and coughs, too. All of this means that the Bénédictine Twist Elixir is just what the doctor ordered when it comes to restoring healthy digestion after an especially rich meal.

ROASTED BEET BORSCHT WITH SOUR CREAM AND VODKA →

In some of Europe's colder regions, such as eastern Europe and Russia, home cooks add shots of vodka to the roasted-beet-based soup, *borscht*, then serve it up steaming hot in mugs to help defrost icy fingers. But no matter where in the world you are, borscht makes a sturdy, curative meal that's the perfect remedy for damp, frigid weather. (Plus, borscht is a versatile devil: This soup can also be chilled, making for a healthy, refreshing meal in the hot summer months.) Here, it's served up hot in shot glasses with just a nip of vodka for a diminutive yet restorative winter warmer. Serve to your chilly crowd *après*-ski.

INGREDIENTS

_ 3 POUNDS (1.4 KG) OF BEETS,
ROASTED AND PUREED (CUT THE
BEETS INTO CHUNKS, AND ROAST IN
A 350°F (175°C) OVEN FOR 1 HOUR
OR UNTIL COOKED THROUGH. THEN
PUREE THEM IN A BLENDER OR FOOD
PROCESSOR UNTIL SMOOTH.)

_ 6 CUPS (1.5 L) STRONG BEEF
BROTH (OR MORE TO TASTE, IF
YOU PREFER A THINNER SOUP)

_ FRESHLY GRATED
HORSERADISH, TO TASTE

_ VODKA

_ SOUR CREAM

DIRECTIONS

Add the beef broth to the pureed beets, using a bit more or less broth depending on how you prefer the soup's consistency. Then mix in the horseradish, a little at a time, to taste. Carefully spoon the mixture into individual shot glasses (be careful: the bright-red beet puree stains fabrics). Add 1 medicine-dropperful of vodka to each shot glass. Top each with a small dollop of sour cream. Dig in, and let this Russian elixir perform its healing work upon body and soul. Makes 10 servings, plus leftovers.

- -

SIDENOTE

⇒ **Vodka,** one of the world's most famous clear spirits, takes its name from the Russian phrase *zhiznennaia voda*, or "water of life." It can be made from beets, potatoes, or grain (and connoisseurs consider the grain-based versions to be the best). And, like other spirits, it was often used medicinally in northern and eastern European countries: It was considered to be a powerful curative in its own right, and was also a valuable preservative for dozens of fragile, healing herbs that would otherwise lose their potency during the long winters. Traditionally, it's served neat—for purists, mixers are unthinkable—and ice-cold, too. But it's so delicious when warmed in my Roasted Beet Borscht that I think even the most staunch traditionalists would forgive me! So lift your glass Russian-style and drink to your health. *Ura!*

RUM PUNCH FOR A CROWD

Citrus-laden rum punch was an early—and effective—curative for the evils of heat waves. In Caribbean areas such as Martinique or Haiti, both of which bear influences of French culture and its healing techniques, an apothecary would traditionally prescribe rum-based potions containing locally gathered herbs and spices, plus lashings of aromatic bitters. These healing potions would help soothe anyone who was suffering from the weather—even in the midst of the most oppressive heat and humidity. These medicinal "cocktails" evolved into rum punches, which are still made and enjoyed today. Combining fresh citrus juices with a healthy dose of light rum over ice and a whack of seltzer water, a bowl of punch is a delightful way to refresh and relax a crowd of thirsty revellers. (And it looks darned impressive, too.)

INGREDIENTS

_ 1 BOTTLE OF RUM (750 ML)

_ 1 BOTTLE OF OVERPROOF
(160-190-PROOF) RUM (750 ML)

_ 1 QUART (950 ML) EACH CITRUS JUICES
(SUCH AS ORANGE, GRAPEFRUIT, LEMON,
LIME—FRESHLY-SQUEEZED IS BEST)

_ 1 BOTTLE CLUB SODA (750 ML)

_ 1 TO 2 TABLESPOONS,
ANGOSTURA BITTERS

_ ICE CUBES

DIRECTIONS

Fill a large punch bowl half full with ice. Pour the rum over the ice, adding the fruit juices one at a time, and mix well with a wooden spoon—then replace the spoon with a ladle so your guests can serve themselves. Serves at least 10 to15 parched partygoers.

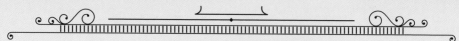

POPPA'S GOT A BRAND NEW BAG

Not every celebration involves a big crowd of rowdy revellers. Sometimes the best parties are the most intimate ones, so if you and a chum or two are in the mood to lift a glass to something special, you're in the market for a round of Poppa's Got A Brand New Bags. Get out your absinthe atomizer—you've got one, right?—and start by spraying two chilled coupe glasses with a sheen of absinthe. Then, you'll want to reach for the best rum you can get your mitts on: I'm a huge fan of Mezan XO Jamaican Rum, which never, ever uses additives like caramel color, glycerin, or extra sugar. Showcase it here with a little maraschino liqueur, broiled citrus juices, and a dash of chocolate bitters: it's luxury in a glass.

INGREDIENTS

_ SPRITZ OF ABSINTHE FROM AN ATOMIZER

_ 2 OUNCES (60 ML) MEZAN
XO JAMAICAN RUM

_ 1/2 OUNCE (15 ML)
MARASCHINO LIQUEUR

_ 1 OUNCE (30 ML) BROILED
GRAPEFRUIT JUICE (SPRINKLE HALF
A GRAPEFRUIT WITH A TEASPOON OF
DEMERARA SUGAR AND BROIL UNTIL
BUBBLY—THEN COOL AND JUICE)

_ 1 OUNCE (30 ML) BROILED
ORANGE JUICE (SPRINKLE HALF
AN ORANGE WITH A TEASPOON OF
DEMERARA SUGAR AND BROIL UNTIL
BUBBLY—THEN COOL AND JUICE)

_ 1/2 OUNCE (15 ML) FRESHLY
SQUEEZED LEMON JUICE

_ CHOCOLATE BITTERS

_ LEMON ZEST TWIST

DIRECTIONS

*Use an atomizer to spray two pre-chilled coupe glasses with absinthe. Then fill a Boston shaker three-quarters full with ice. Add the rum, maraschino liqueur, and fruit juices. Cap and shake hard for fifteen seconds. Strain the mixture into the coupe glasses, and dot each with the chocolate bitters. Garnish each with a lemon zest twist. **Serves 2.***

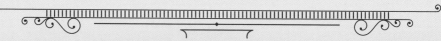

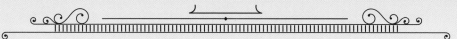

TO THE DISFAVOR OF SOME GENTLEMEN PUNCH

If they consider themselves to be purists, some whiskey-drinking gentlemen and gentlewomen might turn up their noses at the very idea of a whiskey-based punch. Are you one of them? Well, think again: this liquid pleasure trip is elegant, sophisticated, and subtly smoky. Grill your pineapple and citrus fruit before you juice it—the fruit becomes intensely, beguilingly sweet, and complements the smokiness that's the hallmark of Tennessee sipping whiskey. Also, I recommend saving yourself the headache the next morning: Use sparkling mineral water here instead of sparkling wine. You won't miss the wine, since the grilled fruit/whiskey combo gives this Carribeanesque punch all the lift it needs. The grilling and juicing does require a couple extra steps, but it's worth it. Take your time with this recipe, and build each layer of flavor into the punch. Your guests will thank you.

INGREDIENTS

- 6 OUNCES (175 ML) GRILLED PINEAPPLE JUICE (SEE PAGE 312)
- 6 OUNCES (175 ML) GRILLED ORANGE JUICE (SEE PAGE 312)
- 6 OUNCES (175 ML) GRILLED GRAPEFRUIT JUICE (SEE PAGE 312)
- 6 OUNCES (175 ML) SIMPLE SYRUP (SEE PAGE 311)
- ABOUT 16 ICE CUBES MADE FROM FROZEN COCONUT WATER (UNSWEETENED COCONUT WORKS BEST)
- 8 OUNCES (235 ML) TENNESSEE SIPPING WHISKEY
- 2 TO 3 SPRIGS FRESH THYME
- 1 LITER BOTTLE SPARKLING NATURAL MINERAL WATER

DIRECTIONS

Grill and juice the pineapple and citrus fruits. Add the ice to a large punch bowl, and then pour the juices and simple syrup over the ice. Pour in the whiskey and submerge the sprigs of thyme in the fruity mix. Finally, add the sparkling water, and stir gently (you don't want to lose the effervescence of the sparkling water). Let your guests ladle the punch into vintage teacups—and make sure you have enough supplies on hand to whip up another batch. Serves about four gentlepeople.

SARATOGA RACE DAY COCKTAIL

Thanks to its famous horse-racing track and its healing mineral springs, Saratoga Springs in upstate New York has had a reputation for being a playground for the rich and famous since the nineteenth century. During the six weeks that span the end of July and the beginning of September, the town's population mushrooms by as much as six figures, and visiting race- and partygoers have only one thing on their agenda: pleasure. And what's more delightfully indulgent than starting your day with a breakfast cocktail? I envision the Saratoga Race Day Cocktail as the kickoff to a long, lazy day of leisure. Make a batch of them at your next weekend brunch, and serve them alongside eggs Benedict with thick slices of smoked bacon.

INGREDIENTS

_ 3 OUNCES (90 ML) VERY SMOKY SCOTCH WHISKY, SUCH AS LAGAVULIN

_ 3 OUNCES (90 ML) GRILLED TANGERINE SHRUB (SEE PAGE 66)

_ 1 OUNCE (30 ML) CHAMPAGNE OR DRY SPARKLING WINE

_ 2-4 DROPS GRAPEFRUIT BITTERS

DIRECTIONS

Fill a Boston shaker three-quarters full with ice. Add the Scotch whisky and the Grilled Tangerine Shrub, and shake hard for 10 seconds. Place one cube of ice in an old-fashioned glass, and pour the mixture over it. Top with the champagne or sparkling wine, dot with the bitters, and serve. (Have your guests got sore heads this morning? If so, prepare to make a second round.)

THE BROAD REACH

Some of the best parties are the ones you didn't plan on having in the first place. Everyone *should* have gone straight home after happy hour, but all of a sudden—and you're not quite sure how it happened—there are thirteen thirsty people in your kitchen, and you've got to do something about it. But don't panic. If you've got a good bottle of rum on hand, your problem's pretty much solved. Shake up a few batches of The Broad Reach, a simple, rum-based cocktail that's a fabulous crowd-pleaser. It's nothing more than Mezan rum and a good-quality tangerine-flavored mixer, plus a secret ingredient: a dash of white balsamic vinegar. The vinegar acts as a sort of "instant shrub," adding a bracing acidity that makes the Reach incredibly drinkable. This recipe serves two, but go ahead and double—or triple!—it, depending on the size of your crowd.

INGREDIENTS

_ 2 OUNCES (60 ML) MEZAN XO JAMAICAN RUM

_ 2 OUNCES (60 ML) GOOD-QUALITY TANGERINE SODA & COCKTAIL MIXER

_ 1/2 OUNCE (15 ML) WHITE BALSAMIC VINEGAR

_ ANGOSTURA BITTERS

_ TANGERINE SEGMENTS

DIRECTIONS

Combine the first three ingredients in a Boston shaker three-quarters full of ice. Cap and shake hard for 15 seconds. Divide between two ice-filled Collins glasses. Squeeze a tangerine segment over the top of each, then plop it into the glass. Dot with the bitters, and serve immediately. **Serves 2.**

THE JENKS FARM RESTORATIVE →

We've all had those mornings: You had one too many cocktails the night before, you finally hit the sack at some unknown but ungodly hour, and now your stressed-out belly can't stomach your usual cup of coffee—or, heaven help us, food. That's where The Jenks Farm Restorative, a powerful breakfast-time cocktail, comes in. It's a healing concoction of white whiskey and iced coffee laced with heavy cream and sweet vanilla syrup, served over crushed ice—and it's best made by the pitcherful, because it goes down so very quickly and easily. The moonshine provides a little hair of the proverbial dog to calm shattered nerves, while the chilled coffee gets much-needed caffeine into your system, fast. Don't skip the freshly grated nutmeg—inhaling nutmeg's warm, heady scent is like aromatherapy for hangover sufferers.

INGREDIENTS

_ 6 OUNCES (175 ML) WHITE WHISKEY

_ 8 OUNCES (235 ML) HEAVY CREAM

_ 6 OUNCES (175 ML) WHOLE MILK

_ 4 OUNCES (120 ML) BASIC
SIMPLE SYRUP (SEE PAGE 311)
MIXED WITH 2 TEASPOONS REAL
VANILLA EXTRACT, OR TO TASTE

_ 6 OUNCES (175 ML) OLD BLACK
COFFEE (YESTERDAY MORNING'S
COFFEE IS FINE), CHILLED

_ FRESHLY SCRAPED NUTMEG

DIRECTIONS

Combine the first five ingredients in a 32-ounce (1 L) pitcher, and stir well. Fill rocks glasses with crushed ice, and (quickly!) pour this toothsome restorative over the ice. Grate some fresh nutmeg over each drink, and sip to the good health of friends both near and far. **Serves 4** *aching heads.*

SIDENOTE

⇒ **Conquer cream catastrophes.** This may sound terribly basic, but it's a mistake we've all made before. Picture this, and tell me if it doesn't sound familiar: You're in the kitchen or at the bar, and the recipe you're making—like the Jenks Farm Restorative—calls for fresh cream. Happily, you've got a carton to hand, so you toss in the required amount—blissfully unaware that the cream has gone sour on you. Devastated, you have to chuck out the whole drink or dish—and there's nothing more aggravating than waste. There's only one solution: Always, always, always taste your cream before you use it, even if it's within its sell-by date. (Simply smelling it isn't enough: use a clean spoon to place a drop or two on your tongue.) It's such a simple thing, but it's sure to save you time, money, and stress. (You can thank me later.)

DAVID BALFOUR COCKTAIL

Named for the resourceful protagonist of Robert Louis Stevenson's novel, Kidnapped, this refreshing tipple is just as enterprising. Its simple ingredients make it easy to prepare in a flash, and they also travel well in a go-cup, if you want to save your portion of David Balfour for later on. Make your own lemonade with freshly squeezed lemon juice, some cool spring water, simple syrup, and some torn fresh mint—then zest it up with orange bitters and a healthy pour of Irish whiskey. (I recommend trying a few different varieties of orange bitters before you settle on one that really resonates with you: There're lots of versions available on the market.) Mix up a jug of David B. to take with you on your next picnic, barbeque, or trip to the beach: It goes wonderfully with just about all lunchtime noshes.

INGREDIENTS

_ 8 OUNCES (235 ML) IRISH WHISKEY

_ 10 OUNCES (285 ML) FRESH LEM-
ONADE, SWEETENED TO TASTE WITH
BASIC SIMPLE SYRUP (SEE PAGE 311)

_ 1 SMALL BUNCH FRESH MINT, WASHED
WELL AND TORN OR SLAPPED

_ 4 SHAKES ORANGE BITTERS

DIRECTIONS

Fill a pitcher three-quarters full with ice. Add the slapped or torn mint, followed by the Irish whiskey and the sweetened lemonade. Mix gently. Shake the orange bitters over the top—taste for balance, adding more bitters if necessary. Serves 4 picnickers.

DR. SOMERSET'S CURE

In Robert Louis Stevenson's short story, "The Superfluous Mansion," one character inquires of another, "'Have you a drop of Brandy… I am sick.'" It's not an unreasonable request. After all, back in the day, brandy was thought to be medicinal and a restorative—so if you needed an excuse to treat yourself to a brandy-laced cocktail, look no further. Dr. Somerset's Cure features both brandy and French whisky, which is often aged in casks that once held cognac. The result is a softly oaked spirit that's truly the stuff of dreams. Here, it's buttressed by a melange of flavors, including calvados, a bit of inexpensive pomace or marc brandy, roasted apricots, orange segments, and fresh lemon juice. Do mix up a few Cures next time you're hosting a couple close friends for lunch, or at an intimate dinner party.

INGREDIENTS

_ 5 TO 6 ROASTED APRICOTS (SEE
ROASTED STONE FRUITS, PAGE 313)

_ 1 OUNCE (30 ML) SWEET VERMOUTH

_ 1 OUNCE (30 ML) FRENCH WHISKY

_ 1/2 OUNCE (15 ML) CALVADOS

_ 2 ORANGE SEGMENTS (REMOVE
AS MUCH OF THE WHITE
PITH AS POSSIBLE)

_ 1 OUNCE (30 ML) FRESHLY
SQUEEZED LEMON JUICE

_ 1 OUNCE (30 ML) RAW HONEY SIMPLE
SYRUP (SEE PAGE 312-313)

_ 2 TO 3 SHAKES PIMENTO BITTERS

DIRECTIONS

*Add 3 roasted apricot halves to a Boston shaker, and pour the vermouth over them. Using a muddler or the end of a wooden spoon, muddle the apricot halves with the vermouth. Then, add the French whisky and the calvados, and continue muddling, adding the orange segments, the lemon juice, and the Raw Honey Simple Syrup in turns. When the mixture is well combined, divide the mixture between four rocks glasses with one cube of ice in each, and finish with a dash or two of the pimento bitters over the top of each glass. **Serves 4.***

SCURVY KNAVE SHRUB PUNCH

Back in the age of sail, vitamin C–laden fruits, like lemons and limes, were precious cargo: They could keep seagoing men from contracting scurvy, a painful and often fatal disease. Ship cooks would boil lime juice, ginger root, sugar, and vinegar until they formed a thick syrup that, coincidentally, was delicious when mixed with rum. That way, sailors could get a dose of much-needed vitamin C—with a bit of a kick. Use the best rum you can afford: if you use poor-quality industrial-grade rum, you'll feel more than a little seasick the next morning yourself. (And your guests will be wont to give you a bath in the warm bilge water inside the keel of your ship.) A "Scurvy Knave" is a less-than-sympathetic term for someone in the throes of the disease, but don't worry: a cup or two of this potent punch is a sure cure.

INGREDIENTS

_ 4 OUNCES (120 ML) DARK RUM

_ 4 OUNCES (120 ML) LIGHT RUM

_ 4 OUNCES (120 ML) OVERPROOF RUM

_ 6 OUNCES (175 ML) GINGER-LIME SHRUB (SEE PAGE 82)

_ 1 750 ML BOTTLE OF SPARKLING WINE

_ 10 SHAKES PEYCHAUD'S BITTERS

_ 1 JOBO FRUIT (OR 1 TANGERINE)

DIRECTIONS

Combine the rum, Ginger-Lime Shrub Syrup, and sparkling wine in a large punch bowl. Add the Peychaud's Bitters. Lovingly break open the jobo fruit or tangerine and, using your fingers, squeeze its aromatic flesh into the cocktail. Mix well and serve. This is a punch of memorable proportions and serves at least 5 knaves.

THE SQUIRE'S STRAWBERRY-RHUBARB SHRUB →

It's true, the Squire's Shrub does require a couple of extra steps, but I promise it's worth your while: Your patience will be rewarded with a lush, crimson-colored syrup that's straight out of the eighteenth century, when America was in its infancy and early pharmacists would have relied on their gardens to supply the basis for their healing tonics. (Rhubarb has been used as a digestive aid for thousands of years.) There's nothing difficult to it, though, beyond a little extra mixing, and roasting your fruit before making the shrub. The vinegar's high acidity cuts through the sumptuous, charred, caramelized flavor of the roasted strawberries and rhubarb, making it a terribly seductive addition to gin, vodka, and rum-based libations. Use it to make up a couple rounds of the Squire's Shrub Cocktail (see page 310) at your next warm-weather soiree.

INGREDIENTS

_ 2 CUPS (340 G) ROASTED STRAWBERRIES
AND RHUBARB (SEE PAGE 313)

_ 1 CUP (200 G) DEMERARA SUGAR

_ 1 CUP (235 ML) LIGHT
BALSAMIC VINEGAR

DIRECTIONS

Time: 3-4 weeks. *Add the roasted strawberries and rhubarb to a nonreactive bowl. Cover with the sugar, stir to combine, and cover it with plastic wrap. Leave at cool room temperature for 24 hours. Stir frequently during this time to combine as the berries and rhubarb give off their liquid. Place a nonreactive strainer above a second nonreactive bowl, pour the fruit-sugar mixture into the strainer, and use a wooden spoon to mash the mixture in order to release as much liquid as possible. (Reserve the mashed fruit to use in cooking or baking, if you like.) Add the balsamic vinegar to the liquid, stir, and let the mixture sit for a few hours. Funnel into sterilized bottles or jars, and age for 3–4 weeks in the refrigerator. This shrub will last nearly indefinitely, but if it begins to quiver, dance, or speak in foreign languages, throw it out immediately.*

THE SQUIRE'S SHRUB COCKTAIL

Get ready to try another twisted take on the French 75, that timeless combination of gin, champagne, lemon juice, and simple syrup. This version is actually a hybrid of the French 75 and the traditional champagne cocktail, which calls for a bitters-moistened sugar cube, brandy, and a heady top of champagne. Fuse the two together, add a healthy whack of tart, fruity Squire's Shrub, and you've got a cocktail that'll make your guests' knees tremble. In the same way that alchemists of old strove to turn base metals into gold, champagne can turn a plain old Tuesday into a full-on, hat-waving celebration: Be sure to keep a bottle on hand so you can whip these up the next time you find yourself hosting an impromptu shindig. When that happens, make a few batches of the Squire's, if you dare—just keep that bottle of Fernet Branca on hand for the morning after.

INGREDIENTS

- 1 BROWN SUGAR CUBE
- SEVERAL DASHES OF LEMON BITTERS
- 1/2 OUNCE (15 ML) BOTANICAL GIN
- 2 OUNCES (60 ML) SQUIRE'S STRAWBERRY-RHUBARB SHRUB (SEE PAGE 308-309)
- 11/2 OUNCES (45 ML) CHAMPAGNE OR DRY SPARKLING WINE
- L LONG LEMON ZEST TWIST

DIRECTIONS

Add the sugar cube to a champagne flute, and moisten with the lemon bitters. Then add the gin and the Squire's Strawberry-Rhubarb Shrub, and top with champagne. Garnish with a long lemon zest twist. Voila!

Syrups and Infusions

Basic Simple Syrup Add 1 cup (235 ml) of boiling water to 1 cup (200 g) of bar sugar or caster sugar and mix until sugar has dissolved. Let the mixture cool. Keep refrigerated in an airtight container for up to a month.

Berry Vodka Infusion Place 1 cup (145 g) of elderberries in 1/2 cup (120 ml) of blackberry brandy. Add 6 ounces (175 ml) of vodka and combine well. Cover with plastic wrap. Keep the mixture in the refrigerator for 2 days, then puree the mixture in a blender or food processor, and strain it through cheesecloth. Keep refrigerated in an airtight container: It'll last for months.

Blueberry Simple Syrup Simply puree 1 pint (300 g) of blueberries (preferably Maine wild blueberries, if you can get them), then sweeten to taste with Raw Honey Simple Syrup (see above). Let cool. Store in the refrigerator for 1 month.

Bosc Pear "Shrub" Simple Syrup Finely dice 2 Bosc pears, and combine them with 1 cup (235 ml) Basic Simple Syrup (see above), 1/2 cup (120 ml) Japanese rice wine vinegar and 1/2 cup (120 ml) mirin. Add to a small saucepan, and bring to a simmer, then remove from heat, let cool, cover, and let the mixture sit overnight at cellar temperature. Strain, then use in your shrub.

Captain John Silver's Quick Celery Pickle Wash a package of organic celery well, and change the water several times to eliminate any clinging grit. Trim the celery and cut it into small coins. Combine 1/2 cup (120 ml) mirin, 1/2 cup (120 ml) rice wine vinegar, and 1 cup (200 g) of Vietnamese palm sugar: this should be enough to cover the celery. (Add a few slivers of Thai chilies for extra flavor, if you like.) Add 1 teaspoon of black peppercorns, smashed with the side of a chef's knife, and 2–3 lemon zest twists. Cover and refrigerate for 2 days, stirring the mixture daily to ensure that the celery is covered with liquid, and adding more mirin if necessary. Store in an airtight container in the refrigerator for 1 month.

Cardamom Simple Syrup Make a batch of Basic Simple Syrup (above) and pour it into a medium-sized bowl. Add 2 to 3 crushed cardamom pods to the mixture and let it cool. Cover the bowl with plastic wrap, place it in the refrigerator, and let the pods steep in the syrup for 1 to 2 days. Remove the cardamom pods, and keep refrigerated in an airtight container for up to a month.

Cocktail Whisperer's Raw Honey Aromatic Bitters Combine 1 teaspoon gentian extract, 2 tablespoons (30 g) Quassia extract, 2 whole cinnamon sticks, 1–2 (or more, to taste) dried birds-eye Thai chilies with 1/2 ounce (15 g) each freshly grated nutmeg, Chinese five-spice mix, star anise, fennel seeds, and cardamom pods in a very large mixing bowl. Add 375 ml (half of a 750 ml bottle) Spanish sherry (oloroso sherry works best because of its nutty, boldly assertive flavors); 1 750ml bottle of clear grain alcohol, such as Everclear; and 16 ounces (455 g) raw honey. Mix well. Then divide the mixture between two 1-quart (946 ml) Mason jars with tight rubber seals and sturdy glass tops. Store in the fridge or a cool, dark place, and shake vigorously twice daily for 1–2 months. Strain the mixture through cheesecloth to remove the spices, and then funnel into small, sterilized bottles. Use wherever bitters are called for in your food and drink.

Curried Bitters Add 1 teaspoon (5 g) of curry powder to 3 tablespoons (45 g) of Angostura Bitters and mix well. Refrigerate and store indefinitely.

Demerara Sugar Simple Syrup Add 1 cup (235 ml) of boiling water to 1/2 cup (100 g) of Demerara sugar and mix until sugar has dissolved. Let the mixture cool. Keep refrigerated in an airtight container for up to a month.

Easy Home-Cured Cocktail Cherries Add 1 pound (455 g) pitted Ranier or dark cherries to a large, sterilized Mason jar. Cover the cherries with a combination of bourbon and green tea in a ratio of 60% bourbon and 40% green tea. Refrigerate for a month. Store in the refrigerator nearly indefinitely.

Fennel Simple Syrup Make a batch of simple syrup (above) and pour it into a medium-sized bowl. Add 1/4 cup (16 g) chopped fresh fennel to the mixture and let it cool. Cover the bowl with plastic wrap; place it in the refrigerator; and let the fennel steep in the syrup for 1 to 2 days. Strain before using, and keep refrigerated in an airtight container for up to a month.

Ginger Honey Simple Syrup Make a batch of Raw Honey Simple Syrup (see above). Add 1/4 cup (25 g) finely chopped fresh (preferably young) ginger. Pour the mixture into an airtight container, and let it steep in the fridge for a couple days. Strain before using. Use within 2 weeks.

Ginger Syrup Add 1 cup (200 g) of syrup to 1 cup (235 ml) of boiling water. Grate 8 oz. of ginger root into the mixture, and then let it stand for a couple of days. Strain, and now you have ginger syrup. Keep refrigerated in an airtight container for up to a month.

Grilled Citrus Juices To make 1 cup (235 ml) of each citrus juice: Orange: Cut 2 to 3 oranges into 1/2-inch (1.25-cm) thick slices. Place the slices on a grill or grill pan, and cook until char marks appear on the flesh of the fruit. Grapefruit: Cut 1 to 2 grapefruits into 1/2-inch (1.25-cm) thick slices. Place the slices on a grill or grill pan, and cook until char marks appear on the flesh of the fruit. Pineapple: Slice 1 pineapple into wedges 1/2-inch (1.25 cm) thick, removing the rind. Place the slices on a grill or grill pan, and cook until char marks appear on the flesh of the fruit.

TO JUICE: Remove any peel or rind that may remain on the fruit. Cut into pieces small enough to fit into a juicer, and put them one at a time into the juicer. Strain the juices before using. Store them in airtight containers for up to a week.

Healing Herb Simple Syrup Make a batch of simple syrup (above) and pour it into a medium-sized bowl. Place the assorted herbs into a cheesecloth bag and tie tightly with string. Submerge the cheesecloth bag in the simple syrup—let the string hang outside of the bowl, like a teabag, for easy removal—cover the bowl with plastic wrap, place it in the refrigerator, and let the herbs steep in the syrup for 1 to 2 days. Remove the cheesecloth bag of herbs before using. Keep refrigerated in an airtight container for up to a month.

Homemade Grenadine Syrup Combine 2 ounces (60 ml) Basic Simple Syrup, 2 cups (475 ml) pomegranate juice, and 1/4 teaspoon each nutmeg, cinnamon, and cayenne pepper in a medium saucepan. Bring to a simmer, then reduce the heat and continue to simmer for 15 to 20 minutes. Allow the mixture to cool, and then use a funnel to transfer it to a glass bottle. Add no more than four drops of orange water—and, if you like, some overproof rum or vodka for extra zip.

Homemade Lemonade Warm 10 cups (2.4 L) of spring water in a large saucepan until just below simmering. Then add 1 cup (340 g) raw honey, and stir until dissolved. Let cool. Add the juice of 8 lemons. Pour the mixture into a large pitcher, and add a big handful of fresh mint. Chill in the refrigerator for a few hours before serving.

Homemade Whipped Cream Combine 1 pint (473 ml) of heavy whipping cream with 2 tablespoons (26 g) of confectioner's sugar. (To make Coffee Whipped Cream, add 1 tablespoon (13 g) of powdered espresso coffee. To make Cognac Whipped Cream, add a few drops of cognac.) Whip with a whisk until it's a softly creamy, almost pourable, consistency.

Lemon Balm Simple Syrup Make a batch of simple syrup (above) and pour it into a medium-sized bowl. Add 10 to 12 torn lemon balm leaves to the mixture and let it cool. Cover the bowl with plastic wrap, place it in the refrigerator, and let the lemon balm steep in the syrup for 1 to 2 days. Strain before using, and add up to 2 ounces (60 ml) of botanical gin as a preservative, if desired. Keep refrigerated in an airtight container for up to a month.

Luscious Asian Fruit Puree Peel and deseed 1 orange, 1 jackfruit, 1 Asian pear, and 1 starfruit. Puree in a food processor, and then press through a fine sieve to remove any remaining skin or seeds. Store in an airtight container in the refrigerator for up to a week.

Luscious Grilled Lemonade Remove the wax from 8 lemons, and cut them into 1/2 inch (1.3-cm) rounds. Combine 1/2 cup (170 g) raw honey and 1/2 cup (120 ml) water in a bowl, and dip the lemon rounds into the mixture. Sprinkle the lemon rounds with a pinch of sea salt, then char them lightly over indirect heat on a wood grill. Let them cool, then juice them and follow the directions for my Homemade Lemonade, above.

Orange Simple Syrup In a medium saucepan, combine 1 cup (20 g) sugar, 1/2 cup (120 ml) freshly squeezed orange juice (strained), and 2 tablespoons (12 g) grated orange zest, and 1/2 cup (120 ml) water. Simmer, mixing until the sugar has dissolved. Let the mixture cool. Strain before using, and keep refrigerated in an airtight container for up to 2 weeks.

Quick Roasted Tomato-Celery Puree Preheat your oven to 400°F (200°C, or gas mark 6). Slice about 12 ripe tomatoes, and cut the stalks from a package of well-washed celery into coins. Drizzle a little olive oil over the tomatoes and celery, sprinkle them with sea salt, and roast for 1 hour. Let the vegetables cool, and then puree them in a blender.

Quince Puree Preheat your oven to 250°F (120°C, or gas mark 1/2). Cut 1 quince into 1/2-inch (1.25-cm) chunks, and place on a baking tray. (Be careful when slicing the quince: It's rock-hard, and your knife can slip easily, leading to nasty kitchen accidents! Be sure to secure your cutting board first by placing a wet dish towel underneath it.) Roast the quince for at least 4 hours, until soft. When cool, put the quince into a food mill in order to remove the skin and the bitter pits. Reserve as much of the liquid as possible. Refrigerate in an airtight container for up to a week.

Raw Honey Simple Syrup Add 1 cup (235 ml) of boiling water to 1 cup (340 g) raw honey and mix until honey has dissolved. Let the mixture cool. Keep refrigerated in an airtight container for up to a month.

Roasted Stone Fruits Line a baking tray with parchment paper, and preheat your oven to 300°F (150°C, or gas mark 2). Slice 1 pound (455 g) assorted stone fruits, such as peaches, plums, and/or apricots, in half (pits removed). Sprinkle with demerara sugar, and roast slowly for 3 hours. Let the stone fruits cool overnight in as much of their own liquid as possible. Drizzle Raw Honey Simple Syrup (see above) over them to keep moist. Store in an airtight container in the refrigerator for up to a week (any longer and they tend to get fuzzy!)

Roasted Strawberries and Rhubarb First, hull 1 pound (455 g) of strawberries, and wash 1 pound (455 g) of rhubarb stalks. Chop the rhubarb into 1 inch (2.5-cm) chunks. Preheat your oven to 400°F (200°C, or gas mark 6), and place the fruit into a cast-iron roasting pan. Roast for 30 minutes, then reduce the temperature to 300°F (150°C, or gas mark 2) and continue to roast for another 30 minutes. Let cool. Store in an airtight container in the refrigerator for up to a week.

Roasted Tomato Puree Preheat the oven to 400°F (200°C). Line a baking tray with parchment paper. Toss 1 pound (455 g) of grape tomatoes with 2 tablespoons (30 ml) of olive oil and a dash of salt. Arrange the tomatoes on the baking tray, and roast for half an hour. Then turn the heat down to 250°F (120°C) and slow-cook them until melted, about 3 hours. (Keep an eye on them. If they start to burn, turn the heat down, but be patient. You want the tomatoes to melt, not burn.) When the tomatoes are cool enough to handle, puree them either in a food processor or with a mortar and pestle to make a relatively smooth liquid. Add 2 to 4 tablespoons (30 to 60 g) of horseradish (freshly-grated is best, if you can get it), several squeezes of fresh lemon juice, and a dash of celery salt. Store in the refrigerator for up to 3 days.

Root Tea Simple Syrup Combine 4 ounces (120 ml) of organic root tea liqueur with 1/2 cup (100 g) bar sugar and 1 cup (235 ml) boiling water. When the sugar has dissolved, let the mixture cool, and keep refrigerated in an airtight container for up to a month.

Rose-Infused Simple Syrup Place 2 to 3 organic red rose petals into a cheesecloth bag and tie tightly with string (use organic rose petals only). Pour 1 cup (235 ml) simple syrup into a small bowl, then submerge the cheesecloth bag in bowl; cover it with plastic wrap; and store in the refrigerator over-night. Remove the cheesecloth bag before using. Alternatively, combine 1 tablespoon (15 ml) of rosewater (be sure to use the edible kind!) with 1 cup (235 ml) of simple syrup in a small bowl, and store in the refrigerator overnight before using. Keep refrigerated in an airtight container for up to a month.

Rosemary Simple Syrup Make a batch of Basic Simple Syrup (see above). Crumble a handful of rosemary leaves, place them in a cheesecloth bag, and submerge the bag in the Basic Simple Syrup. Let the mixture cool. Remove the cheesecloth bag, pour the mixture into an airtight container, and store in the fridge for up to 1 month.

Spicy Ginger Honey Simple Syrup Make a batch of Raw Ginger Honey Simple Syrup (see above), and add 1/2 teaspoon cayenne pepper. Pour the mixture into an airtight container, and let it steep in the fridge for a couple days. Strain before using. Use within 2 weeks.

Spicy Pickled Cucumber Garnish Slice a European cucumber lengthwise. Combine with 1/2 cup (120 ml) white vinegar, a few shards of sliced red chiles, 1 tablespoon (15 g) sugar, and 1 teaspoon sea salt. Cover tightly and store in the fridge overnight. Pour off the marinade, and use the pickled cucumber slices as garnishes for your cocktails.

Spicy Simple Syrup In a medium saucepan, combine 2 cups (400 g) of sugar with 1 cup (235 ml) of water and bring to a boil, mixing until the sugar has dissolved. Let the mixture cool. Add a tablespoon of chopped poblano and/or ancho chiles. Pour the mixture into an airtight container, and let it steep in the fridge for a couple days. Strain before using. Use within 2 weeks.

The Best Hot Chocolate Mix 1/2 cup (100 g) of the best-quality bittersweet chocolate powder (ideally, seventy-five percent cocoa) with 1 cup (235 ml) whole milk and 1/2 cup (115 g) heavy cream. Over a low heat, slowly whisk the mixture until it reaches a smooth consistency, and sweeten to taste with Basic Simple Syrup (see above). Finish with a pinch of freshly grated nutmeg.

Vietnamese Fizzy Lemonade Chop 2 to 3 preserved lemons (available in Asian supermarkets). Add them to a pitcher, combine with 4 tablespoons (52 g) of sugar, a 1/4 teaspoon sea salt, and top with fizzy water to taste.

How To Sterilize a Bottle: Using a pair of rubber-coated metal tongs, submerge the bottle in boiling water for 2 minutes. Remove the bottle, empty it of water, and let cool.

ABOUT THE AUTHOR

WARREN BOBROW

WARREN BOBROW, "THE COCKTAIL WHISPERER," IS THE CREATOR OF THE POPULAR BLOG COCKTAILWHISPERER.COM AND THE AUTHOR OF APOTHECARY COCKTAILS, WHISKEY COCKTAILS AND BITTERS & SHRUB SYRUP COCKTAILS.

Warren has taught classes on spirits and cocktails all over the world, including an advanced class on rum at the Moscow Bar Show. He's taught the fine art of social media and food writing at the New School in New York as well as classes on creative cocktails and mocktails at Stonewall Kitchen in Maine.

Warren has written hundreds of articles on cocktails and food for Chilled Magazine, Saveur, Whole Foods/Dark Rye, Total Food Service, Eater, Voda, Serious Eats, Foodista, Distiller, Sip and Beverage Media as well as many other international outlets. He has also written for the Oxford Encyclopedia: Gotham issue and the Sage Encyclopedia of Food Issues.

Warren was a 2010 Ministry of Rum judge and was the only American food journalist asked to participate in Fete de la Gastronomie, a nationwide celebration of French cuisine in Burgundy.